CORPORATE LAW AND SUSTAINABILITY FROM THE NEXT GENERATION OF LAWYERS

Corporate Law and Sustainability from the Next Generation of Lawyers

Edited by

Carol Liao

McGill-Queen's University Press
Montreal & Kingston • London • Chicago

ISBN 978-0-2280-1131-6 (cloth)
ISBN 978-0-2280-1132-3 (paper)
ISBN 978-0-2280-1309-9 (ePDF)
ISBN 978-0-2280-1310-5 (ePUB)

Legal deposit third quarter 2022
Bibliothèque nationale du Québec

Printed in Canada on acid-free paper that is 100% ancient forest free (100% post-consumer recycled), processed chlorine free

Financé par le gouvernement du Canada | Funded by the Government of Canada | Canada

Canada Council for the Arts

We acknowledge the support of the Canada Council for the Arts.

Nous remercions le Conseil des arts du Canada de son soutien.

Library and Archives Canada Cataloguing in Publication

Title: Corporate law and sustainability from the next generation of lawyers / edited by Carol Liao.

Names: Liao, Carol (Law professor), editor.

Description: Includes bibliographical references and index.

Identifiers: Canadiana (print) 20220232717 | Canadiana (ebook) 20220233039 | ISBN 9780228011316 (hardcover) | ISBN 9780228011323 (softcover) | ISBN 9780228013099 (PDF) | ISBN 9780228013105 (ePUB)

Subjects: LCSH: Corporation law—Canada. | LCSH: Sustainable development—Law and legislation—Canada. | LCSH: Social responsibility of business—Law and legislation—Canada.

Classification: LCC KE1389 .C665 2022 | LCC KF1414 .C665 2022 kfmod | DDC 346/.71066—dc23

This book was typeset by Marquis Interscript in 10.5/13 Sabon.

Contents

PART TWO CSR AS RISK MANAGEMENT IN INDUSTRY PRACTICE

PART THREE CORPORATE ACCOUNTABILITY AND REGULATION

Foreword

This is a timely and much-needed collection. Young people and the generations that come after them will bear the brunt of the climate crisis and other environmental ills. Not surprisingly, it is they who feel most acutely the urgent need for action, who cannot help but consider the prospect of a world destroyed within their lifetimes. We need to hear from them, whether in the form of global climate protests by school children, youth-led litigation to reign in fossil fuel companies, leadership by young activists, like Greta Thunberg, or – as in the case of this collection – scholarly analyses from next generation lawyers.

What you are about to read is thrillingly unique, not only because of the demographic of its contributors, but also because of its focus on corporate law as a site of contestation. The seemingly technical and apolitical character of corporate law often serves to belie its profound impact on the world and its role in fomenting social and environmental crises. We readily see areas like environmental law, natural resources policy, and Aboriginal rights as reflecting and driving politics and policy. But the laws that constitute corporations and markets (capitalism, in other words) are somehow presumed natural and inevitable, the surface upon which politics happens, but not in themselves political. Legal scholars have long worked to deconstruct these distinctions – famously, legal realists, like Robert Hale and Morris Cohen and, later, critical legal studies scholars, like Duncan Kennedy – but they persist nonetheless.

That is why this volume is so important. It brings corporate law into the open, makes it visible, and draws direct and strong connections between it and the environmental crises we now face. Introduced and led by the deft hand of Dr Carol Liao, the contributors to this volume provide new perspectives on the legal, regulatory, and governance frameworks that constitute corporate capitalism, and that are, therefore, implicated in a myriad of pressing issues, including climate change, environmental degradation, social injustice, boardroom diversity, global supply chain management, transnational business and human rights, decolonization, and Indigenous rights. The contributions transcend old, tired debates with fresh, critical inquiries into key issues where corporate law and social and environmental values and interests meet. Overall, this collection is nothing short of a tour de force, addressing some of the most pressing issues in corporate law and sustainability, and indeed of our time.

There is a surfeit of rigorous analysis, thorough research, and cogent writing. But what comes through most strongly, time and again, in these contributions are authenticity and desire for a society that is ethical and good. These are the perspectives and pleas of young people, at the start of their legal careers, in the midst of a precarious period in human history, and a global pandemic. Their questioning of core legal structures challenges, probes, and deepens understanding. Their skepticism about corporate power and corporations' relentless campaigns to convince us they have now become good actors, reveal and inspire a profound hope that through rigorous analysis and revelation of truth, we can begin to build a better world.

Joel Bakan
Author and filmmaker of *The Corporation*
and *The New Corporation*

Acknowledgments

The motivation for this book came as I listened to a diverse group of young lawyers share their ideas on how to change the world. It occurred to me then that these were some of the most refreshing ideas on corporate law that I had heard in a long time. Time and experience can make one lose sight of the forest for the trees, and there is nothing more humbling and rewarding than having the next generation teach you something. As the editor of this volume, I extend my gratitude to these contributors who stuck it out through countless drafts and whose energy inspired this book.

Thank you to my editor Jacqueline Mason, who let me pitch this outside-of-the-box idea to her and took a chance on me and this group of young professionals. Her commitment to and enthusiasm for this project over the years was essential in it ever seeing the light. I am grateful to the two anonymous peer-reviewers whose early excitement over the book confirmed we had something special; their comments to initial drafts were invaluable. I also thank Kathleen Fraser and the team at McGill-Queen's University Press for their support in the final stages of the book.

Several current and former law students (including some contributors) helped me ensure the quality and academic rigour of this collection. Their exceptional research and editorial assistance were indispensable and I thank them: Lisa Chaudhry, Yu-Ting (Andy) Chen, Austin Darling, Ariyana Dhawan, Blair Feltmate, Julia Fyfe, Jaden Lau, Stephanie Lee, Oludolapo Makinde, Kirsten Saikaly, Erica Sandhu, Pawanpreet Sran, Asha Young, and Sherry Yu. Generous funding from the Social Sciences and Humanities Research Council, the Peter A. Allard School of Law, and the UBC Sauder School of

Business enabled their contributions and is gratefully acknowledged. I also received institutional support from the Centre for Business Law, the Peter P. Dhillon Centre for Business Ethics, and the Canada Climate Law Initiative, three organizations that do critically important work at the intersection of corporate law, business ethics, sustainability, and climate change. Sincere gratitude to my colleagues at these organizations whose imprints in business education and legal scholarship have been foundational influences in the framing of this book.

We are eighteen months into this COVID-19 pandemic, living in a surreal time with no modern precedent. My thanks to friends and colleagues that have kept our communities together online, and in person when COVID-19 protocols allowed it, and whose conversations on sustainability, corporate law, social justice, legal education, and the state of the world were immensely helpful: Patricia Barkaskas, Brenna Bhandar, Ryan J. Black, Ljiljana Biuković, Gordon Christie, Daryl Dujon, Alexandra Flynn, Sara Ghebremusse, Camden Hutchison, Asha Kaushal, Johnny Mack, Lori Mathison, Shona McGlashan, Debra Parkes, Victor V. Ramraj, Lee Schmidt, Beate Sjåfjell, Anne Uteck, Stepan Wood, and Margot Young. Thank you to my long-time friends with a shared passion for sustainability and sisterhood: Christine Bergeron, Stephanie Garrett, Christie Stephenson, and Anne Wittman. Profound thanks as well to Sonja Dula, Susan Higgs, and Michelle Robichaud who have kept me grounded over the years.

This book, and indeed, my academic career, never would have materialized without the love and ongoing encouragement of my family. In particular, thank you to Susan Su-Ling Liao, Steve Kuo-Chin Liao, Diana Liao, Roger Liao, Heather Fogden, Dan Fogden, Simon Jay, William Wei-Le Jay, Kerbie Reader, Lawrence Chen, Yuri Tei, and Patricia Carlton. Finally, to the four loves of my life and companions in this pandemic, Kyle Fogden and our three daughters, Lucy Hai-Le Fogden, Skye Hai-Ling Fogden, and Hannah Hai-Mei Fogden: life is beautiful and hopeful each day because of you. As these pages amplify the voices of young leaders during a time of intersecting global crises, I hope that a sustainable future in this greater-than-human world can happen within our lifetimes.

Carol Liao
Vancouver, BC, Canada
xʷməθkʷəy̓əm (Musqueam) Territory

Abbreviations

BEPS	Base Erosion and Profit Shifting
BHP	Broken Hill Proprietary Company Limited
BHR	business and human rights
CEDAW	Convention for the Elimination of All Forms of Discrimination Against Women
CEO	chief executive officer
CMIS	Common Material Issues
CNCA	Canadian Network for Corporate Accountability
CORE	Canadian Ombudsperson for Responsible Enterprise
CPA	corporate political activity
CPR	Canadian Pacific Railway Limited
CRTC	Canadian Radio-television Telecommunications Commission
CSP	corporate social performance
CSR	corporate social responsibility
CTSCA	*California Transparency in Supply Chains Act*
DPA	Deferred Prosecution Agreement
ESG	environmental, social, governance
FTSE	Financial Times Stock Exchange
GAAR	General Anti-Avoidance Rule
GEO	Global Environmental Outlook
GP 29	Guiding Principle 29
GRI	Global Reporting Initiative
IARD	International Alliance for Responsible Drinking
ICA	International Cooperative Alliance
IMI	Investable Market Index
KLD	Kinder, Lydenberg, Domini & Co.

KRA	Kenyan Revenue Authority
LLC	limited liability company
MLI	Multilateral Convention to Implement Tax Treaty-Related Measures to Prevent Base Erosion and Profit Shifting
MNC	multinational corporation
NAP	National Action Plan
NCP	National Contact Point
NDP	New Democratic Party
NGO	non-governmental organization
NHS	New Haven School
OECD	Organisation for Economic Co-operation and Development
OGM	operational-level grievance mechanism
P3	public-private partnership
PCSR	political corporate social responsibility
RAS	Reported Actions towards Sustainability
SAFE	Simple Agreement for Future Equity
SBB	social benefit bond
SCC	Supreme Court of Canada
SCUS	Supreme Court of the United States
SIB	social impact bond
SOE	state-owned enterprise
SPV	special purpose vehicle
SRI	socially responsible investment
SSCM	sustainable supply chain management
TNC	transnational corporation
TRC	Truth and Reconciliation Commission
UNDRIP	United Nations Declaration on the Rights of Indigenous Peoples
UNIPCC	United Nations Intergovernmental Panel on Climate Change
UNSDGS	United Nations Sustainable Development Goals
UNWEP	United Nations Women's Empowerment Principles

CORPORATE LAW AND SUSTAINABILITY FROM THE NEXT GENERATION OF LAWYERS

For Kyle, Lucy, Skye, and Hannah

INTRODUCTION

The Millennial Generation and the Post-pandemic Future of Corporate Law and Sustainability

Carol Liao

REIMAGINING OUR POST-PANDEMIC FUTURE

This book began prior to the COVID-19 pandemic and goes to press as the World Health Organization records over 209 million confirmed cases of COVID-19 to date, including over 4.4 million deaths.[1] Vaccines are being distributed disproportionately around the world, with wealthy countries beginning to administer third boosters while half of the world remains unvaccinated,[2] "variants of concern" are causing global unease,[3] and the prospect of COVID-19 soon becoming an endemic disease seems to be eluding us. Our global society has adapted to a new normal and the long-term impacts on local, national, and international business sectors are still unknown, other than to say they will be profound.

At the onset of COVID-19 and the wave of unprecedented lockdowns across countries, the pandemic was described as a "portal"[4] and "The Great Reset" for humankind.[5] Now, with "no end in sight,"[6] COVID-19 is the "inequality virus"[7] and "a test of our systems, values, and humanity."[8] In the wake of this pandemic, our world is going to be redefined as the time before and the time after. Our understandings on the role of business and law in advancing environmental, social, and economic sustainability are going to be reformulated post-pandemic, whether we like it or not. The open-ended question is what that reformulation will entail.

Future pandemic risks are inseparable from climate change, as deforestation and biodiversity loss force animals to migrate out of their natural habitats, increasing infectious zoonotic disease risk in humans.[9] In 2019, the United Nations Intergovernmental Panel on Climate Change (UNIPCC) estimated that we have until the year 2030 to mitigate the most catastrophic effects of global warming, the effects of which are already being experienced.[10] In 2021, the UNIPCC updated its assessment, finding that temperatures are rising faster than anticipated, climate change is "widespread, rapid, and intensifying," and we must engage in transformational change across industries and institutions.[11] Beyond immediate environmental impacts, calls for authentic corporate sustainability and increased demands for social and racial justice are forcing fundamental shifts in how companies behave in the marketplace.[12] In a time of global climate strikes and extinction rebellions, a growing chorus of state leaders, institutional investors, and even bankers are issuing urgent warnings to businesses regarding their role in the age of the Anthropocene, our epoch in history where significant human-driven changes have impacted the structure and functioning of the Earth.[13] Corporate social responsibility (CSR) has traditionally been regarded as voluntary practices exercised within the purview of corporate discretion. Now, legal and regulatory frameworks are adapting in response to changing expectations and the saturated arena of CSR scholarship has found new grounding in the law.

Over a decade ago, Dirk Matten and Jeremy Moon described the difficult prospect of defining CSR, noting how CSR had become an "essentially contested concept" with relatively open rules of application and "an umbrella term overlapping with some, and being synonymous with other, conceptions of business-society relations."[14] They saw how CSR was increasingly becoming a dynamic phenomenon.[15] Fast forward to present day, and the CSR movement has fractured and reinvented itself around the globe, attempting to shed much of its baggage from critics of the movement[16] while being recast under a plethora of names – clean capitalism; stakeholder capitalism; green or eco-business; social enterprise; values-driven business; environmental, social, governance (ESG); triple bottom line; corporate purpose; and its most prominent transformations in academic scholarship under the fields of business and human rights (BHR), and corporate law and sustainability, to name a few. Beate Sjåfjell and Benjamin Richardson have noted weaknesses in CSR terminology, stating how "[t]he problematic nature of CSR in its voluntary form and the 'greenwashing' that is done under its guise are some of the reasons that one may be reticent about using the concept at all."[17] As CSR trends continue to propagate within the backdrop of looming climate catastrophe, corporate boards and executives need to be oriented to a new reality – that the integration of sustainability into business practices is increasingly becoming a legal obligation and not a choice. It is also an ethical obligation to our future generations.

The UNIPCC observes that one of the challenges in limiting global warming to no more than 1.5 degrees Celsius above pre-industrial levels is "the governance capacity of institutions to develop, implement and evaluate the changes needed within diverse and highly interlinked global social-ecological systems" and that "[p]olicy arenas, governance structures and robust institutions are key enabling conditions for transformative climate action."[18] CSR as a field is being reframed as risk management, and regulatory and legislative reforms are occurring in real time in response to ever-increasing public consciousness of climate change and other social and environmental risks. To date, over 1,850 climate lawsuits have been lodged around the world.[19] Increased BHR litigation is being levelled against corporations, including specifically towards large multinational corporations operating outside their central office home states.[20] The growing tide of lawsuits against governments and corporations has led to ripple effects in legislation and industry standards. The Canadian federal government's endorsement of the Task Force on Climate-related Financial Disclosures is but one example of the accelerating trajectory in corporate accountability within legal and regulatory frameworks.[21] As sustainable business practices increasingly shift from voluntary activities to mandatory obligations from corporations, there must be active scholarly and community engagement in this transition.

The new field of corporate law and sustainability is gaining important footholds within academic scholarship. Sjåfjell and Christopher Bruner note how in 2020, "the sustainability-related study of corporate law and corporate governance is firmly established as a field ... [and] is one of the most dynamic and significant areas of law and policy in light of the convergence of crises that we as a global society face."[22] Sjåfjell provides a recent and holistic definition of corporate sustainability:

> When business in aggregate creates value in a manner that is (a) *environmentally* sustainable in that it ensures the long-term stability and resilience of the ecosystems that support human life,

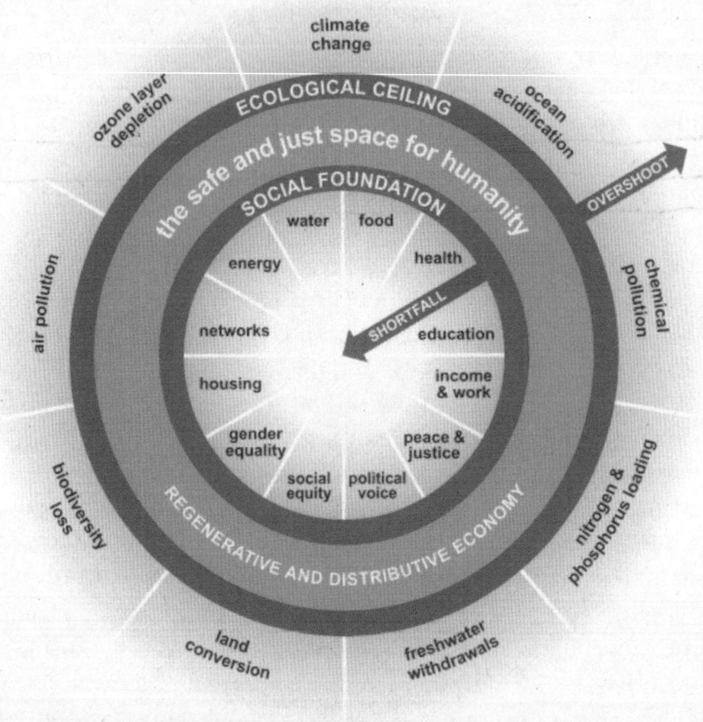

Figure 0.1 The planetary boundaries and social foundations. Kate Raworth, *Doughnut Economics: Seven Ways to Think Like a 21st Century Economist* (2017).

> (b) *socially* sustainable in that it facilitates the respect and promotion of human rights and of good governance, and
> (c) *economically* sustainable in that it satisfies the economic needs necessary for stable and resilient societies.[23]

In combination with growing movements in social finance and the rapid spread of ESG and responsible investment principles, impact investing, etc., we are seeing the development of new theoretical and methodological approaches that undergird this dynamic field of law.

The notable shift in academic dialogue has been to identify and recognize the "business case" perspective of CSR as a path-dependent and "weak" form of sustainability that is insufficient in addressing the foundational changes needed to meet climate targets by 2030.[24] Thus, references in this book to CSR are in reference to that definition, as an outdated and essentially contested concept in desperate need of improvement.

In the 2020 state-of-the-art collection, *The Cambridge Handbook for Corporate Law, Corporate Governance and Sustainability*, sixty corporate law scholars around the world prescribed to a new and integrated way of understanding corporate sustainability employing new economic approaches to act as a compass for human progress (see figure 0.1). In Kate Raworth's doughnut economics model,[25] our planet's environmental ceiling consists of nine planetary boundaries advanced by Johan Rockström et al., beyond which lie unacceptable environmental degradation and potential tipping points in Earth systems.[26] The twelve dimensions of the social foundation are derived from internationally agreed minimum social standards, as identified by the world's governments in the United Nations Sustainable Development Goals (UNSDGs) in 2015.[27] Between social and planetary boundaries lies an environmentally safe and socially just space in which all of humanity can thrive. Sjåfjell and Bruner note how real corporate sustainability "must ultimately involve corporate legal and governance structures promoting practices that contribute to and, at a minimum, do not undermine society's potential for achieving the overarching of sustainability," which they define as "securing the social foundation for humanity everywhere, now and in the future, within the ecological limits of our planet."[28] Raworth's new economic approach has gained the attention of the United Nations General Assembly and has forced a reconsideration of past economic theories of growth, requiring traditionally "free" assets of natural resources to be viewed by corporations as assets within a circular economy, meaning a regenerative system where product lifecycles operate in a closed loop.[29]

Doughnut economics is still an embryonic approach and, in many ways, unfinished; further development of Raworth's model is necessary in the context of corporate law and governance. Raworth's model and challenge to growth-focused economics has been particularly relevant in the onset of COVID-19 and the related lockdowns and stay-at-home orders that have circulated unevenly around the world.[30] Energy consumption and greenhouse gas emissions will rebound to pre-COVID-19 levels when economies gradually re-open, as already demonstrated by rebounds in countries that have loosened economic, factory, and mobility restrictions.[31] Negative environmental effects have also been observed and exacerbated during the crisis, such as increases in residential emissions and energy usage, increases in organic waste from lowered agricultural exports, increases in businesses reverting to wasteful practices, and the weakening of certain state environmental regulations.[32] The next few decades mark a critical period in domestic and international legal and regulatory reform as legislators and industry set their sights on a post-pandemic world.

THE NEXT GENERATION OF LAWYERS

The millennial generation, described as those born between 1981–96 and "the first generation to come of age in the new millennium," with Generation Z following closely behind, have grown up in an era far different from previous generations.[33] Environmental and social crises have defined much of their adult lives, along with the recurrent message that time is of the essence.[34] Amid populist nationalism and mounting geopolitical risks, the growing anxiety held by millennials regarding the fate of the world is well documented.[35] The COVID-19 pandemic is now also permanently etched into their adult lives.

In the Anthropocene, we are seeing an intergenerational moral storm: future generations will bear the greatest share of the burden created by climate change and entrenched social inequities but they are not the ones currently in positions of significant power to make impactful or transformative decisions about it.[36] This book aims to give voice to a group of young lawyers offering new and critical perspectives on the burgeoning field of corporate law and sustainability. As planetary problems have intergenerational effects, the solutions and paths forward must also include intergenerational voices.[37] Millennials are rising in power at a critical juncture in the Earth's climate history, and their perspectives on business and law stand apart from those who have been trained under traditional, and often relatively narrower, views of what constitutes change. The chapters in this book are presented from the angle of those who will be on the cusp of power too late in our planetary tipping points. They will most likely hold senior positions in the workforce after 2030; yet the short window of time to radically reduce emissions and significantly limit global warming will invariably be closed by then.[38] Legal scholarship should amplify voices from the millennial generation now, not a decade from now.

As they come of age during a time of environmental, social, and economic upheaval, millennials are often perceived as having a stronger connection and involvement with social issues. Notably, this connection presents itself in consumer and employment practices, as millennials have reportedly placed higher value on sustainable activities.[39] Studies show that this generation, dubbed as "civic-minded," widely believe that companies have a responsibility to contribute positively to society.[40] This belief in the importance of social responsibility has been recorded as notably higher than previous generations and presents itself through increased rates of volunteering, increased likelihood to pay more for sustainable products, and a high willingness to either reward or punish companies based on their contributions to society.[41] For instance, a 2017 study on CSR reported that 91 per cent of millennials surveyed were willing to support organizations that employed CSR practices.[42] Despite a higher propensity to value sustainable initiatives, it is important to note that the millennial generation is not prepared to accept any version of CSR as beneficial and often view CSR activities as simply an exercise in improving companies' reputations. A survey conducted by Deloitte in 2018 reported that millennials are becoming increasingly concerned with the true motivations underlying a corporation's CSR initiatives.[43] Specifically, initiatives based largely in resource provisions or monetary donations are viewed with more skepticism as they are perceived as business advancement strategies, rather than true commitments to society.[44] Recognizing, of course, that millennials do not share a set of identical beliefs and there is diversity across a generation, millennials have tended to develop more meaningful connections to the topic of climate change and sustainability, particularly given their investment in the future, and, overall, value climate and sustainability issues more significantly than previous generations.

The role of young lawyers in advancing social change and transformation is another aspect to consider in this new field of corporate law. Where access to justice concerns abound, lawyers in many ways are the keepers – and gatekeepers – of the law. Whether ideal or not, lawyers are participants, influencers, and powerful agents in the creation, interpretation, and application of the law. Yet by virtue of their training, lawyers – and perhaps corporate lawyers in particular – are taught to be risk-averse. Often, they are the ones advising against innovation and change, favouring tradition, precedents, and caution.[45] That must change in this climate emergency. The range of essays within this collection challenge the status quo in our legal profession across several pressing topics in the field of corporate law and sustainability, examining cutting-edge issues with a level of thoughtfulness and urgency that demands attention from policymakers and scholars alike.

This collection of voices from lawyers of the millennial generation is excerpted from a period when it is not too late for theories and ideologies to be redrawn. This collection offers a diverse but harmonious range of voices calling for bona fide corporate accountability within our legal and regulatory frameworks, infused with innovative new ideas and challenges to further the dialogue in corporate law and sustainability. The power of new perspectives unburdened by tradition means the dynamism of environmental, social, and economic sustainability will continue to evolve as it intersects and melds with the law in the coming years. The imperative of including voices from the millennial generation across political and scholarly dialogues must be emphasized within our collective goal of limiting global warming to 1.5 degrees Celsius above pre-industrial levels. A multifaceted, complex problem requires multifaceted solutions, and, in the context of corporate law and governance, there is a great deal of work to be done.

Throughout the chapters, common threads of legitimacy, authenticity, and accountability are woven within the topics. The UNSDGs, which form the social foundation in Raworth's model and include ensuring human rights, enhancing gender equality and women's empowerment, building resilient infrastructure, promoting sustainable industrialization, fostering innovation, and creating sustainable consumption and production patterns – all the while operating within the environmental ceiling of our planetary boundaries – are thematic within these chapters. Part one, "Governing and Financing Responsible Business," begins with an exploration into the internal governance and financing mechanisms to actualize corporate sustainability within business practices. In chapter 1, Sherry Yu questions the paradox between corporations that implement CSR policies while simultaneously raising executive compensation and argues that legitimacy of the former and continued inflation of the latter cannot coexist. Blair Feltmate challenges the colonial business corporation model in chapter 2, proposing that the cooperative ownership structure is better aligned to provide Indigenous communities with social and economic benefits. Next, while gender diversity in corporate boardrooms is widely agreed upon as a good governance practice, why have years of supposed policies to improve gender representation on boards only produced incremental change? Oludolapo Makinde tackles that question in chapter 3, employing a comparative analysis across jurisdictions and assessing the arguments for and against soft and hard law quotas to examine the feasibility of mandatory quotas in solving the gender diversity problem. Finally, in chapter 4, Saul Wang presents an innovative potential solution to the problem of raising capital for social impact bonds by proposing a crowdfunding framework based on Morteza Farajian and Brian Ross's public-private partnership model.

Part two, "CSR as Risk Management in Industry Practice," analyzes the corporate law and sustainability discourse within the context of CSR and its role and usage as a risk management tool within specific industries. Here, the authors present case studies on companies that have implemented CSR policies within their industries and offer important insights on how corporations can be held accountable for their actions both locally and abroad. Asha Young provides an in-depth examination on the "Bell Let's Talk" mental health initiative spearheaded by Canada's largest telecommunications company in chapter 5, reflecting on the implications of changing risk registers beyond traditional legal mechanisms due to the onslaught of social media. In chapter 6, Megan Parisotto emphasizes the importance of responsible lobbying in today's political climate where the relationship between the fossil fuel industry and political parties is at the forefront, acknowledging that in the transition to a net-zero carbon economy, uncomfortable discussions on mitigating factors during this "in-between" period are still necessary. In chapter 7, Catherine L.H. Lee pointedly questions whether the alcohol industry can ever give rise to socially responsible corporations given the nature of the business and, using Matten and Moon's implicit-explicit CSR framework, offers policy recommendations relevant across controversial industries. Selena Chen then weighs in on the efficacy of CSR initiatives implemented by fast fashion retailers in their complex, cross-border supply chains in chapter 8, and finds that a transition from passive sustainability reporting to a proactive effective disclosure system is needed.

Part three, "Corporate Accountability and Regulation," extends the discourse on corporate law and sustainability into methods of ensuring corporate accountability and the development of regulatory approaches to address accountability, including in the global arena. In chapter 9, Bikaramjit S. Sandhu demonstrates how shareholder activism, traditionally a solely profit-focused tactic, is becoming a viable tool to pressure corporations toward integrating ESG policies into their infrastructure. Julie Liang provides a refreshing analysis of tax avoidance practices in chapter 10, suggesting that aggressive tax planning poses a social problem that should be addressed by authentic corporate sustainability approaches, and she offers proposals for how corporations and governments can work together to mitigate this problem. Erica Sandhu critically examines the role and responsibilities of the federal government's Canadian Ombudsperson for Responsible Enterprise (CORE) in chapter 11. She explores what is necessary for the CORE to be effective in addressing human rights abuses committed by Canadian corporations abroad, providing early lessons for state governments. Part three concludes with Cristina Borbely powerfully recounting the significant governance gap surrounding business and human rights abuses committed by transnational corporations in chapter 12, reflecting on how corporate accountability for human rights violations is not achieving the same progress as the recognition of discretionary CSR as an international norm.

The field of corporate law and sustainability is in its nascent years, but far more global in nature, and growing at a formidable pace in light of our environmental and social catastrophes. Our institutions and leaders must be challenged to do better, and corporations must be held accountable in preserving the planet on which we all reside, including addressing their role in perpetuating the deep social inequalities entrenched within our systems. Voluntary *and* regulatory action is necessary – it is a fictitious debate when these positions are viewed as dichotomous, as each informs the other and ultimately can raise the bar on legal, international, and customary standards. Yet regulatory capture,[46] failures in implementation, failures in oversight, and failures in upending the status quo make for an indeterminate planetary future. Too often those in positions of power who have caused institutional failures, or at least profoundly benefited from them, are also those purporting to provide solutions.[47] We make conscious decisions on whose voices are heard and whose interests are prioritized. Time will tell if long-held norms in corporate law and governance that favour existing power structures can be meaningfully transformed. This next decade for our planet, and the next decade in the field of corporate law and sustainability, is a profoundly important period. Let us ensure we are listening to those groups that will be most impacted by our failures.

NOTES

1 World Health Organization, "WHO Coronavirus (COVID-19) Dashboard," accessed 20 August 2021, https://covid19.who.int.

2 World Health Organization, "WHO Director-General's Opening Remarks at the Media Briefing on COVID-19," 4 August 2021, https://www.who.int/director-general/speeches/detail/who-director-general-s-opening-remarks-at-the-media-briefing-on-covid-4-august-2021; "The WHO is Right to Call a Temporary Halt to COVID Vaccine Boosters," *Nature,* 17 August 2021, https://www.nature.com/articles/d41586-021-02219-w.

3 Centers for Disease Control and Prevention, "Delta Variant: What We Know About the Science," 19 August 2021, https://www.cdc.gov/coronavirus/2019-ncov/variants/delta-variant.html; World Health Organization, "Tracking SARS-CoV-2 Variants," last modified 25 August 2021, https://www.who.int/en/activities/tracking-SARS-CoV-2-variants.

4 Arundhati Roy, "The Pandemic is a Portal," *Financial Times*, 3 April 2020, https://www.ft.com/content/10d8f5e8-74eb-11ea-95fe-fcd274e920ca.

5 World Economic Forum, "The Great Reset," 3 June 2020, https://www.weforum.org/great-reset.

6 William A. Haseltine, "COVID-19, No End in Sight," *Forbes,* 17 August 2021, https://www.forbes.com/sites/williamhaseltine/2021/08/17/covid-19-no-end-in-sight.

7 Zara Liaqat, "Why COVID-19 is an Inequality Virus," *Policy Options,* 30 April 2021, https://policyoptions.irpp.org/magazines/april-2021/why-covid-19-is-an-inequality-virus.

8 Michelle Bachelet and Filippo Grandi, "The Coronavirus Outbreak is a Test of our Systems, Values and Humanity," *The UN Refugee Agency,* 12 March 2020, https://www.unhcr.org/news/latest/2020/3/5e69eea54/coronavirus-outbreak-test-systems-values-humanity.html.

9 Centre for Climate, Health and the Global Environment and Harvard T.H. Chan School of Public Health, "Coronavirus, Climate Change, and the Environment," last modified 6 July 2020, https://www.hsph.harvard.edu/c-change/subtopics/coronavirus-and-climate-change.

10 Valérie Masson-Delmotte et al., eds., "Global Warming of 1.5° C," Intergovernmental Panel on Climate Change, 2019, https://www.ipcc.ch/sr15/.

11 IPCC, "Climate Change Widespread, Rapid, and Intensifying," 9 August 2021, https://www.ipcc.ch/2021/08/09/ar6-wg1-20210809-pr; IPCC, "AR6 Climate Change 2021: The Physical Science Basis," accessed 20 August 2021, https://www.ipcc.ch/report/ar6/wg1.

12 David A. Lubin and Daniel C. Esty, "The Sustainability Imperative," *Harvard Business Review* 88, no. 5 (May 2010): 42–50.
13 Masson-Delmotte et al., "Global Warming," 543.
14 Dirk Matten and Jeremy Moon, "'Implicit' and 'Explicit' CSR: A Conceptual Framework for a Comparative Understanding of Corporate Social Responsibility," *Academy of Management Review* 33, no. 2 (April 2008): 3.
15 Ibid.
16 See e.g. S. Prakash Sethi, "Dimensions of Corporate Social Performance: An Analytical Framework," *California Management Review* 17, no. 3 (Spring 1975): 58.
17 Beate Sjåfjell and Benjamin J. Richardson, eds., *Company Law and Sustainability: Legal Barriers and Opportunities* (Cambridge University Press, 2015), 315.
18 Masson-Delmotte et al., "Global Warming," 71.
19 "About," Climate Change Litigation Database, last modified 17 September 2020, http://climatecasechart.com/about.
20 Andrea Hearon, Maysa Zorob, and Stephanie Regalia, "Corporate Human Rights Litigation: Trends from 200 Seminal Lawsuits," *Business & Human Rights Resource Centre*, 8 December 2020, https://www.business-humanrights.org/en/blog/corporate-human-rights-litigation-trends-from-200-seminal-lawsuits.
21 Task Force on Climate-related Financial Disclosures, last modified 20 July 2021, https://www.fsb-tcfd.org.
22 Beate Sjåfjell and Christopher M. Bruner, eds., *The Cambridge Handbook of Corporate Law, Corporate Governance and Sustainability* (Cambridge: Cambridge University Press, 2020), 3.
23 Beate Sjåfjell, "When the Solution Becomes the Problem: The Triple Failure of Corporate Governance Codes," SSRN, University of Oslo Faculty of Law Legal Studies, 24 August 2016, 28.
24 Sjåfjell and Bruner, *Cambridge Handbook*, 7.
25 Kate Raworth, *Doughnut Economics: Seven Ways to Think Like a 21st Century Economist* (Vermont: Chelsea Green Publishing, 2017).
26 Johan Rockström et al., "Planetary Boundaries: Exploring the Safe Operating Space for Humanity," *Ecology and Society* 14, no. 2 (November 2009): 32, http://www.ecologyandsociety.org/vol14/iss2/art32.
27 United Nations Sustainable Development Goals, "17 Goals to Transform Our World," 13 August 2021, https://www.un.org/sustainabledevelopment.
28 Sjåfjell and Bruner, *Cambridge Handbook*, 4, xxiii.
29 European Commission, "Closing the Loop, An EU Action Plan for the Circular Economy," 12 February 2015, https://eur-lex.europa.eu/legal-content/EN/TXT/?uri=CELEX:52015DC0614.

30 Dieter Helm, "The Environmental Impacts of the Coronavirus," *Environmental and Resource Economics* 76, no. 1 (May 2020): 21–38.
31 Manuel A. Zambrano-Monserrate, María Alejandra Ruano and Luis Sanchez-Alcalde, "Indirect Effects of COVID-19 on the Environment," *Science of the Total Environment* 728, no. 1 (August 2020): 1–4.
32 Loujain Kurdi, "COVID-19, Climate & Environment: The Answers to Your Questions," *Greenpeace*, 29 March 2020, https://www.greenpeace.org/canada/en/story/30174/covid-19-climate-environment-the-answers-to-your-questions; UN Environment Programmed, "Record Global Carbon Dioxide Concentrations Despite COVID-19 Crisis," 11 May 2020, https://www.unep.org/news-and-stories/story/record-global-carbon-dioxide-concentrations-despite-covid-19-crisis.
33 Michael Dimock, "Defining Generations: Where Millennials End and Generation Z Begins," *Pew Research Center*, 17 January 2019, https://www.pewresearch.org/fact-tank/2019/01/17/where-millennials-end-and-generation-z-begins.
34 Joelle Thomas, "Climate Change and Millennials: The Future Is in Our Hands," *Scientific American*, 8 December 2015, https://blogs.scientificamerican.com/guest-blog/climate-change-and-millennials-the-future-is-in-our-hands.
35 Deloitte, "The Deloitte Global Millennial Survey 2019," 20 May 2019, https://www2.deloitte.com/content/dam/Deloitte/global/Documents/About-Deloitte/deloitte-2019-millennial-survey.pdf.
36 Stephen M. Gardiner, "A Perfect Moral Storm: Climate Change, Intergenerational Ethics and the Problem of Moral Corruption," *Environmental Values* 15, no. 3 (August 2006): 397–413.
37 Leah Davidson, "Intergenerational Commitments Are Critical to Protecting Future Climate Leaders," *OpenGlobalRights*, 2 November 2017, https://www.openglobalrights.org/intergenerational-commitments-are-critical-to%20protecting-future-climate-leaders.
38 Masson-Delmotte et al., "Global Warming," c. 3.
39 Olivia Johnson and Veena Chattaraman, "Conceptualization and Measurement of Millennial's Social Signaling and Self-Signaling for Socially Responsible Consumption," *Journal of Consumer Behaviour* 18, no. 1 (November 2018): 32–42.
40 Teresa McGlone, Judith Winters Spain, and Vernon McGlone, "Corporate Social Responsibility and the Millennials," *Journal of Education for Business* 86, no. 4 (April 2011): 195–200.
41 Ibid., 196.
42 Seoyeon Kim and Lucinda Austin, "Effects of CSR Initiatives on Company Perceptions Among Millennial and Gen Z Consumers,"

Corporate Communications: An International Journal 25, no. 2, (November 2019): 299–317.

43 Tashfeen Ahmad, "Corporate Social Responsibility: A Value-Creation Strategy to Engage Millennials," *Strategic Direction* 35, no. 7 (May 2019): 5–8.

44 Ibid.; Kim and Austin, "Effects of CSR," 300.

45 Jordan Furlong, "Why Lawyers Don't Innovate," *Law21,* 20 August 2013, https://www.law21.ca/2013/08/why-lawyers-dont-innovate.

46 George J. Stigler, "The Theory of Economic Regulation," *Bell Journal of Economics and Management Science* 2, no. 1 (Spring 1971): 3–21; for modern examples see David G. Tarr, *The Political, Regulatory and Market Failures That Caused the US Financial Crisis* (World Bank, 2010), https://elibrary.worldbank.org/doi/abs/10.1596/1813-9450-5324.

47 Joel Bakan, *The New Corporation: How "Good" Corporations are Bad for Democracy* (London: Allen Lane, 2020).

PART ONE

Governing and Financing Responsible Business

I

Reconciling Corporate Social Responsibility with Executive Compensation

Sherry Yu

Across North America, chief executive officers (CEOs) and other top executives of leading corporations exist in a different subset of the economy, sheltered from financial hardships that befall the average worker throughout the lifetime of their career. In 2017, the Canadian Centre for Policy Alternatives remarked on how, "[o]ver the past 10 years, compensation for Canada's 100 highest paid CEOs has proven to be resilient in nature, weathering all kinds of economic storms, and continually breaking new highs."[1] A review of CEO compensation in Canada between 1998 and 2015 shows an increase in average earnings of 178 per cent for the country's top one hundred CEOs.[2] At the same time, the average Canadian wage has not only failed to come even close to that of the corporate top one hundred, but the gap is widening.[3]

More recently, a 2018 report on the same topic finds that Canadian CEOs continue to earn pre-2008 financial crisis levels of compensation; in a particularly sobering statistic, it calculates that the average Canadian top one hundred CEO will have made the average Canadian worker's entire salary by 10:57 AM on 2 January of that same year.[4] To put things in perspective, that year pay actually fell for the average Canadian worker after inflation was taken into account, but the country's top one hundred CEOs managed to beat the trend and enjoyed an average pay raise of 8 per cent.[5] In fact, in 2020, at the height of the unprecedented COVID-19 pandemic where the federal government was spending billions of dollars in support for workers, most of Canada's top CEOs received increased pay.[6] What is perhaps most disheartening about these facts is that the corporations behind them are the same voices advocating the loudest against measures to close the pay gap, such as raising the minimum wage and expanding the Canada Pension Plan.[7] Meanwhile, CEOs of these corporations are pulling in salaries averaging over CA$1 million with bonuses averaging double base pay, and for the richest CEOs, shares and stock options on top of everything.[8] In other words, excessive executive compensation is a problem for everyone because the income inequality represented by the growing wage gap "has been a consistent reminder that there is enormous wealth circulating through the economy – it is simply not making its way into the hands of the average worker."[9]

Before proceeding to discuss the implications of corporate social responsibility (CSR) for executive compensation, it is helpful to first contextualize this chapter needing to challenge the limitations of CSR as used by corporations. Many theories of CSR currently exist in academic scholarship, but the theory that holds the greatest relevance for the purposes of this chapter is that CSR should be striving for "good corporate citizenship"[10] and "strong" (meaning, actual) sustainability practices.[11] The rationale behind good corporate citizenship theory is that, since corporations are recognized under law as being separate legal personalities, the logical next step is to situate corporations in society as citizens next to natural persons, and with similar rights and duties.[12] Corporations, therefore, have responsibilities to other persons in society just as individuals do, and CSR policies may be viewed by some as one of the ways in which these responsibilities are carried out. The question then remains: are excessively high levels of executive compensation contrary to "good citizenship"?

The intuition, at least initially, is that corporations that allow executive compensation to rise to astronomical levels or award bonuses worth more than base salary will tend to have weaker CSR policies with lower rates of successful implementation. This intuition may be based on a variety of reasons, including the pragmatic fact of budget allocations being directed away from CSR initiatives or the tendency to attract risk-seeking managers who are only concerned with the bottom line (to the detriment of other stakeholders). This chapter is interested in a third potential reasoning: an inherent incompatibility of values underlying ethical business, on the one hand, and perceived overcompensation of high-level employees, on the other hand. Although the two often coexist in the form of lofty CSR goals alongside incredibly generous executive compensation programs, in theory, they should not; their coexistence likely points to a lack of integrity in the company's CSR policies. The reason this hypocrisy goes largely unchecked seems to be because the two business components – CSR and executive compensation – are not often looked at in tandem. CSR aspirations to date have primarily been concerned with accounting for the human and environmental waste incurred in the process of providing products and services to society. While it is obvious why such issues should have prompted the need for CSR and its various iterations, it no longer makes sense to limit the application of CSR principles to correcting only the externalities of doing business. The "corporate veil" serves not only to protect business individuals from unlimited liability but it also creates an artificial partition between a corporation's internal structures of corporate governance and its external policies of CSR and related matters, such that the two are generally viewed as being separate entities. This legal fiction, in turn, allows for inherent inconsistencies to develop between a corporation's corporate governance processes and its CSR targets, to the predictable end that the latter is frustrated. Excessive executive compensation is but one symptom of this disease.

This chapter will proceed as follows: section 1 of this chapter provides a brief overview of the existing literature on the relationship between CSR and executive compensation, and then examines the proxy statements of three top one hundred corporations in Canada for the philosophies underlying their executive compensation programs. Section 2 evaluates the strengths and weaknesses of three different mechanisms for control on unreasonable executive compensation. The chapter concludes in section 3 with calls for the greater integration of sustainable corporate governance practices as a response to rising levels of executive compensation and a reminder of the importance of legitimacy when using CSR-type policies as tools for change.

COMMONLY PROVIDED JUSTIFICATIONS FOR EXECUTIVE COMPENSATION LEVELS

In their 2013 study on the link between CSR and executive compensation, Patti Collett Miles and Grant Miles found that there is a significant correlation between perception of a company as a good corporate social performer and rate of executive compensation; companies that are rated as being good corporate social performers will generally have lower rates of executive compensation than companies that are not.[13] They interpret this finding as suggesting that good corporate social performers are more likely to keep executive compensation in check, and note that it should not be interpreted as good corporate citizenship being punished because the average level of compensation in their sample of US companies was around US$8 million even by conservative computations.[14] On the latter point, researchers acknowledge that executives rewarded at such high levels of compensation likely produce diminishing marginal returns on additional pay with respect to motivation – more pay does not necessarily generate more incentive. This point is important because when executive compensation reaches levels where the marginal rate of return to corporations (and arguably marginal utility to executives as well) begins to diminish, it becomes harder to justify continuing or even increasing pay at those levels by citing financial performance benefits, which is the oft-cited rationale.

It is worthwhile to note that Miles and Miles' study also looked at the perception of good social performance, ultimately concluding that pay may have been sacrificed at those companies with high corporate social performance (CSP) ratings for the "intangible rewards of being seen as good corporate citizens and treating all employees fairly."[15] While perception does not necessarily serve as an accurate proxy for reality, in this case, where executive compensation was indeed kept in check, it may not be useful to parse motivations. Ye Cai, Hoje Jo, and Carrie Pan came to a similar conclusion in their 2011 study, finding that both CSR and employee relations are inversely associated with CEO compensation.[16] Most notably, they concluded that "the CSR-executive compensation nexus of socially responsible firms is indeed different from that of socially irresponsible firms, suggesting that the top management of the US socially responsible firms, on average, care more for their employees and have better self-control rather than follow the path of greed."[17] More recently, Claude Francoeur et al. found that "environmentally friendly" companies tend to pay their CEOs less total compensation, of which incentive-based compensation (i.e., shares and stock options) form a smaller percentage.[18] These studies all point to a clear correlation between various indicators of CSR performance and levels of executive compensation – high levels of the latter are generally incompatible with the former.

Another grouping of studies on the topic looks at the effects of corporate governance structures underlying executive compensation decisions on CSR, and vice versa. Interestingly, Ming Jian and Kin-Wai Lee found in their 2015 study that the relationship between CSR investment and CEO compensation is consistent with the value destruction hypothesis, such that total CSR investment by a CEO cannibalizes total compensation levels and the effect is more pronounced at companies with stronger corporate governance.[19] On a superficial level, these results appear to contradict the conclusion reached by Miles and Miles that the negative correlation between perception of good corporate social performance and rate of executive compensation is not indicative of punishment. However, once the researchers broke down total CSR investment into normal and abnormal levels, they found that, in fact, normal levels of CSR investment are rewarded while abnormal levels are penalized.[20] This effect is again more pronounced in companies with stronger corporate governance,[21] leading to the conclusion that a discerning board of directors will tolerate and even encourage CSR investment up to a point, but that they still view CSR as a means to an end – presumably the bottom line. Similarly, Karen Maas found that even when CSP targets are incorporated into decisions about executive compensation, they do not necessarily result in better CSP.[22] Importantly, she notes that:

> Based on these findings, we must face the possibility that the use of CSP targets in executive compensation and CSP improvement might not be related (or might be only weakly related) in firms, even when these firms claim an explicit linkage between these two variables. The notion of a limited effective relationship is an important one as it contributes to the ongoing quest whether CSP targets are a sign of corporate responsibility or just window dressing ... This finding is consistent with the logic that certain governance mechanisms are a response to external pressures ... instead of an attempt to improve performance. A similar situation might well prevail in the context of CSP links to top executive compensation. Faced with pressures for accountability and legitimacy in a world where CSR issues are increasingly important, with specific pressures for compensation linkages from activist shareholders, social investing funds, and other stakeholders, compensation committees might respond by explicitly using CSP targets in executive compensation and rest satisfied with this initiative.[23]

The results of these studies can be interpreted to support the proposition that it is not the strength of corporate governance that requires work, but the values and culture informing it – these requisite "right" conditions likely already exist in Miles and Miles' good corporate social performers. Walid Ben-Amar, Nadia Smaili, and Eustache Ebondo Wa Mandzila suggest in their 2014 study that the existence of a positive relationship between quality of executive compensation disclosures and a company's social responsibility empowers stakeholders to demand greater transparency, thereby limiting rent-seeking behaviour from managers.[24] However, this link is problematic because it assumes a causal relationship where one has not been proven; it is more likely the case that transparency and social responsibility are both determined by an exogenous variable than that improved transparency causes greater social responsibility.

To get a snapshot of the justifications commonly given by corporations for their executive compensation programs, the most recent proxy statements of three top one hundred corporations in Canada will be used as a sample: Bausch Health Companies Inc.[25] (formerly Valeant Pharmaceuticals) (Bausch), Rogers Communications Inc.[26] (Rogers), and Canadian Pacific Railway Limited (CPR).[27] Note that Bausch and CPR provide for say-on-pay voting while Rogers does not, and all three companies benchmark their executive compensation programs against a peer group. In the section of the proxy statement that describes the company's compensation philosophy, Bausch states, "[o]ur compensation program is intended to link executive compensation to long-term business [meaning, financial] performance, while providing compensation opportunities that are competitive as compared to our peers and align the interests of our executives with those of our shareholders."[28] Similarly, Rogers "fosters a 'pay-for-performance' culture by placing strong emphasis on incentive compensation for its executives"[29] and cites attracting talent in a competitive environment as well as aligning management's interests with those of shareholders.[30] CPR asserts a belief in "paying for performance" and "aligning management's interests with those of our shareholders."[31] Although CPR's proxy statement does not explicitly reference the market in its compensation objectives section, as mentioned above, the company also uses peer group benchmarks to set its executive compensation levels.[32] These statements from the three companies can be distilled down to three main underlying values: (1) pay-for-performance; (2) stay on top of market competition; and (3) mitigate agency costs.

It is highly doubtful whether executive compensation is truly proportionate to financial performance in most cases or even whether the pay structure is an effective incentive for boosting financial performance. Despite more than a decade of studies challenging – and in some cases, disproving – the pay-for-performance paradigm, it remains the most oft-cited reason for why executives take home millions in compensation every year. Expanding on this point, Bausch explains that its promotion of pay-for-performance rests upon a belief that "incentive pay appropriately rewards executives for their contribution to our overall performance"[33] – a sentiment that the other two companies echo. As others have argued, the trend towards using share-based compensation to reward past financial performance can actually be seen as contradictory to the principle of pay-for-performance because stock markets are forward-looking and largely outside of executives' control.[34] The goal of being competitive with the market is equally fallacious because it assumes that market value is equivalent to true value; in the case of executive compensation where market value has become grossly inflated, that is certainly not true and assuming as such only serves to entrench a problematic status quo. In terms of mitigating agency costs, it is correct, in theory, that principal-agent concerns inherent in a corporate structure can be moderated by giving executives a stake in the company; however, it is questionable whether this is an adequate justification for excessive executive compensation. The concept of using shares to align management and shareholders' interests is reasonable, but the magnitude of the incentive pay being awarded to executives is disproportionate to this reasoning. Finally, while it is promising that Bausch and CPR have voluntarily signed on to say-on-pay voting, the important caveat is that these votes are non-binding – as discussed further in the next section.

MECHANISMS FOR CONTROL

The widening pay gap between senior executives and the average worker remains both an indicator of income inequality in North America, as well as elsewhere around the world, and one of its contributing factors. Simply mandating a cap on executive compensation and similar measures is likely to yield results comparable to those of other attempts to regulate business practices: superficial compliance and exploitation of loopholes. In the US, corporations are required to make certain disclosures to the US Securities Exchange Commission regarding executive compensation under s. 953 of the *Dodd-Frank Wall Street Reform and Consumer Protection Act* (*Dodd-Frank Act*)[35] – most notably, a disclosure of CEO-to-median worker compensation. The idea behind the disclosure requirement is to exert public pressure upon corporations to reduce the pay gap between the CEO and the workers. However, a corporation that wishes to reduce the CEO-to-median ratio can simply outsource work and increase part-time positions.[36] It then follows that a legislated disclosure or cap on CEO-to-median ratio may result in reduced workers' pay or full-time job opportunities instead of reducing CEO pay, which is exactly the opposite of what the CEO salary cap was intended to achieve. No such disclosure requirement exists in Canada, but s. 953 seems to have done little to curb the even higher levels of executive compensation in the US since the *Dodd-Frank Act*'s enactment in 2010.[37] Greater disclosure, by way of transparency or insight or otherwise, is thus an unpromising solution. The real problem is not so much with poor regulation as it is with problematic corporate mentalities. As long as our primary focus in doing business continues to be finding the path of least resistance to the bottom line (single or otherwise), compliance issues will remain merely obstacles along the path. Without more meaningful disruption, the market for executive compensation will continue to perpetuate the inflated status quo. As the 2018 Canadian Centre for Policy Alternatives report on executive compensation in Canada notes: "[i]t is unlikely that any one measure – to increase transparency in executive compensation, for example, or make minor changes to tax measures – will curtail overall growth in CEO pay."[38] This next section will look at three potential mechanisms for control on growth of executive compensation: (1) pay-for-performance; (2) shareholder activism (say-on-pay); and (3) a minimum "living" wage.

Pay-for-Performance

As discussed earlier, executive compensation is commonly justified by tying pay to performance:

> For years, apologists for highly paid CEOs have peddled the line that their pay is a reward for good performance ... The notion that modern executive compensation systems are tied to corporate performance is as resilient in the face of evidence to the contrary as the compensation itself is to everything from economic recession to political pressure to shareholder activism.[39]

If calibrated appropriately, financial performance metrics, in theory, could be used to limit and standardize executive compensation. In fact, according to Esra Burak's 2018 study, people can and do express displeasure with high CEO pay while at the same time approving of performance-based rewards; his findings indicate that "the slope of the pay and performance function may be at issue rather than a hard limit on pay."[40] Nevertheless, the practical reality is that the current pay-for-performance model used by corporations in designing executive compensation programs does not accord with the rest of society's idea of proportionality, and so the appropriate slope of the pay and performance function is not struck. This failure is due in large part to the increasingly popular practice of paying executives primarily with company stock, which, as previously alluded to, is not the best performance metric upon which to base compensation levels. Particularly with stock options, executives who are given this form of incentive pay will be tempted to prioritize short-term volatility of share prices over long-term growth of the company, which ironically is also counterproductive to the agency theory function of incentive pay.[41] Also problematic is the fact that a significant percentage of so-called performance pay may in fact be completely divorced from performance metrics, as many compensation contracts guarantee at least 80 per cent of "performance" pay regardless of how the company's stock performs.[42]

A particularly big disconnect appears in the performance pay plot when the gender pay gap is considered. Already, women constitute only 4 per cent of Canadian CEOs and 10 per cent of senior executives; even after making the cut into the male-dominated C-suite, women make CA$0.68 on the dollar relative to their male colleagues.[43] The gender pay gap at the executive level is largely driven by disparities in incentive pay, but as this is occurring within the same company facing the same share prices, the performance argument comes up short. Not only does excessive executive compensation oppress other stakeholders, but also it can be discriminatory towards the people who receive it – both effects are clearly contrary to CSR ethics.

Other studies conducted on pay-for-performance include Kiridaran Kanagaretnam's empirical evidence that even financially stagnant companies pay their CEOs with stock options and that pay-performance sensitivity for these companies is predictably low.[44] In addition, Michael Cooper, Husevin Gulen, and Raghavendra Rau concluded from their findings that "CEOs who accept high long-term incentive pay are, on average, overconfident and engage in value destroying activities that result in lower future operating performance and stock returns."[45] Results from these studies tend to challenge the integrity of the pay-for-performance justification, both as a legitimate motivating factor behind executive compensation decisions and as an effective incentive to align corporate interests. By contrast, Scott Wallsten advances the argument that, pursuant to agency theory, an efficient compensation program should rightly incentivize CEOs to take risks while insulating them from unintended negative effects on share price.[46] Assuming this logic is valid, pay-performance sensitivity analyses should, therefore, be adjusted to allow for this insulation.[47] The counter argument to this, of course, would be that agency theory alone cannot be enough to justify the gross inequalities brought about by rising levels of executive compensation.

Shareholder Activism

In the US, publicly traded companies are required by s. 951 of the *Dodd-Frank Act* to grant shareholders an advisory vote on executive compensation programs, known as say-on-pay. Again, no such mandate exists in Canada. Nevertheless, many Canadian companies have voluntarily elected to provide for say-on-pay at their annual general meetings; by 2013, over 120 companies had adopted say-on-pay voting and the Canadian Coalition for Good Governance has suggested the adoption of an annual vote by all boards.[48] The idea that shareholder activism can be utilized to constrain excessive executive compensation is very promising and certainly a step in the right direction, but it is subject to a number of limitations, the most obvious of which is the non-binding nature of say-on-pay votes. The hope, of course, is that in today's age of globalization and powerful media, companies will need little more incentive than the potential for public shaming to change problematic practices as the public can often exert greater pressure than even a contractual promise. However, the strength of this assumption can vary across industries and the assumption itself runs into problems as well: are shareholders an appropriate proxy for the public, and how activist are shareholders, anyway?[49] Several studies have been conducted to evaluate the efficacy of say-on-pay. As say-on-pay voting has been mandatory in the US since the *Dodd-Frank Act*'s enactment in 2010, this chapter will look at the issue primarily in the US context.

In the first few years after say-on-pay became the law in 2010, researchers and industry alike were optimistic about its potential to disrupt the executive compensation paradigm. Steven Balsam et al. found that in the period leading up to the first say-on-pay vote, affected companies reduced executive compensation ahead of the vote in hopes of securing a higher approval rate.[50] They noted that the reduction was greater in companies that had previously overpaid their CEOs and that a noticeable shift was made towards greater use of performance-based compensation.[51] For the first two years of say-on-pay voting, Marinilka B. Kimbro and Danielle Xu presented evidence in support of the proposition that, despite the advisory nature of the vote, shareholders did in fact vote disapprovingly of excessive CEO compensation and that boards responded accordingly.[52] In terms of the effects of a negative voting outcome, it was found that the market-to-book value ratio was significantly lower for companies that failed say-on-pay votes[53] and that higher CEO pay-performance sensitivity was correlated with positive voting outcomes.[54] Particularly encouraging is the finding that, for both director and say-on-pay voting,

> CSR strengths are positively associated with shareholder support for both director nominees and for executive compensation ... Overall, these results indicate that shareholders may view CSR performance favorably and may be more supportive of boards and management when a company has stronger CSR performance.[55]

Generally, the prospects for say-on-pay voting in the US were looking good in the first few years of the 2010s; the assumption that companies would take these votes seriously was holding true and there was evidence that shareholders were voting based at least in part on CSR considerations.[56]

Unfortunately, a more recent empirical study by Thomas Hemphill conducted over a five-year period indicates that shareholders are not as "activist" as we believe them to be regarding say-on-pay, and, in fact, they do not share the general public's opinion about executives being overcompensated.[57] Hemphill acknowledges the powerful potential of say-on-pay voting as a mechanism for control but is ultimately forced to come to the conclusion that shareholders as a whole are satisfied with executive compensation programs – since 2011, shareholders have approved these programs at an approval rate of 92 per cent.[58] These results are certainly disheartening, but also unsurprising given the conspicuous lack of significant downward pressures on executive compensation in the US. In the UK context, it was also found that "in cases of excessive CEO pay, a remuneration report that is obscurely written is associated with lower say-on-pay voting dissent."[59] The intentional use of obfuscation is, therefore, another concern that should not be overlooked in implementing say-on-pay voting. Of course, different institutional contexts means that the results of these studies may not necessarily hold true in Canada, but lessons from other countries' experiences are nonetheless instructive.

Minimum "Living" Wage

A final and radical potential mechanism for control, one that is in line with CSR principles of good corporate citizenship and sustainability, is the concept of a minimum living wage for all workers. In 2015, the CEO of Gravity Payments, Inc., a Seattle-based credit card processing company, announced that he would be imposing a salary floor of US$70,000 for every one of the company's employees, and that he would be cutting his own salary from US$1 million down to US$70,000 in order to help fund the initiative.[60] In order to correct what he had come to realize was an injustice, Dan Price took it upon himself to adjust his own executive compensation program and use the freed up funds to invest in activities geared towards the company's long-term growth – cultivating a strong workforce and inspiring public confidence. Of course, along with the outpouring of public support, he received some backlash and encountered logistical problems as well: some employees quit, new people had to be hired to handle the sudden influx of inquiries into the company, and his brother/co-founder sued him for lack of consultation on decisions.[61] Despite the setbacks, Gravity Payments has flourished since 2015, doubling revenues and pursuing steady organic growth.[62]

However, this one success story of CSR-inspired corporate governance includes several limitations for broader implementation. For one, the context here is unique in that this is a family-run, privately held company of which Price is both CEO and co-founder. Agency costs were largely not an issue for Price, and it is highly questionable whether such a move would be appropriate for public companies with dispersed ownership and more complicated corporate governance structures. Price acknowledges these doubts as well; his minimum wage idea may not work across all industries and it is likely not scalable everywhere to the same degree due, in part, to his first-mover advantage.[63] But that is not to say that something similar could never be achieved under other circumstances. The key lesson that should be gleaned from the example of Gravity Payments is that disrupting the status quo is not only possible but also necessary and doing so will require a sustainability-oriented business mindset.

CONCLUSION: INTEGRATION OF SUSTAINABILITY AND CORPORATE GOVERNANCE

Even with the rise in popularity of CSR and the emergence of increasingly comprehensive disclosure requirements across all industries, few gains have been achieved in the way of real change in areas of income inequality, accountability, and sustainability. In this context, CSR and corporate governance should not be seen as two distinct concepts but as two gears from the same machine, the function of which is to facilitate the long overdue integration of business and ethics. CSR as a collection of (largely aspirational) policies and programs has failed to achieve this integration because it offers band-aid solutions to what is a systemic disorder – the idea that the internal structuring of corporations is a purely business matter and, therefore, immune to scrutiny for soft issues such as social responsibility. Instead of treating corporate governance as a series of mechanisms and controls and CSR as a collection of policies and programs, there should be a rethinking of both such that the latter is a set of guidelines and principles that the former is designed to embody and carry out. Only once the two have been harmonized and refocused on the same goal – socially responsible and sustainable business practices – can CSR and its iterations regain legitimacy in both practice and perception.

Throughout the discussion about the relationship between CSR and executive compensation, the notion of legitimacy has played an important validating role. Despite the literature establishing a clear link between the strength of a company's sustainable activities and its levels of executive compensation, not much has been done about this powerful insight. Immensely influential companies continue to perpetuate the old rhetoric of pay-for-performance against share-based metrics even though its underlying logic has been unravelled time and again. Several mechanisms for control have the potential to fix the broken market for executive compensation, but each also invariably runs into the enforcement problem created by the lack of a corporate governance structure designed according to sustainability principles. Real change requires changing mindsets not mechanisms, but as this can often be an insurmountable task, the truly practical solution may be to simply clean house and install into positions of power, individuals who already possess the right mindset attuned to ways of ethical business. Of course, this is not to downplay the difficulty of such an undertaking; dislodging the entrenched ruling class of the corporate world will be a long and arduous process, but it is probably our best – and only – shot at realizing an economy in which CSR is a reality and not just a buzzword.

NOTES

1 Hugh Mackenzie, "Throwing Money at the Problem: 10 Years of Executive Compensation," Canadian Centre for Policy Alternatives, 3 January 2017, 5, https://www.policyalternatives.ca/ceo2017.

2 Ibid.

3 For CEO versus average wage pay ratios 2008–15, see ibid., 10.

4 David Macdonald, "Climbing Up and Kicking Down: Executive Pay in Canada," Canadian Centre for Policy Alternatives, 2 January 2018, 4, https://www.policyalternatives.ca/publications/reports/climbing-and-kicking-down.

5 Ibid.

6 David Milstead, "Most of Canada's Top CEOs Saw Pay Climb as COVID-19 Hit Economy," *The Globe and Mail,* 5 July 2021, https://www.theglobeandmail.com/business/article-in-a-year-of-covid-19-ceos-pocket-more-pay.

7 Mackenzie, "Throwing Money."

8 Macdonald, "Climbing Up." A significant source of other compensation comes from "golden parachute" retirement packages; in 2016, six men alone took home CA$80.1 million of the CA$124.5 million paid out to the one hundred richest CEOs in the category of "other compensation" (11).

9 Ibid.

10 See Domènec Melé, "Corporate Social Responsibility Theories" in *The Oxford Handbook of Corporate Social Responsibility*, edited by Andrew Crane et al. (Oxford University Press 2008), 22–8.

11 Beate Sjåfjell and Christopher Bruner, *The Cambridge Handbook of Corporate Law, Corporate Governance and Sustainability* (Cambridge: Cambridge University Press, 2020), 3.

12 CSR theories focused on corporate social performance are also caught by this definition.

13 Patti Collett Miles and Grant Miles, "Corporate Social Responsibility and Executive Compensation: Exploring the Link," *Social Responsibility Journal* 9, no. 1 (March 2013): 86.

14 Ibid.

15 Ibid.

16 Ye Cai, Hoje Jo, and Carrie Pan, "Vice or Virtue? The Impact of Corporate Social Responsibility on Executive Compensation," *Journal of Business Ethics* 104, no. 2 (December 2011): 159.

17 Ibid., 171.

18 Claude Francoeur et al., "Green or Greed? An Alternative Look at CEO Compensation and Corporate Environmental Commitment," *Journal of Business Ethics* 140, no. 3 (February 2017): 439.

19 Ming Jian and Kin-Wai Lee, "CEO Compensation and Corporate Social Responsibility," *Journal of Multinational Financial Management* 29 (February 2015): 63.

20 Ibid.

21 Ibid.

22 Karen Maas, "Do Corporate Social Performance Targets in Executive Compensation Contribute to Corporate Social Performance?," *Journal of Business Ethics* 148, no. 3 (March 2018): 573.

23 Ibid., 581.

24 Walid Ben-Amar, Nadia Smaili, and Eustache Ebondo Wa Mandzila, "Corporate Social Responsibility and the Quality of Executive Compensation Disclosures," *Journal of Applied Business Research* 30, no. 2 (February 2014): 625, 630–1.

25 Bausch Health Companies Inc., "Corporate Social Responsibility Report," September 2018, https://www.bauschhealth.com/Portals/25/PDF/BauschHealth-CSR-Report.pdf.

26 Rogers Communications Inc., "2017 Corporate Social Responsibility Report," 2017, https://about.rogers.com/wp-content/uploads/2018/06/2017-Rogers-CSR-Report-en.pdf.

27 Canadian Pacific Railway Limited, "Corporate Sustainability Report 2016," 2016, https://www.cpr.ca/en/about-cp-site/Documents/cp-csr-2016.pdf.

28 Bausch Health Companies Inc., "Executive Compensation and Related Matters: Compensation Discussion and Analysis," Investis Digital, 18 March 2019), https://ir.bauschhealth.com/corporate-governance/sec-filings.

29 Rogers Communications Inc., "Notice of 2019 Annual General Shareholder Meeting and Information Circular," February 2019, 31,

https://1vjoxz2ghhkclty8c1wjich1-wpengine.netdna-ssl.com/wp-content/uploads/2019/02/Circl.pdf.

30 Ibid.

31 Canadian Pacific Railway Limited, "Notice of Annual Meeting Proxy Circular 2019," accessed 1 March 2020, 24, https://www.cpr.ca/en.

32 Rogers, "Notice of 2019 Annual General."

33 Bausch, "Executive Compensation."

34 Mackenzie, "Throwing Money," 17; Macdonald, "Climbing Up," 13.

35 *The Dodd–Frank Wall Street Reform and Consumer Protection Act*, Pub.L. 111–203, H.R. 4173.

36 Alex Edmans, "Why We Need to Stop Obsessing Over CEO Pay Ratios," *Harvard Business Review*, 23 February 2017, https://hbr.org/2017/02/why-we-need-to-stop-obsessing-over-ceo-pay-ratios.

37 See Lawrence Mishel and Jessica Schieder, "CEO Compensation Surged in 2017," Economic Policy Institute, 16 August 2018, https://www.epi.org/publication/ceo-compensation-surged-in-2017.

38 Macdonald, "Climbing Up," 5.

39 Mackenzie, "Throwing Money," 16–17.

40 Esra Burak, "Is the Sky the Limit? Fair Executive Pay as Performance Rises," *Social Problems* 65, no. 2 (May 2018): 211.

41 Macdonald, "Climbing Up," 13.

42 Ibid.

43 David Macdonald, "The Double-Pane Glass Ceiling: The Gender Pay Gap at the Top of Corporate Canada," Canadian Centre for Policy Alternatives, 2 January 2019, 3–4, https://www.policyalternatives.ca/publications/reports/double-pane-glass-ceiling.

44 Kiridaran Kanagaretnam, Gerald J. Lobo, and Emad Mohammad, "Are Stock Options Grants to CEOs of Stagnant Firms Fair and Justified?," *Journal of Business Ethics* 90, no. 1 (November 2009): 147–59.

45 Michael J. Cooper, Huseyin Gulen, and P. Raghavendra Rau, "Performance for Pay? The Relation between CEO Incentive Compensation and Future Stock Price Performance," SSRN, last modified 2 December 2016, 5, https://papers.ssrn.com/sol3/papers.cfm?abstract_id=1572085.

46 Scott J. Wallsten, "Executive Compensation and Firm Performance: Big Carrot, Small Stick," Stanford Institute for Economic Policy Research, March 2000, 3.

47 Ibid., 11.

48 Matt Orsagh, "'Say on Pay': How Voting on Executive Pay Is Evolving Globally – and Is It Working?," *Market Integrity Insights*, CFA Institute,

26 December 2013, https://blogs.cfainstitute.org/marketintegrity/2013/12/26/say-on-pay-how-votes-on-executive-pay-is-evolving-globally-and-is-it-working.

49 For more on shareholder activism, see Bikaramjit S. Sandhu, "The Return of Robin Hood: A New Kind of Shareholder Activism," chapter 9 of this book.

50 Steven Balsam et al., "The Impact of Say-on-Pay on Executive Compensation," *Journal of Accounting and Public Policy* 35, no. 2 (Spring 2016): 164.

51 Ibid.

52 Marinilka Barros Kimbro and Danielle Xu, "Shareholders Have a Say in Executive Compensation: Evidence from Say-on-Pay in the United States," *Journal of Accounting and Public Policy* 34, no. 6 (Winter 2015): 37–8.

53 Xiaoli Yuan, Wenguang Lin, and Ebere A. Oriaku, "Executive Compensation, Financial Performance and Say on Pay Votes," *International Journal of Business & Economic Development* 5, no. 1 (March 2017): 85.

54 Ibid.; Denton Collins, Blair B. Marquardt, and Xu Niu, "Equity-Based Incentives and Shareholder Say-on-Pay," *Journal of Business Finance & Accounting* 46, nos. 5–6 (Summer 2019): 739–61.

55 Charles P. Cullinan, Lois Mahoney, and Pamela B. Roush, "Are CSR Activities Associated with Shareholder Voting in Director Elections and Say-on-Pay Votes?," *Journal of Contemporary Accounting & Economics* 13, no. 3 (December 2017): 226.

56 For similar findings in say-on-pay countries, see Ricardo Correa and Ugur Lel, "Say on Pay Laws, Executive Compensation, Pay Slice, and Firm Valuation around the World," *Journal of Financial Economics* 122, no. 3 (December 2016): 500–20.

57 Thomas A. Hemphill, "Say-on-Pay Voting: A Five-Year Retrospective," *Business and Society Review* 124, no. 1 (Spring 2019): 69–70.

58 Ibid.

59 Reggy Hooghiemstra, Yu Flora Kuang, and Bo Qin, "Does Obfuscating Excessive CEO Pay Work? The Influence of Remuneration Report Readability on Say-on-Pay Votes," *Accounting and Business Research* 47, no. 6 (2017): 720.

60 See "The Gravity of the $70K Decision," Gravity Payments, last modified 22 January 2021, https://gravitypayments.com/thegravityof70k. For more on how these events unfolded, see Paul Keegan, "Here's What Really Happened at That Company That Set a $70,000 Minimum Wage," *Inc. Magazine*, November 2015, https://www.inc.com/magazine/201511/paul-keegan/does-more-pay-mean-more-growth.html.

61 Nicholas Kristof, "The $70,000-a-Year Minimum Wage," *The New York Times*, 30 March 2019, https://www.nytimes.com/2019/03/30/opinion/sunday/dan-price-minimum-wage.html.

62 Ibid.

63 Ibid.

2

Decolonizing and Reinvigorating Economic Development in Indigenous Communities Through Cooperative Ownership

Blair Feltmate

As part of the colonial experiment, advancing colonial powers throughout the world have oppressed and excluded Indigenous Peoples nearly to the point of extinction. It has been estimated that after first contact with European settlers, almost 80 per cent of Indigenous Peoples worldwide have been killed.[1] James (Sa'ke'j) Youngblood Henderson notes how there has been "probably more genocide, ethnocide, and extinction of tribal or ethnic groups than in any time in history" in relation to the advancement of colonial ideas and power over Indigenous Peoples throughout the world.[2] Genocide has advanced in Canada in a variety of ways as colonizers "created new orders, hierarchies, and governments by military or political force, believing in the superiority of Europeans over the colonized, the masculine over the feminine, the adult over the child, the historical over the ahistorical, and the modern or 'progressive' over the traditional."[3] Of note is the manner in which colonial ideas of capitalism and individualism were forced onto the natural pattern of Indigenous life supplanting collectivism and community. This displacement was conducted economically through policies of exclusion, codified in the *Indian Act*, that created immense burdens for Indigenous Peoples to overcome to continue practicing their culture and pursue social thriving.[4]

This chapter advocates for the implementation of the cooperative business structure as an alternative to traditional economic development for Indigenous communities. Cooperative ownership offers a sustainable, resilient, and purpose-driven structure that has the potential to align with Indigenous values, democratize ownership of lands and resources, and support efforts to move away from economic development rooted in colonial structures. The primary function of a cooperative is to help communities achieve better social and economic outcomes, whereas boards of directors of corporations are designed to pursue the "best interests of the corporation" with stakeholder interests and benefits to social welfare as ancillary outcomes.[5] Indigenous Peoples throughout the world struggle to survive and often face poverty. The situation is no different in Canada where, by many metrics, Indigenous Peoples are struggling with less than satisfactory social outcomes. Traditional economic development is not optimized to improve social and economic outcomes for people.[6] Cooperatives are designed to create better social and economic outcomes for their members and in turn the communities for those members to live, work, and thrive.

This chapter is not implying to be an authority on decision-making for Indigenous Peoples. Instead, it is a reflection on the colonial nature of corporate law and advising to better inform the exercise of self-determination of Indigenous Nations and subsequent choices that may follow. In turn, it also means that with respect to operating within planetary boundaries, it is the decision and responsibility of Indigenous Peoples to consider their contribution to harms that may be brought upon Earth – including potential detrimental effects of mining projects with large companies on Indigenous lands, for instance. With the rise of Indigenous green energy projects continuing into our post-pandemic recovery,[7] the cooperative is an alternative approach that may better suit some of these communities, depending on what their goals may be.

This chapter thus champions the idea that the current political and legal climate is ripe for a rethinking of traditional social and economic development and can advance the cooperative structure as an effective model for disruptive innovation.[8] The first section introduces the concept of the cooperative, assessing the potential benefits and providing a brief snapshot of the role cooperatives play in the Canadian economy. The next section examines the relationship between Indigenous communities in Canada and settler Canadians and defines Indigenous cooperatives, as well as analyzes traditional economic development models for Indigenous communities in Canada. The third section identifies how Indigenous Peoples in Canada have re-appropriated the cooperative form to build grassroots, locally driven organizations that create better social and economic outcomes for Indigenous Peoples.

The final section responds to potential challenges and limitations to the cooperative structure in this context and recommends best practices for developing Indigenous cooperatives in Canada. Cooperatives are uniquely positioned to meet the holistic social and economic development needs of Indigenous communities in British Columbia (BC) as they are designed to serve the primary function of meeting community needs.

BRIEF OVERVIEW OF COOPERATIVE OWNERSHIP IN CANADA

The Government of Canada defines the cooperative as "a legally incorporated corporation that is owned by an association of persons seeking to satisfy common needs such as access to products or services, sale of their products or services, or employment."[9] Cooperatives serve many functions but are generally categorized into the following types: consumer cooperatives, producer cooperatives, worker cooperatives, and multi-stakeholder cooperatives.[10] The cooperative business structure is flexible and designed to improve social and economic outcomes for communities.

The International Cooperative Alliance (ICA), which identifies as "the independent association that unites, represents and serves cooperatives worldwide,"[11] defines cooperatives as: "people-centered enterprises owned, controlled and run by and for their members to realize their common economic, social and cultural needs, and aspirations."[12] The principles of cooperatives, as defined by the ICA, further elucidate the characteristics of a cooperative and its distinction from other legal entities. The seven principles of the cooperative movement identified by the ICA are as follows: (1) voluntary and open membership; (2) democratic member control and equal voting rights; (3) member economic participation to the capital of their cooperative; (4) autonomy and independence to preserve the democratic power; (5) education, training, and information on the nature and the advantages of the cooperative; (6) cooperation among cooperatives locally, nationally, and internationally; and (7) concern for the sustainable development of the community.[13] These principles have been incorporated into the *Canada Cooperatives Act*.[14]

Purpose is a key distinguishing characteristic of a cooperative. Antonio Fici notes that while there are business structures that can be regarded as neutral regarding purpose, this is not the case for cooperatives.[15] Fici defines the legal characteristics of other business structures as: "legal personality, limited liability, transferable shares, delegated management … and investor ownership" whereas a cooperative is defined by the seven ICA principles but specifically the pursuit of a purpose.[16] Fici breaks down purpose into two components "the ultimate purpose of benefitting members" and "the carrying out of a particular activity to fulfill this purpose."[17] It is in this purpose-driven approach where the primary function of a cooperative, to serve communities and meet community needs, emerges.

While being defined by its principles, a cooperative remains a very flexible organization. Like any organization, it is a frame into which an entrepreneur or a community can place their values and their objectives – whatever these values they may be.[18] The ability to flexibly pursue specific community goals and aspirations touches on the core value of the cooperative model, which is to mobilize local resources to improve social and economic outcomes for communities. In the Indigenous context, this often takes the form of sustainable development designed to improve self-governance, self-determination, and ownership within communities. Cooperative models offer a "complementary approach to community development" and function to build better social and economic outcomes for individuals and communities regardless of what the community intends to achieve.[19]

There are four particular benefits of the cooperative model worth noting. First, cooperatives have been shown to be more resilient than other business structures. For example, between 2009–10, as the global economy was recovering from the financial crisis of 2008, the cooperative sector "outpaced the national economy in terms of value-add GDP growth, job growth, and increase in household income."[20] Second, social purpose is embedded into cooperatives through the mandatory principles listed in relevant cooperative statutes. Third, they are democratic and transparent. Fourth, and potentially the most important to this analysis, is that they create circular economies with feedback loops that support communities to thrive. Although cooperatives are underutilized in Canada,[21] they remain a key component of the Canadian economy. In 2015, Innovation, Science and Economic Development Canada conducted a study on the 7,887 incorporated non-financial cooperatives in Canada on the nature of cooperatives in Canada.[22] They found cooperatives were responsible for CA$44.1 billion in revenue, issued 765 million in patronage dividends to their members and communities, produced 101,567 full- and part-time jobs, and had 9.1 million members.[23] The vast majority of these cooperatives were headquartered in Quebec (36 per cent), Ontario (23 per cent), and Saskatchewan (11 per cent).[24] Per the same study, there were 592 cooperatives headquartered in BC in 2015, and of these BC cooperatives, 328 responded to the study.[25] Reporting cooperatives headquartered in BC were responsible for CA$1.7 billion in revenue, employed 4,948 people, and had 4,974 members.[26] These numbers reflect how, for millions of Canadians and thousands of British Columbians, cooperatives are an essential part of their everyday life.

INDIGENOUS ECONOMIC DEVELOPMENT WITHIN SETTLER COLONIALISM

To identify the role of colonialism in the development of Indigenous cooperatives, and Indigenous economic development in general, it is important to acknowledge colonialism itself. Two types of colonialism apply in Canada: standard colonialism and settler colonialism.[27] Standard colonialism is resource- and labour-based. The invading state wishes to extract resources in the most efficient way possible through accessing land by force and exploiting the labour of the people on the land.[28] Settler colonialism is a larger project that requires the redrawing of the national pattern of an area through the removal of people or their culture, the establishment of sovereignty by the invading state, and the permanent settlement of colonizers – in our case, the permanent settlement of European immigrants.[29] Settler colonialism is an imposed structure – not an event – and as such its tentacles reach deep into our society today.

Indigenous economic development occurs in a colonial, capitalist structure. One of the insidious consequences of this dual structure is the "proliferation of strictly economic organizations that divorced themselves from social, environmental or cultural goals."[30] Despite advancements in Canadian corporate law and a renewed interest in corporate social performance, the corporate form in Canada is still characterized in this manner. The divorce from social, environmental, and cultural considerations is still apparent and abiding, as can be shown through resource extraction projects that have devastated regions by their very nature, or the callous disregard for environmental safeguards when dealing with toxic waste.[31] Failing to consider social, environmental, and cultural goals has been significantly more pronounced when the impacts of these failings are felt solely by rural and Indigenous communities.

Today, Indigenous Peoples living within Canada's borders are categorized by Canada into three groups: First Nations, Inuit, and Métis peoples, who account for 4.9 per cent of the population of Canada and 5.8 per cent of the population of BC.[32] Indigenous economic development has proceeded mostly with a consideration beyond profit. While not always the case, it has been found that "[I]ndigenous entrepreneurial responses ... include more holistic reintegration and combinations of social, environmental, and cultural goals with economic goals."[33] Indigenous economic development corporations often play a dual role in their community, functioning as the profit-earning arm while also delivering key services. In a study of the development of Indigenous cooperatives, Ushnish Sengupta writes that Indigenous entrepreneurs have "multiple goals in addition to self-sufficiency" and the following four purposes can be identified as characteristics of Indigenous entrepreneurship: (1) ending dependency through economic self-sufficiency; (2) controlling activities on traditional lands; (3) improving the socioeconomic circumstances of Aboriginal peoples; and (4) strengthening traditional culture, values, and language.[34] These four purposes can be achieved through several different business structures. Economic development in Indigenous communities is often fulfilled through a complex legal structure that involves an intricate mix of corporations and partnerships designed to maximize profit to the band, minimize taxation, and reduce liability.[35] Economic development in this form creates increased wealth intended to produce better social and health outcomes for Indigenous communities. Furthermore, the pursuit of wealth in a manner divorced from social and health benefits still provides an indirect approach to producing social and health benefits for these communities.

Although difficult to define, researchers have generally accepted that Indigenous cooperatives are defined as "formally incorporated co-operatives where the majority of the members are Indigenous" and Indigenous values are implemented "in its long-term strategy and operations."[36] Further, Indigenous cooperatives can be identified by the presence of economic, social, environmental, and cultural goals often called the "quadruple bottom line."[37] Indigenous values are unique to each community although there are common threads that can be identified, and they are dynamic, adjusting over time to external influence and internal dynamism. Indigenous cooperatives play a key role in structuring the provision of goods and services to Indigenous communities and are "one type of organizational tool in a broad toolkit" to manage economic development in Indigenous communities.[38]

While there are greater numbers of Indigenous Peoples in southern Canada, there is greater concentration of Indigenous Peoples, mostly Inuit, in the North. Indigenous Peoples make up 85.9 per cent of the population of Nunavut, 50.7 per cent of the population of the Northwest Territories, and 23.3 per cent of the population of Yukon.[39] The concentration of Indigenous Peoples in the North is of value to the discussion of cooperative ownership as it provides a potential explanation for why this group has been able to exert greater influence over their political and economic institutions and have adopted the cooperative structure to a greater extent than in the South.[40] Formal cooperative models of social and economic development have also been part of Indigenous development in the Prairie provinces more so than on the West or East Coast.[41] The first formally incorporated Indigenous cooperative in Canada was established in Saskatchewan in 1945, and the first formally incorporated Inuit cooperative was established in 1959.[42] Northern and southern cooperative models are slightly different. Northern cooperatives often establish a broad suite of services and provide goods in multiple areas whereas southern cooperatives are often for a single purpose.[43] It is important to acknowledge that there are a very large number of Indigenous organizations that align with cooperative principles but are not formally registered as cooperatives under Canadian or provincial statute, and Sengupta provides the following examples: "Indigenous drumming and singing groups, artist collectives, and some Indian band-owned businesses."[44]

Glen Sean Coulthard, a Yellowknives Dené political scientist, in his book *Red Skin, White Masks* identifies a main critique of economic development in Indigenous communities.[45] Reduced to its barest form is the statement that capitalism is inherently counter to Indigenous ways of living. In studying the resistance to the Mackenzie Valley Pipeline by the Yellowknives Dené people, Coulthard notes how there are fundamental distinctions between Indigenous and Western philosophies that ought to lead to a rejection of capitalist notions of wealth and approaches to land and resource development.[46] Citing Vine Deloria Jr, Coulthard points to how Western societies "derive meaning from the world in historical or developmental terms, thereby placing *time* as the narrative of central importance,"[47] whereas

"American Indians hold their lands – places – as having the highest possible meaning, and all their statements are made with this reference point in mind."[48] Coulthard argues that understanding land or place as "simply some material object of profound importance to Indigenous cultures" is insufficient; rather, place ought to be understood as "a way of knowing, of experiencing and relating to the world and with others."[49] This significant difference between ways of living forms a critique of the Indigenous pursuit of economic development by harnessing the value of land. Land is not property. Capital accumulation in this way, according to Coulthard, is an affront to Dené ways of living.[50]

COOPERATIVE DEVELOPMENT IN INDIGENOUS COMMUNITIES IN CANADA

Today, it may be hard to see the cooperative model as a tool of colonial oppression. Lauded for their democratic principles and commitment to social good, cooperatives are often seen as legal structures that can help distribute wealth and build community. However, their history has not always been so rosy. Cooperatives were used in empire building by the British, relied on indentured labour in some instances, actively excluded or ignored Indigenous Peoples, and were complicit in the displacement of Indigenous Peoples to secure land for farming.[51] Sengupta's research found that, for example, Barbadian cooperative sugar factories relied on indentured labour from India, and Scottish and Finnish immigrants in Canada excluded Indigenous communities as they attempted to bolster their own economic position in British dominated industries.[52] Further, the trading patterns of British cooperatives in the commonwealth led to a clearing of usable farmland of the Indigenous populations to meet the demand for food back in Great Britain. While their intention was to provide low-cost food for impoverished people in their home country, they did so with a disregard for the lives and rights of individuals impacted by their need for farmland.[53]

While the ICA was founded as a tool to disrupt class hegemony, it was formed by British elites. As a result, the ICA carried with it colonial and racist beliefs that led "to either outright exclusion, often coerced or restricted labour use of Indigenous populations by cooperatives."[54] Sengupta provides a specific example of one of these elites, Earl Grey who "had Christian beliefs that extended to virtues of cooperative production for poorer sections of society both in Britain and for White colonial settlers, virtues that however did not extend to local Indigenous populations whom he considered to be 'savages.'"[55] This colonial history creates concerns about the ability for cooperatives to be a useful tool in the decolonizer's toolkit. Sengupta argues that settler cooperative advocates have failed to acknowledge and have outright revised the history of cooperatives as a social good. Rather, they were a response by new immigrants to monopolies set up by the British ruling class and political elites. They did not acknowledge race in a comprehensive way and actively did not include nor intend to benefit Indigenous communities.

Settler cooperatives in North America failed to properly account for the collective land and human rights of Indigenous Peoples; however, contemporary, community-led organizations have re-appropriated the cooperative form with Indigenous values, enabling it to be a useful and culturally appropriate tool for economic development within Indigenous communities. Marcelo Vieta explains that there has been a resurgent form of "new co-operativism" that is not "tied to state nor capital-centric interests but strives to move beyond them for an alternative form of community development."[56] Vieta's assertions are supported by a study identifying that cooperatives in Canada represent a distinct approach to community economic development that addresses the specific needs of specific groups of peoples, aims to meet the needs of members not outside groups, and operates as part of a larger network.[57] The network component is of particular relevance to rural, small Indigenous cooperatives because a broader network can bring economies of scale, expertise, and social connection that would otherwise be unavailable.[58] Another study by Lou Ketilson and Ian MacPherson suggests that cooperatives can offer certain advantages for community development in Indigenous communities, finding that Indigenous leaders prefer economic development "conceived of as a process that takes into account the history, collective aspirations, economic diversity, and underlying realities of each Aboriginal community."[59] Further, in their view, the cooperative model conforms well with this approach.[60]

Hope for this model emerges today, with Sengupta noting that the cooperative form has been adapted and re-appropriated into an "effective tool of decolonization by Indigenous communities in the contemporary context."[61] There is no better time for Indigenous communities that are pursuing economic development to consider the cooperative model. First, leaders and activists within Indigenous communities have wrestled significant power from the state in the last several years.[62] Second, changes in Canadian policy and law governing Indigenous Peoples, most notably the adoption of the United Nations Declaration on the Rights of Indigenous Peoples (UNDRIP) in response to the Truth and Reconciliation Commission (TRC) Report, provide greater autonomy for communities to make decisions about their economic and social development without such significant interference from the state.[63] Third, we are experiencing a climate crisis that requires a rethink of business as usual. We need to enable innovative approaches in response to climate challenges and Indigenous communities have historically been at the forefront of climate protection. They are well-positioned to be leaders in innovative solutions to this transformational challenge.

Resurgence and Declaration of Autonomy

Idle No More is an Indigenous movement that began in the winter of 2012 and has been considered the most "far-reaching grassroots Indigenous mobilization in the country since the contestation of the … White Paper of 1969."[64] Sparked by proposed alterations to the *Indian Act* and a drastic reduction in environmental regulations through a federal omnibus bill, Bill C-45, the Idle No More movement began with a small group of women in the Prairies educating people on the implications of decreased environmental regulation. The movement gained notoriety when Chief Theresa Spence of the Attawapiskat Cree Nation (Āhtawāpiskatowi ininiwak) began a hunger strike to denounce housing conditions on her reserve and in support for the movement of the Prairie women.[65] This movement, although sparked by specific concern over Bill C-45, has been identified as a catalyst for the actualization of Indigenous Peoples in coming to "see themselves as subjects capable of altering the structures of society."[66] Further, this movement gaining support throughout the country was a major contributor to altering the political rhetoric of the 2015 federal election in Canada. Prime Minister Justin Trudeau was elected on promises to reinstate a nation-to-nation relationship with Indigenous communities in this country.[67] It can be argued that this firm campaign stance would not have been taken without the direct action of mobilized Indigenous Peoples across this country chanting, "Idle no more!"[68]

Following those campaign promises, the federal government committed to a nation-to-nation relationship with Indigenous Peoples in Canada.

The TRC Report recommends "establishing and maintaining a mutually respectful relationship between Aboriginal and non-Aboriginal peoples in this country," stressing the necessity of forming an "awareness of the past, acknowledgment of the harm that has been inflicted, atonement for the causes, and actions to change behaviours."[69] UNDRIP affirms the inherent collective and individual human rights of Indigenous Peoples. Canada removed its objector status in 2016 and expressed full support for the implementation of UNDRIP within the existing legal structure and the *Constitution Act 1982*.[70] On 21 June 2021, UNDRIP received Royal Assent and came into force.[71] UNDRIP is important in this discussion of economic development because it establishes certain rights for Indigenous communities to control, manage, and profit from their lands and resources. Articles 3 and 4 establish that Indigenous Peoples have a right to economic self-determination.[72] Article 20 further defines their economic and cultural sovereignty by stating the right to "maintain and develop their own political, economic and social systems or institutions, to be secure in the enjoyment of their own means of subsistence and development and to engage freely in all their traditional and other economic activities."[73] Article 26 provides that "Indigenous peoples have the right to the lands, territories, and resources which they have traditionally owned, occupied or otherwise used or acquired."[74] The enshrinement of these rights has the potential to help secure tenure over traditional territory and enable the pursuit of prosperity through the development of lands and resources. Whether this occurs in the way this document codifies is up to the federal government.

In addition to these recent policy changes, there have been changes to Aboriginal law over the past several years that have far-reaching impacts on Indigenous communities' abilities to pursue economic and social development without interference from the federal government. Three changes to highlight for the purposes of this chapter are: the *Tsilhqot'in Nation v. British Columbia* decision in 2014,[75] the *First Nations Land Management Act*,[76] and the modern-day treaty process.[77] On 28 November 2019, the legislature gave royal assent to Bill-41, which integrated BC law with UNDRIP, making it the first province since Canada endorsed UNDRIP.[78] There are countless other ways in which the relationship between the Crown and Indigenous Peoples have developed, but these provide a snapshot of the dynamism of this field and the continued devolution of prescribed, limited power to Indigenous communities.

Climate Crisis Requiring a Rethink of "Business as Usual"

Introducing the Global Environmental Outlook (GEO) edition 6, co-chairs Joyeeta Gupta and Paul Elkins issued this ultimatum to humanity:

> Choose a challenging but navigable path towards a new golden age of sustainable development as envisaged by the United Nations Agenda 2030 in which human hunger and poverty are consigned to history through the sustainable use of Earth's resources and the natural environment that leaves no one behind OR continue with current trends and practices, which will lead to a losing struggle against environmental disruptions, which threaten to overwhelm large parts of the world.[79]

Humanity currently exists in this ultimatum. Indigenous communities in Canada face this impossible decision most directly as they are often both at the forefront of environmental degradation and rising sea levels and, in certain communities, responding to economic crises. The global COVID-19 pandemic itself has laid bare the disproportionate vulnerability of Indigenous populations in the face of these ongoing and potential future crises.

Doubling down on the crises humanity is facing, GEO edition 6 warns that "the ecological foundations of human society and natural systems that support other species and provide invaluable ecosystem services are in great danger."[80] Acknowledging the consequences of human activity, GEO identifies that "human activities are causing increasing amounts of pollution, to the extent that is now recognized as the biggest single risk to human health worldwide."[81] They suggest that "continuing to live on the brink of or outside of ecological limits, from the global to the local, will make it dramatically more difficult to achieve prosperity, justice, equity, and a healthy life for all ... The need for humanity to remain within the planetary boundaries' safe operating space and the need to eradicate poverty and accelerate social and economic development are linked by the concept of a 'safe and just space for humanity.'"[82] The global climate crisis and its interconnected relationship with poverty cannot be overstated.

To respond to these transformational challenges requires rethinking the entire economy and the way in which business structures support this economy. It requires a rethink of business as usual. Kate Raworth identifies one key component of approaching these challenges in an innovative manner. She refers to it as "design to distribute" – meaning designing economies and business structures that are far more distributive of the value that they generate "going beyond redistributing income to exploring ways of redistributing wealth, particularly the wealth that lies in controlling land, enterprise, technology, knowledge and the power to create money."[83] Raworth describes redistribution of land as "one of the most direct ways to reduce national inequalities,"[84] while further providing examples in West Bengal, Japan, and South Korea.[85] Declarations of sovereignty and changes in the legal landscape in Canada have begun the process of redistributing land back to its original stewards – the Indigenous Peoples that have lived on this land since time immemorial.

Cooperatives and cooperative-like structures have been formally around for hundreds of years, and informally for thousands of years, but, despite their age, they represent an innovative solution that is sufficiently flexible to the changing objectives of communities while meeting the challenges posed by the climate crisis in placing "purpose" at the forefront of decision-making. Entrepreneurs, lawyers, and business owners are being forced to reconsider our economy due to broader social movements and compelling critiques from scholars like Raworth. They are ripe to be convinced to try new models for economic development, thus enabling a cooperative approach to emerge as a potential solution to build better social and economic outcomes for communities.[86]

BUILDING A SUCCESSFUL INDIGENOUS COOPERATIVE SYSTEM

It is possible to develop a cooperative culture in Canada that helps unlock the ability for Indigenous communities to thrive in a manner that aligns with Indigenous law, promotes ecological integrity, and has the potential to build sustainable economies within Indigenous communities. In 2017, the Centre for the Study of Co-operatives released the final report of their cooperative innovation project – a research project that analyzed rural Indigenous community cooperatives in Alberta. This report found that the cooperative model is feasible in rural Indigenous communities as a "locally-driven solution to address[ing] unmet needs."[87] Cooperatives can work in this context. Yet barriers to this development remain. This section will address the barriers that a successful cooperative must overcome then identify recommendations for best practices in cooperative development for Indigenous communities.

There are major hurdles to adoption of the cooperative system by more Indigenous communities. Ketilson identified the difficulty produced by policy and regulations rooted in the *Indian Act*. She notes how the complicated political and policy environment acts as a general barrier to economic and community development.[88] Further hurdles include the lack of education on models of cooperative development that incorporate Indigenous law and culture; concerns over power and control of lands, resources, and economic activity; funding limitations; and the challenge of maintaining a large membership base in rural Indigenous communities as there is often not enough people to create effective economies of scale.[89] These issues present themselves in a variety of ways, and rather than identifying one solution or a suite of solutions to each barrier, I have aggregated a set of principled approaches to Indigenous cooperative development and practical guidance that form a set of three general recommendations. Ultimately, the key to cooperative development is to listen to the unique needs of the community and respond appropriately. The flexibility and purpose-driven nature of cooperatives lend themselves to this listen-and-respond approach.

Recommendation One

In order for an Indigenous cooperative to be successful, it must incorporate Indigenous Knowledge into the cooperative form.[90] Successful Indigenous cooperatives have been able to re-appropriate the cooperative structure, stripping it of its colonial history, and use it as another tool to achieve broad community goals. Sengupta shares a story from Mi'kmaw Elder Albert Marshall to highlight how these distinct ways of living and knowing can be used together to create better cooperatives: "'two-eyed seeing' refers to learning to see from one eye with the strengths of Indigenous knowledge and ways of knowing and from the other eye with the strengths of Western knowledges and ways of knowing … and learning to use both these eyes together for the benefit of all."[91]

It is important to note that this is a significant and difficult request and requires non-Indigenous cooperative experts to understand the insufficiency of their knowledge and create space for Indigenous Knowledge and individuals to lead the process. An example of combining the formal structure of the cooperative with Indigenous Knowledge is the NeechiFood Cooperative Limited (Neechi) in Winnipeg, a multi-stakeholder-owned cooperative that provides "healthy, affordable food to the community" including groceries, catering, baked goods, and an Aboriginal arts store.[92] Neechi aligns with the practice of placing food as a cultural and community linchpin. Further, Neechi provides traditional, cultural foods that reconnect people to their traditional food systems by helping to reduce food insecurity and reclaim an element of cultural identity.[93] The connection and revitalization of Indigenous Knowledge of the role of food and food systems in culture is an integral component of Neechi's success.

Recommendation Two

For an Indigenous cooperative to achieve its goals, the developers must hone their expertise or have access to experts specializing in the unique legal complexities of Indigenous communities as they relate to the *Indian Act* and other legislation that governs the economic development, governance, land, and membership of Indigenous life. The key is direct mentorship and support from a network of cooperatives that have navigated these tricky legal situations.[94] Furthermore, these cooperatives can benefit from "vigorous co-op development at the community level and focused effort at the pan-provincial level to leverage economies of scale and connect the Western Canadian co-operative community."[95] In addition, lawyers practicing in Indigenous economic development ought to be educated on the potential benefits of cooperative structures to provide holistic benefit to Indigenous communities.

Recommendation Three

To be successful, Indigenous cooperatives must acknowledge the colonial history of the cooperative structure to avoid the mistakes of the past and ensure that they strip cooperatives of colonial vestiges. Leaders must "ensure that cooperative solutions to complex problems are deeply aware of and examined through the lenses of oppression, including class, race, and gender, in order to ensure that a cooperative solution to a problem for one group of people does not adversely impact another group of people."[96]

Sengupta notes that "increased awareness among cooperative and community development practitioners of the troubled history of cooperatives in the lives of Indigenous peoples can help prevent repeating some of the historical injustices" that have occurred as a result of ignorant and reckless development of cooperatives on Indigenous land.[97] Indigenous communities seeking to re-establish communal and collective ways of being through the cooperative form are often the most aware of the insidious nature of capitalism and assimilative attempts by the Crown. Non-Indigenous practitioners and individuals not directly connected to the community must be vigilant not to dominate discussions with capitalist and colonial-centric ideas and values.

These recommendations are not exhaustive but pose the key considerations for the creation of successful Indigenous cooperatives to benefit Indigenous communities.

CONCLUSION

This chapter advocates that cooperatives are a more direct tool to improve social, health, and economic outcomes in Indigenous communities than the traditional economic development structure of a limited partnership and a corporation. The cooperative business structure has the potential to be a preferable model for Indigenous communities in achieving their economic, social, environmental, and cultural goals. Simply put, the cooperative model is a grassroots approach designed to produce better social and economic outcomes for communities – this is its primary function. As a result, it is uniquely positioned to meet Indigenous economic development needs and begin the process of reducing the livelihood gap between Indigenous Peoples in Canada and settler society. Cooperatives offer a sustainable, resilient, and purpose-driven structure that has the potential to align with Indigenous values, democratize ownership of lands and resources, and support efforts to move away from economic development rooted in colonial structures.

NOTES

1 James (Sa'ke'j) Youngblood Henderson, *Indigenous Diplomacy and the Rights of Peoples: Achieving UN Recognition* (Saskatoon: Purich Publishing 2008), 17. See also Alexander Laban Hinton, *Annihilating Difference: Anthropology of Genocide* (University of California Press 2002).

2 Henderson, *Indigenous Diplomacy*, 17.

3 For a full discussion of the cultural genocide that occurred in Canada see Tamara Starblanket, *Suffer the Little Children: Genocide, Indigenous Children, and the Canadian State* (Clarity Press 2018).

4 *Indian Act Revised Statutes of Canada* 1998, c.I-5, https://laws-lois.justice.gc.ca/eng/acts/i-5.

5 BCE *Inc. v. 1976 Debentureholders* [2008] 3 SCR 560 at para 82, 2008 SCC 69. This interpretation seems to equate "best interest of the corporation" with a shareholder-centric business approach, which is contrary to the BCE *v. 1976 Debentureholders.*

6 Henderson, *Indigenous Diplomacy*, 28.

7 Frank Davis and John Beaucage, "Indigenous-Led Green Energy Partnerships Will Move Us Forward," *The Globe and Mail*, 20 July 2021, https://www.theglobeandmail.com/business/commentary/article-indigenous-led-green-energy-partnerships-will-move-us-forward.

8 This argument does not claim that the cooperative is a better model for maximizing profit, reducing taxes, and minimizing liability than the complex limited partnership structures commonly used by First Nations governments, as they tend to satisfy those objectives. The chapter advances the argument that a cooperative structure is a more direct and potentially more effective structure to improve social, health, and economic benefits in Indigenous communities.

9 Innovation, Science and Economic Development Canada, Government of Canada, "Information Guide on Co-operatives," last modified 27 August 2018, https://www.ic.gc.ca/eic/site/106.nsf/eng/h_00073.html.

10 Ibid.

11 International Cooperative Alliance, accessed 13 August 2021, https://www.ica.coop.

12 Cliff Mills and Will Davies, *Blueprint for a Co-operative Decade*, International Cooperative Alliance, 2013, https://www.ica.coop/en/media/library/blueprint-cooperative-decade.

13 These principles are embedded in s. 7 of the *Canada Cooperatives Act* and loosely adopted into s. 8 of BC's *Cooperative Association Act*, *Statutes of British Columbia* 1999, c.28.

14 *Canada Cooperatives Act*, *Statues of Canada* 1998, c.1.

15 Antonio Fici, "The Essential Role of Cooperative Law," *The Dovenschmidt Quarterly* 4, (2014).

16 Antonio Fici, "An Introduction to Cooperative Law," in *International Handbook of Cooperative Law*, edited by Dante Cracogna, Antonio Fici, and Hagen Henrÿ (Berlin: Springer-Verlag 2013), 21.

17 Ibid., 18.

18 In many ways, the cooperative functions very similarly to a corporation. Fici identifies that cooperatives limit liability in much the same ways as a corporation, through asset partitioning with "liquidation protection and member limited liability" (ibid., 16). The similarities between a co-operative entity and a corporation are an important feature in understanding the legal benefits and limitations of incorporating cooperatives into community and economic development approaches for First Nation, Inuit, and Métis peoples.
19 Oluwabusola Oluwatodimu Olaniyan et al., *The Co-operative Model Advances Indigenous Development: A Case Study of the Neechi Co-operatives Limited* (Quebec: International Summit of Cooperatives 2016), https://community-wealth.org/sites/clone.community-wealth.org/files/downloads/the%20coop%20model.pdf.
20 George Karaphillis, Fiona Duguid, and Alicia Lake, "Economic Impact of the Canadian Co-Operative Sector (2009 and 2010)," *International Journal of Social Economics* 44, no. 5 (May 2017): 643–52.
21 Robert Yalden et al., *Business Organizations: Practice, Theory and Emerging Challenges,* 2nd ed. (Toronto: Emond 2018), 533.
22 Innovation, Science and Economic Development Canada, Government of Canada, "Co-operatives in Canada in 2015," last modified 18 October 2018, https://www.ic.gc.ca/eic/site/106.nsf/eng/h_00151.html. The data references the 63 per cent of co-operatives that responded to the request for information.
23 Ibid., 3, 4.
24 Ibid., 5.
25 Ibid.
26 Ibid., 8, 9.
27 Edward Cavanagh and Lorenzo Veracini, eds., *The Routledge Handbook of the History of Settler Colonialism* (London: Routledge 2016), 15.
28 Ibid.
29 Ibid.
30 Ushnish Sengupta, "Indigenous Cooperatives in Canada: The Complex Relationship Between Cooperatives, Community Economic Development, Colonization, and Culture," *Journal of Entrepreneurial and Organizational Diversity* 4, no. 1 (2015): 125.
31 See e.g., Dirk Messiner, "Mount Polley Mine Disaster 5 Years Later; Emotions, Accountability Unresolved," *CBC News*, 4 August 2019, https://www.cbc.ca/news/canada/british-columbia/mount-polley-mine-disaster-5-years-later-emotions-accountability-unresolved-1.5236160.
32 The Daily, Statistics Canada, "Aboriginal Peoples in Canada: Key Results from the 2016 Census," 25 October 2017, https://www150.statcan.gc.ca/n1/daily-quotidien/171025/dq171025a-eng.htm.

33 Ibid.
34 Sengupta, "Indigenous Cooperatives," 128.
35 Yalden et al., *Business Organizations*, 257.
36 Sengupta, "Indigenous Cooperatives," 126.
37 Ibid.
38 Ibid., 127.
39 Ibid.
40 Sengupta, "Indigenous Cooperatives," 126; Isobel M. Findlay, "Nuna Is My Body: What Northerners Can Teach about Social Cohesion," in *Co-operative Canada: Empowering Communities and Sustainable Businesses*, edited by Brett Fairbairn and Nora Russell (Vancouver: UBC Press 2014), 43.
41 Lou Hammond Ketilson, "To See Our Communities Come Alive Again with Pride: Reinventing Co-Operatives for First Nations' Needs," in *Co-operative Canada: Empowering Communities and Sustainable Businesses*, edited by Brett Fairbairn and Nora Russell (Vancouver: UBC Press 2014), 213.
42 Sengupta, "Indigenous Cooperatives," 127.
43 Ibid.
44 Ibid., 122.
45 Glen Sean Coulthard, *Red Skin, White Masks: Rejecting the Colonial Politics of Recognition* (Minneapolis: University of Minnesota Press 2014), 60.
46 Ibid.
47 Glen Coulthard, "Place Against Empire: Understanding Indigenous Anti-Colonialism," *Affinities: A Journal of Radical Theory, Culture, and Action* 4, no. 2 (Fall 2010), 79.
48 Ibid.
49 Coulthard, *Red Skin, White Masks*, 61.
50 Ibid.
51 Sengupta, "Indigenous Cooperatives," 133–7.
52 An alternative view is that cooperatives have historically been used as a tool for racial minorities to exert control over industries that were elite-dominated and through this, reclaim their cultural identities. Examples include Chinese housing cooperatives in Vancouver, which were used to avoid racist housing and rental policies, and Japanese fishing cooperatives, which were created to control working conditions in the fisheries. See ibid.
53 Sengupta, "Indigenous Cooperatives," 134.
54 Ibid.
55 Ibid.
56 Marcelo Vieta, "The New Cooperativism," *A Journal of Radical Theory, Culture, and Action* 4, no. 1 (Summer 2010), 1.

57 Fairbairn and Russell, *Co-operative Canada*, 11.

58 Ibid.

59 Lou Hammond Ketilson and Ian MacPherson, *A Report on Aboriginal Co-operatives in Canada: Current Situation and Potential for Growth*, Centre for the Study of Co-operatives, University of Saskatchewan, 2001, 4.

60 Ibid.

61 Sengupta, "Indigenous Cooperatives," 134.

62 This has been done, amongst other things, through legal challenges that have solidified Aboriginal Title such as *Tsilhqot'in Nation v. British Columbia* [2014] 2 SCR 257, 2014 SCC 44; and increased self-government and self-determination of Indigenous Peoples through the modern-day treaty process.

63 Government of Canada, *Honouring the Truth, Reconciling for the Future: Summary of the Final Report of the Truth and Reconciliation Commission of Canada*, IR4-7/2015E-PDF, Truth and Reconciliation Commission of Canada, 2015, https://publications.gc.ca/collections/collection_2015/trc/IR4-7-2015-eng.pdf; United Nations, *United Nations Declaration on the Rights of Indigenous Peoples*, A/RES/61/295, 2007, https://undocs.org/A/RES/61/295.

64 Jeffrey R. Webber, "Idle No More: An Introduction to the Symposium on Glen Coulthard's Red Skin, White Masks," *Historical Materialism* 24, no. 3 (2016): 4.

65 Ibid.

66 Ibid., 7.

67 John Paul Tasker, "Trudeau Promises New Legal Framework for Indigenous Peoples," *CBC News*, 14 February 2018, https://www.cbc.ca/news/politics/trudeau-speech-indigenous-rights-1.4534679.

68 "The Legacy of Idle No More Put InFocus," *Aboriginal Peoples Television Network*, 22 January 2020, https://www.aptnnews.ca/national-news/the-legacy-of-idle-no-more-put-infocus.

69 Government of Canada, *Honouring the Truth*.

70 For a thoughtful discussion of how best to implement UNDRIP see: Brenda L. Gunn et al., "UNDRIP Implementation: Braiding International, Domestic and Indigenous Laws," Centre for International Governance Innovation, 31 May 2017, https://www.cigionline.org/publications/undrip-implementation-braiding-international-domestic-and-indigenous-laws.

71 Government of Canada, "Backgrounder: United Nations Declaration on the Rights of Indigenous Peoples Act," last modified 19 July 2021, https://www.justice.gc.ca/eng/declaration/about-apropos.html.

72 United Nations, *Declaration on the Rights of Indigenous Peoples*.

73 Ibid.

74 Ibid.
75 *Tsilhqot'in Nation v British Columbia* [2014] 2 SCR 257, 2014 SCC 44.
76 *First Nations Land Management Act, Statutes of Canada* 1999, c. 24.
77 BC Treaty Commission, "BC Treaty Commission," accessed 13 August 2021, http://www.bctreaty.ca.
78 BC Legislation on the Declaration on the Rights of Indigenous Peoples, "British Columbia's Historic Declaration on the Rights of Indigenous Peoples Act," accessed 26 August 2021, https://www.bcdripa.org.
79 United Nations Environment, Paul Ekins, Joyeeta Gupta, and Pierre Boileau, eds., *Global Environment Outlook – GEO-6: Healthy Planet, Healthy People* (Cambridge: Cambridge University Press, 2019), xxviii.
80 Ibid., 4.
81 Ibid.
82 Ibid.
83 Kate Raworth, *Doughnut Economics: Seven Ways to Think Like a 21st Century Economist* (Vermont: Chelsea Green Publishing 2017), 23.
84 Ibid., 129.
85 Ibid.
86 Mills and Davies, *Blueprint for a Co-operative Decade*, 2.
87 Co-operative Innovation Project, "Co-operative Innovation Project – Executive Summary," accessed 24 April 2019, 1, https://ccednet-rcdec.ca/sites/ccednet-rcdec.ca/files/executive-summary-cip.pdf; Co-operative Innovation Project, "Co-operative Innovation Project Overview," accessed 24 April 2019, https://coopinnovation.files.wordpress.com/2016/01/overview-cip.pdf.
88 Ketilson and MacPherson, *A Report on Aboriginal Co-operatives in Canada*, 4.
89 Ketilson, "To See Our Communities," 209–32.
90 Sengupta, "Indigenous Cooperatives," 146.
91 Ibid., 123.
92 Olaniyan, *A Case Study*, 4.
93 Ibid., 6.
94 Co-operative Innovation Project, "Executive Summary," 8.
95 Ibid., 1.
96 Sengupta, "Indigenous Cooperatives," 147.
97 Ibid.

3

Gender Diversity on Corporate Boards: Much Ado About Mandatory Quotas?

Oludolapo Makinde

Directors play a crucial role in piloting a company's affairs. It is for this reason that corporate governance scholars advocate for diversity on the board – bringing together persons with varying skillsets, competencies, and backgrounds, including across genders, ethnicities, and races, etc., who altogether help the company make sound business decisions.[1] Although board diversity as a whole is generally encouraged, gender diversity in particular has received global attention in the wake of the #MeToo movement;[2] racial diversity has also garnered attention in response to the Black Lives Matter movement and broader discussions on global racial justice.[3] While discussions on racial board diversity are only just beginning to take hold, on the issue of gender diversity, corporate boards are now encouraged – and in some cases, mandated – to have a gender-balanced board. Institutional shareholders have also been active in driving change, being known to deny approval to board or management decisions where the board consists of all-male directors.[4]

Despite the intense pressures to increase gender diversity on boards over the years, adequate traction has not been gained in practical terms. Statistics derived from a 2018 study reveal that, based on an analysis of approximately 8,648 companies in forty-nine countries, women hold only 16.9 per cent of board seats, 5.3 per cent of board chair positions, and 4.4 per cent of CEO positions globally.[5] Although some measure of success has been attained with about 78.7 per cent of MSCI ACWI (Morgan Stanley Capital International All Country World Index) companies having at least one woman,[6] and 32.1 per cent having at least three women on their board (as of 16 October 2018),[7] much still needs to be done to achieve genuine diversity and inclusion in the boardroom. For example, even though women are increasingly being appointed to boards, they often have short tenures and are unlikely to hold powerful positions such as the position of chairperson.[8] The nature of the challenge ahead has been aptly quantified by Sharon Thorne, Chair of Deloitte Global, who notes:

> If the global trend continues at its current rate of an approximately 1 percent increase of women on boards per year, we will be waiting more than 30 years to achieve global gender parity at the board level. And even then, actual parity is likely to be concentrated to the few countries that are currently making concerted efforts to overcome this issue, leaving several regions lagging behind.[9]

In a bid to address this issue, several countries across the world have adopted varying measures ranging from "soft law" or voluntary quotas, inclusion of diversity principles in corporate governance codes and disclosure rules, and establishment of mandatory quotas. Of these measures, mandatory quotas have been the most controversial with arguments being advanced for and against their use. Accordingly, this chapter aims to examine the viability of mandatory quotas in relation to soft law and codes of corporate governance principles, in solving the lack of gender diversity problem.

COMPARATIVE JURISDICTIONAL APPROACHES TO ENHANCING GENDER DIVERSITY

The lack of gender diversity on corporate boards is not a problem peculiar to any one country, but a widespread international issue. As such, states have adopted varying approaches to achieve gender parity. On one hand, while certain states have adopted a soft law approach in prescribing voluntary gender quotas, others have included gender diversity principles in corporate governance codes requiring disclosures on a "comply-or-explain" basis, which would require companies to comply with the code or provide reasons for not doing so,[10] or an "apply-and-explain" basis, which assumes compliance with the relevant codes and requires companies to outline steps taken to comply with set out principles.[11] Still others have taken the significant step of mandating gender quotas for corporate boards. These approaches and their success rates are considered in turn.[12]

Soft Law Gender Quotas

In a bid to increase gender equality on corporate boards, in 2007, the Spanish government enacted the *Gender Equality Act,* which required all companies to have at least 40 per cent of each gender on their boards by 2015.[13] The *Gender Equality Act* also stipulates that compliant companies will obtain preferential treatment when government contracts are awarded. This gender quota system is termed "soft law" because there is no punishment for non-compliance; rather, rewards are given for compliance. As such, the quotas merely serve as suggestions or at best, recommendations that urge companies to take action towards having a gender-balanced board.[14] Results-wise, a study involving 767 Spanish firms revealed that only about 9 per cent of firms complied with the quota and that the reward of preferential treatment in awarding public contracts only motivated companies whose businesses were hinged on government contracts.[15] However, although only 9 per cent met the prescribed quota, there was an increase in the number of female directors from 6.8 per cent in 2005 to 11.6 per cent in 2014.[16] As of 2018, women held 23.2 per cent of corporate directorships in Spain.[17]

In 2010, the Kenyan government adopted a slightly different approach towards gender diversity in state-owned enterprises (SOEs) by enshrining in the constitution the requirement for all SOEs to have not more than two-thirds of each gender on corporate boards.[18] There are, however, no sanctions for non-compliance.[19] Also, there has been some power tussles in Kenya with its Parliament refusing to enact the *Constitution of Kenya (Amendment) Bill 2018*, which seeks to act on the constitutional provision requiring that each gender not hold more than two-thirds of board positions.[20] Despite this, according to a 2015 Board Diversity Report prepared by the African Development Bank, which analyzed diversity policies in twelve African countries, Kenya has the highest number of women directorships in Africa, with women holding 19.8 per cent of all directorships,[21] and also recorded an increase in the number of female directorships on SOE boards from 15 per cent to 20 per cent in 2010 and 2012, respectively.[22]

Similar results have been found in other jurisdictions employing soft law quotas. In Malaysia, the government issued a policy in 2011 that required at least 30 per cent women directorships to be achieved by 2016, but again without any sanctions for non-compliance.[23] This target was not attained in 2016, as women only held 15.3 per cent of corporate directorships at the time.[24] As a result, the government extended the target deadline to 2020,[25] and as of 2018, women make up 21.9 per cent of directorships in the country.[26] Netherlands also enacted soft law quotas in 2013 that required at least 30 per cent composition of each gender without any threat of sanctions.[27] The law basically adopts a comply-or-explain approach, requiring companies who fail to meet the quota target to explain the reason for such failure and indicate steps to be taken to achieve a gender-balanced board in the future.[28] In addition, the law was issued for a fixed period of time and lapsed on 1 January 2016, as the government had envisaged that the prescribed quota would have been achieved.[29] It is generally accepted that this Dutch law was largely unsuccessful because it did not achieve the 30 per cent quota target. As of 2018, women held 24.9 per cent of directorships in the Netherlands.[30]

The *Indian Companies Act 2013* also requires listed companies and public companies with a paid-up share capital above one hundred rupees or a turnover of over three hundred rupees to have at least one female director on their boards.[31] There has also been relative success with this initiative as statistics show that the number of women on boards has increased from 5 per cent in 2012[32] to 12.3 per cent in 2014.[33] As of 2018, women held 14 per cent of all directorships and 100 per cent of companies had one or more women on their boards.[34] However, despite the increase over the years, the number of women directorships still falls below the global average of 17.9 per cent.[35] There has also been concern that a majority of women appointed to boards in India are family members of promoters because India predominantly consists of family-owned, public-listed companies.[36] The quota has also not achieved critical mass as only 11.4 per cent of companies have more than three women on their boards.[37]

In Finland, the 2016 *Act on Equality between Women and Men* mandates equal composition of women and men in government offices and SOEs.[38] The Government Action Plan for 2016–19 for Gender Equality also requires listed SOEs and public companies to achieve a 40 per cent representation of women and men on corporate boards.[39]

The MSCI Index records an increase from 29.9 per cent in 2016[40] to 33.7 per cent female directorships in 2017 and 34.5 per cent in 2018.[41] Overall, 100 per cent of companies have at least one woman on their board while 76.9 per cent have three or more women.[42]

In all, from the multi-country analysis discussed above, we see that soft law quotas have, in most cases, helped to marginally increase the number of women on corporate boards. Also, many states were unable to meet the targeted quota within the expected timeframe.[43] Scholars have therefore suggested that soft law quotas are more effective in the short term as they serve as a looming statutory threat that propels companies to aim for gender parity.[44]

Inclusion of Gender Diversity Principles in Corporate Governance Codes

The inclusion of gender diversity principles in corporate governance codes is another approach that has been applied in certain countries.[45] In these cases, either a "comply-or-explain" or an "apply-and-explain" approach is put in place. A multi-country analysis of this approach and their consequential results is discussed below.

The UK's Code of Corporate Governance employs a comply-or-explain disclosure requirement which mandates companies to establish a gender diversity policy and disclose steps taken to achieve gender parity.[46] Companies are equally required to disclose reasons for non-compliance. Key reforms concerning gender diversity in the UK commenced in 2011 with the Lord Davies Review, which recommended that companies aim for at least 25 per cent women directors by 2015 as opposed to the 12.5 per cent representation in 2010.[47] In 2016, a government backed Hampton-Alexander Review was set up to achieve the target of having at least 33 per cent women directors on boards of Financial Times Stock Exchange (FTSE) 350 companies by 2020.[48] As of December 2020, women held over 34 per cent of all directorships in the UK, effectively meeting the quota target.[49] The Hampton-Alexander Review also mentions that further progress is required "building diversity into the executive pipeline."[50]

In Canada, amendments to National Instrument 58-101 *Disclosure of Corporate Governance Practices* in 2014 requiring Toronto Stock Exchange listed companies to disclose steps and policies put in place to increase female representation on boards has also contributed to the gradual increase of women on boards as well as in senior management positions. In 2016, women held 19.4 per cent of board positions, and as of May 2019, 28 per cent of companies had one woman on their boards and 15.2 per cent had more than one woman, while all-male boards still accounted for 58 per cent of board directorships.[51] Amendments made to the *Canada Business Corporations Act* in May 2018 also require the annual disclosure of steps taken to ensure gender parity as well as representation of Aboriginal peoples, persons with disabilities, and visible minorities.[52]

In South Africa, the King IV Report on Corporate Governance 2016 provides for board diversity.[53] This report recommends that the board should comprise "an appropriate balance of knowledge, skills, experience, diversity, and independence."[54] Boards are also required to disclose compliance based on an apply-and-explain approach that assumes compliance with all the principles set out in the Code and does not give room for non-compliance. It is estimated that as of 2018, women hold about 24.6 per cent[55] of directorship positions in South Africa, compared to 7.1 per cent in 2004.[56] The Johannesburg Stock Exchange also now requires boards of listed companies to disclose their gender and race diversity targets as well as steps taken towards achieving the set target.[57]

The 2018 Hong Kong Listing Rules and Corporate Governance Code requires listed companies to disclose diversity policies that have been put in place and indicate measurable goals on how diversity would be enriched within the organization – this requirement in particular is targeted for independent non-executive directors.[58] The listing rules, however, appear to have had no effect as the percentage of female directors dropped from 11.3 per cent in 2017 to 11 per cent in 2018.[59]

In Mexico, the 2018 Code of Best Practices of Corporate Governance issued by the Mexican Business Council includes suggestions for enhancement of diversity and requires listed companies to report annually on their compliance with this Code.[60] Similar to Hong Kong, little progress has been recorded with the percentage of female directorships falling from 7.5 per cent in 2017 to 7.3 per cent in 2018.[61] However, 57.7 per cent of companies are recorded to have at least one woman on their board.[62]

The above analysis on the effect of gender diversity principles and disclosure requirements contained in corporate governance codes generally reveals that the outcome is not substantially different from that of soft law quotas. The UK appears to be an outlier, having recorded substantial success in achieving the 33 per cent target without implementing mandatory quotas. This result suggests that it may be useful to study the UK model and its efficacy in meeting gender targets without the use of mandatory quotas.

Mandatory Gender Quotas

As an alternative to soft law gender quotas, some other countries have taken a firmer stand by adopting mandatory gender quotas. Unlike soft law quotas, mandatory quotas prescribe sanctions such as fines or possibly delisting for non-compliance of gender quota requirements.

The very first of the national mandatory gender quotas occurred in 2003 when Norway required that boards of public companies be comprised of at least 40 per cent of each gender by 2008.[63] Sanctions ranging from fines to delisting from the stock exchange were stipulated as punishment for non-compliance, and all companies complied by the deadline.[64] Although the quota was achieved in 2008 (coming a long way from merely 6 per cent in 2002),[65] the number of female directorships recently fell from 42.2 per cent in 2017 to 39.6 per cent in 2018.[66] There have also been conflicting studies on the effect of Norway's quota system. Some studies allege that it has led to the recruitment of many inexperienced women, which negatively affected stock prices.[67] On the other side of the divide, studies also show that there have been fewer employee reductions and better stakeholder engagement outcomes.[68]

In Belgium, a mandatory quota was put in place in July 2011, and became effective September of that same year, requiring large, listed companies to have one-third representation of both genders by 2017 and for small and medium-sized listed companies by 2019.[69] The law prescribes that where a certain gender is underrepresented, subsequent director appointments must be of that gender; otherwise, such an appointment will be invalid. An additional sanction relating to suspension of board members' benefits also applies to listed companies.[70] In 2010, women only made up 7.7 per cent of corporate directorships and, following implementation of the quota, representation increased substantially to 30.4 per cent in 2017[71] and 31.1 per cent in 2018.[72] Studies also show that despite initial criticism and fears concerning the quota legislation, Belgian companies have now embraced gender diversity initiatives and are paying better attention to staffing and board recruitment exercises.[73]

Mandatory quotas were also introduced in France in 2011 with the law requiring at least 40 per cent representation of each gender in both listed companies and private companies (with assets worth €50,000,000 and over five hundred employees) by January 2017.[74] Sanctions for non-compliance included the nullification of director appointments and non-payment of board attendance fees.[75] With the issuance of the law, the number of female directorships increased from 12.7 per cent in 2010 to 16.6 per cent in 2011.[76] In 2018, there were 41.2 per cent women directors.[77]

In Italy, Law 120 of 12 July 2011, "Gender Balance on the Boards of Listed Companies," was passed and became effective in August 2011.[78] The law required boards and statutory auditors to give the less represented gender one-fifth of the board seats. The law also provides that if a listed company is found to be in disregard of the law, a company may be granted a four-month grace period to comply.[79] If following this, the company still fails to comply, a fine between €100,000–€1,000,000 will be levied.[80] Companies are thereafter given another three months within which to comply with the law and failure to do so will lead to the replacement of the board.[81] As of 2018, women occupied about 35 per cent of directorships in Italian companies,[82] which is a long way from the 3.6 per cent representation in 2010.[83]

On 30 September 2018, California passed legislation requiring public companies with their head office in California to have at least one woman on their board by the end of 2019 and companies with five directors will need to have at least two female directors.[84] The law also prescribes a fine of US$100,000 for first time violation and US$300,000 for subsequent incidences of non-compliance. [85] This law makes California the first state in the US to establish a gender diversity quota for corporate boards. There have been several objections to the enactment of the law, chief of which revolves around the potential violation of constitutional provisions on freedom from discrimination based on gender.[86] A study conducted by the MSCI ESG Research LLC in 2018 reveals that about fifty-one MSCI ACWI IMI (Investable Market Index) companies have male-dominated boards and were unlikely to meet the 2019 deadline to have at least one woman on their board.[87]

Overall, it appears that mandatory quotas have been effective in driving up the number of women on boards in countries where it has been utilized. Although the effect of same in the US is yet to be seen, from the results achieved by European countries that adopted this system, the likelihood is high that similar results will be realized in California. There is, however, slight concern – as is evidenced from the Norwegian analysis, that mandatory quotas are not sufficient to maintain the required threshold of female directorships.

BREAKING DOWN THE MANDATORY GENDER QUOTA DEBATE

Due to its controversial nature, this section will summarize and consider many of the arguments that have been put forward in support of and against the implementation of mandatory quotas to increase gender diversity on corporate boards.

Arguments in Favour of Mandatory Gender Quotas

SOCIAL JUSTICE AND EQUALITY

One key reason given by advocates of gender diversity quotas is the promotion of social justice and equality.[88] Quotas are essentially targeted at addressing the historical discrimination of women that continues to this day and reverberates in corporate boardrooms. Thus, quotas are measures put in place by states in keeping with their commitment to enhance gender equality, as required under the United Nations Convention for the Elimination of All Forms of Discrimination Against Women (CEDAW), which many countries have ratified.[89] As Güler Turan notes, "quotas are by definition temporary measures, aimed at eradicating an inequality that has built up over time. Once that is done, the quotas will be lifted in accordance with the principle of equal treatment as it is interpreted by international courts of human rights."[90]

Mandatory quotas, therefore, are seen as a firm commitment to social justice, equality, and the enhancement of the right of every person to equal treatment and equal outcomes.[91] It is believed that equal treatment is achieved by putting measures in place that help provide underrepresented persons with more opportunities than others, which effectively balances the scale.[92] As seen in the first section of this chapter, countries with the highest number of women on corporate boards are those that have implemented mandatory quotas, and there is ample research to support this view.[93]

PRODUCES EXPONENTIAL RESULTS

The multi-country analysis in the first section also reveals that mandatory quotas are immensely effective in driving up the number of female directorships in Europe. In the case of Norway, female directorships increased by 33.6 per cent from 2002–18.[94] Similarly, a 23.4 per cent increase was recorded in Belgium,[95] 28.5 per cent in France[96] and 31.4 per cent in Italy.[97] These results have, therefore, put Europe at the forefront of achieving gender diversity in corporate boardrooms. It is expected that similar results will be achieved in California, as preliminary analysis conducted by 2020 Women on Boards reveals that the number of women on corporate boards with headquarters in California increased from 17.4 per cent in 2018 to 21.1 per cent as of June 2019.[98] More so, these results indicate that mandatory quotas are more effective in enhancing gender diversity compared to soft law gender quotas and diversity policies included in corporate governance codes.

ENHANCES OVERALL GOVERNANCE AND DECISION-MAKING

Research suggests that increasing the number of women on corporate boards enhances overall governance and the quality of decision-making processes. This position has been supported by Lynda Gratton and Lamia Walker who assert that a gender-balanced board "delivers optimal performance in most areas that drive innovation."[99] Having more women on boards, however, is just half the task. To reap the full benefits of diversity, it is important that more *independent* female directors are appointed to corporate boards, as opposed to family members of promoters or existing corporate officials. Mandatory quotas could prove to be veritable tools in this respect. For example, in Norway it was found that most of the female directors appointed following mandatory quota legislation were independent directors who were not affiliated to the company or to management.[100] Further research suggests that having a critical mass of about three or more women on boards produces "more robust deliberation, disruption of groupthink, more effective risk management, higher quality monitoring of management, and more systematic work."[101]

ESTABLISHES MEASURABLE AND ENFORCEABLE GENDER PARITY GOALS

Arguments similarly can be made to the effect that unlike soft law quotas and diversity principles and policies, mandatory quotas establish gender parity goals that can be measured, monitored, and enforced. In some of the cases discussed previously in this chapter, such as in relation to Malaysia and the Netherlands, soft law quotas were deemed unsuccessful as they failed to achieve set targets. Although soft quota targets are measurable, since soft law quotas are devoid of sanctions, they cannot be enforced. Both domestic and international communities are aware of the need to put measures in place to promote gender diversity in all sectors.[102] As such, governments have adopted either soft law quotas, the inclusion of gender diversity principles in corporate governance codes, or mandatory quotas to signify their commitment towards a more gender-balanced world. While the first two approaches may be sufficient to signify this commitment, more concrete tools like mandatory quotas seem necessary to achieve the gender parity goal.

NEXT STEP WHEN OTHER MEASURES FAIL

Typically, many countries are more inclined to adopt soft law quotas or diversity policies at the onset in the hopes that either one or the other, or both, would be sufficient to enhance gender diversity. When these measures fall short of expectations, countries then turn to mandatory quotas as a tool of last resort. In 2016, the Canadian Minister for Innovation, Science and Economic Development indicated that mandatory quotas would be the next step if the diversity policies issued for listed companies do not lead to an increase in female directorships.[103] In his words, Minister Navdeep Bains stated: "We want to send a clear signal that diversity is important and you need to explain what your diversity policies are and we feel that will start moving the needle … But in a few years, if we don't see meaningful results – then we will re-evaluate our position and look at all other options at that time."[104]

Similarly, in explaining the rationale behind the quota legislation, California's governor Jerry Brown indicated that, although mandatory quotas were controversial, prior attempts to substantially enhance gender diversity had been largely unsuccessful thus enacting mandatory quotas was inevitable.[105] In his words, the governor states, "there have been numerous objections to this bill and serious legal concerns have been raised … I don't minimize the potential flaws that indeed may prove fatal to its ultimate implementation. Nevertheless, recent events in Washington, DC – and beyond – make it crystal clear that many are not getting the message."[106]

As such, one observes that in countries where prior approaches of soft law quotas, diversity principles, or a mixture of both have not provided the desired results, mandatory quotas are being considered as the next logical step.

Arguments Against Mandatory Gender Quotas

FEAR OF DISCRIMINATION AND TOKENISM

A common fear expressed by opponents of mandatory quota legislation is that it is unconstitutional, as it works contrary to constitutional provisions that enshrine the right to freedom from gender-based discrimination. In California, there is the live concern that the California law will not survive judicial contest concerning its constitutionality.[107] This concern has also been expressed concerning Germany's quota legislation as scholars have suggested that it may be in breach of the principle of equal treatment, and that there is a high probability that it may not withstand judicial review. [108]

Also related to this is the fear of tokenism. Directors and scholars alike have expressed concerns that mandatory quotas will only lead to the appointment of token female directors –coined "golden skirts" – who will likely sit on multiple boards and be over boarded.[109] However, results from varying countries reveal that this may not be so in all cases. Evidence from Norway shows that this fear was not realized.[110] Norway's experience is in contrast to the results gleaned from India, where women who were family members of promoters or managerial officers were appointed following the enactment of soft law quotas.[111] Thus the tokenism challenge may be more likely experienced in countries with a preponderance of family-owned businesses, like India, and is less a function of the quota system adopted.

MIXED FIRM PERFORMANCE EFFECTS

Another objection posed against mandatory quotas is that there have been mixed firm performance effects, that is, in terms of the company's financial health. Marion Hutchinson and Siri Terjesen respectively, believe that the inclusion of women on boards increases the earnings forecast of publicly listed companies, and can potentially increase firm revenue.[112] On the other hand, scholars like Kenneth Ahern and Amy Dittmar have argued that increased membership of women on corporate boards via the quota system have negatively impacted the stock price of public listed companies.[113] In the same vein, another group of economists have argued that the effect of the quota system on companies is unclear;[114] while still others find that the quota system has had no effect whatsoever.[115] A possible reason for these varying conclusions is that it may be difficult to solely assess the impact of gender diversity on firm performance because a myriad of other factors affect and contribute to firm performance.

NO "TRICKLE-DOWN" EFFECT

Opponents of the mandatory quota approach have also argued that such quotas only result in an increase in the number of women on boards but not in executive positions.[116] They explain that board appointments are usually made both internally through promotions of persons within the executive and externally through the appointment of outside directors. As a result, mandatory quotas only affect the recruitment of independent directors but do not trickle down to securing executive or managerial positions for women.[117] This phenomenon is often referred to as the "pipeline problem," that is, a situation wherein the number of women within the internal pool has not increased in the same manner as the number of women on boards.[118] This concern has been corroborated by a number of studies. For example, in one study, Bertrand et al. found that "overall, seven years after the board quota policy fully came into effect, we conclude that it had very little discernible impact on women in business beyond its direct effect on the women who made it into boardrooms."[119] Some scholars have thus suggested that additional measures may be needed to solve the pipeline problem.[120] However, it seems that these concerns downplay the importance of independent directors to the company. Independent directors not only play a crucial role in safeguarding the independence of the board, but they also bring in diverse skill sets, networks, and perspectives which enhance board diversity.[121] That is why corporate governance codes and policies often require boards to recruit more independent directors.[122] It is, therefore, commendable that mandatory quotas have been successful in increasing the number of independent directors on corporate boards.

DIVERTS ATTENTION FROM OTHER KEY ASPECTS OF BOARD DIVERSITY

Critics have also argued that prioritizing gender will be detrimental to other areas of diversity such as race, ethnicity, skills, etc. [123] They explain that it would be absurd to similarly prescribe mandatory quotas for these other diversity elements and that doing so will amount to governments micro-managing businesses, which would stifle board efficiency and effectiveness.[124] According to Maggie Philbin, a UK television and radio personality who advocates for diversity in the technology industry, "if we address all diversity, other things would start to fall in place as well, whereas if we simply focus on getting more women into companies, we're not going to achieve what we really need to achieve. We still won't have diversity, we'll have gender diversity, but we won't have real diversity."[125]

These concerns are particularly acute in times like these where the Black Lives Matter movement has caused global concern about systemic racism. The movement has given rise to more prominent calls for racial diversity within public and private sectors, and more particularly on corporate boards.[126] For example, statistics from a 2018 study reveal that women of colour account for 4.6 per cent of corporate directorships on Fortune 500 companies.[127] These statistics explain why critics argue that mandatory quotas divert from the attainment of a truly diverse board. The question as to how to pragmatically achieve this preferred holistic diversity, however, requires much consideration and is yet to be satisfactorily answered.

RESULTS ARE UNSUSTAINABLE

In addition to the previous arguments discussed above, opponents of mandatory quotas have also asserted that they are unsustainable because, as temporary measures, they do not produce lasting results.[128] For example, in the case of Norway, there has been a decline in female directorships from 42.2 per cent in 2017 to 39.6 per cent in 2018; Italy equally recorded a decline from 35.8 per cent to 35 per cent in 2017 and 2018, respectively.[129] These declines have led to concerns about the ability of mandatory quotas to sustainably enhance gender diversity. However, the concerns may be premature considering that this decline is not widespread across other countries that have adopted mandatory quotas, and that countries with soft law quotas like Spain have recorded similar declines (24 per cent in 2017 to 23.6 per cent in 2018).[130]

NO ROOM FOR MERIT

Mandatory quotas are affirmative action tools, and thus several arguments made against affirmative action have also been applied to mandatory quotas. There is concern that prioritizing gender as a yardstick for board recruitment would result in hiring unqualified or less qualified candidates to the board and usurp the place of merit in the recruitment process.[131] In response to this assertion, some scholars have pointed out that "merit and quotas are not mutually exclusive but that in fact, quotas are essential to a meritocratic system."[132] Furthermore, research reveals that in countries where mandatory quotas were implemented, this fear was not realized.[133] The merit versus diversity argument has led to the assertion from advocates of mandatory quotas that there is "a hostility towards quotas in countries that don't have them."[134]

A WAY FORWARD

From the multi-country analysis discussed in this chapter, we see that mandatory quotas have been predominantly utilized in Europe to substantially increase female directorships. The state of California in the US has also gotten on board with this approach, and it is hoped that similar results will be recorded therein. Although no state was able to meet the targeted quota within expected timeframes, soft law quotas have only led to marginal increases. This lackluster performance explains why they are often regarded as short-term tools.[135] It is also probable that soft law quotas are more suitable for small scale groups like Crown corporations in Quebec, Canada, where soft law requiring Crown corporations to be equally comprised of men and women was enacted in 2006 and the quota was achieved by the 2011 timeframe.[136] The same type of results also appear to pertain to gender diversity principles included in corporate governance codes; that is, with the exception of the UK (having made substantial progress towards its 33 per cent female representation target by the 2020 deadline). Overall, unlike the other two approaches, in all instances where mandatory quotas were employed, the number of female directors increased exponentially by the stipulated deadline. Particularly, statistics reveal that as of October 2018, companies in Norway, Italy, and France are the only MSCI ACWI Index companies with at least an average of three women on their board.[137]

The effect of implementing mandatory quotas becomes more visible from a qualitative analysis of its impact. During a qualitative study analyzing the experiences of women who have benefited from the Norwegian quota, one of the study participants made the following profound statement:

> I have so much experience; I have worked in the industry for more than 20 years. Still no one thought of contacting me to be on boards ... It is because they have their own networks. With

> the gender representation law, I have been given the opportunity to prove myself. The law has opened for women, women who were not in the immediate network. Now nomination committees have to choose "untraditional" and that is a good thing, it is fair. Until now, it's been more like "I'll call Ola, I know him. He has experience and he is good, he is close to 80 but so what."[138]

The above statement lends to the argument that mandatory quotas have largely been successful in disbanding the "old boys club" and creating better opportunities for women to apply their skills and experiences on corporate boards.

Furthermore, the responses to mandatory quota outcomes, particularly in terms of mixed performance results and lack of trickle-down effect, seem to downplay a key benefit derived from imposing mandatory quotas – which is the significant increase in the number of women on corporate boards. This outcome is yet to be achieved by soft law approaches. More so, research shows that many of the perceived harmful effects of mandatory quotas were not experienced in Norway and perhaps there are some unwarranted fears of the unknown held in countries that do not have mandatory quotas compared to countries that do.

Care must be taken when critiquing the effectiveness or otherwise of mandatory quotas, so as not to perceive the legislative tool as a magic wand, which would holistically eradicate gender inequality at all levels and close the gender gap. Gender inequality is a product of decades of continuous discrimination that has substantially marginalized women and it cannot be solved by a singular legislation. Therefore, although it may not be the final solution, establishing mandatory quotas may be a step in the right direction.

In addition, the implication of current research studies on mandatory quotas suggests governments and regulators all over the world cannot sit back and hope quota legislation will resolve decades of inequality that has been meted out to women. While mandatory quotas will be sufficient to drastically enhance representation of women on boards, it is also necessary to put measures in place to ensure the representation of women in management and senior management positions. As researchers have pointed out, commitment to diversity policies, training of directors, and promotion of a culture of female participation in corporate boards is necessary to effectively address the deep-rooted causes of gender inequality.[139]

Jean Du Plessis et al. adequately captured the solution when they stated that "a change in cultural attitudes, so that the advantages of diversity are recognized and female participation encouraged, will increase the quantity of qualified, experienced female directors in a sustainable and productive manner."[140] Another approach could be to adopt specific language in mandatory quota laws that require companies to hire women in both independent and executive director positions. This legislative fix could help address the pipeline problem by ensuring that women are appointed not just as independent directors, but also as top executive directors.[141]

While soft law quotas did lead to a marginal increase in female directorships, it is important to note how within countries that adopted this approach, diversity targets still were not met. Similarly, the inclusion of diversity principles in corporate governance codes also produced marginal benefits in most of the countries identified. In contrast to these two approaches, in all instances where mandatory quotas were utilized, gender diversity targets were met, and female directorships significantly increased. Compelling arguments in favour of mandatory quotas include the probability of deriving exponential results in terms of increasing female directorships, functioning as a measurable and enforceable gender parity tool, signifying a country's commitment to achieving a more gender-balanced world in line with commitments made under human rights instruments such as the CEDAW, and being the next logical step after other measures prove ineffective. Opponents have highlighted concerns relating to mixed performance results and fears that quotas will dethrone merit, or that gender quotas divert attention from other key areas of diversity, produce results that do not trickle down to managerial positions, and are unsustainable in the long run. Notwithstanding arguments against mandatory quotas, the multi-country analysis explored in this chapter shows that of the three methods employed, establishing mandatory quotas has been the most successful. Accordingly, as Beate Sjåfjell points out, "boardroom gender diversity has such a positive effect that it should be sought to be achieved, through mandatory legislation if necessary."[142] Nonetheless, it is important that we do not rely solely on mandatory quotas as a holistic solution to bridging the gender divide. Diversity trainings, cultural attitudinal changes, board diversity policies, and better awareness are still necessary to ensure that women not only occupy board seats, but also have seats at the managerial level. Initiatives such as the United Nations Women's Empowerment Principles (UNWEP), which seek to encourage business leaders across the world to sign on to and observe seven key principles geared towards enhancing gender equality in the "workplace, marketplace and community," are equally important and beneficial initiatives.[143] It is, however, imperative that companies and CEOs go beyond signing the UNWEP's Statement of Support, and do more to establish tangible targets and accountability measures geared towards closing gender gaps.[144]

NOTES

1 See e.g., Michael Adams, "Board Diversity: More than a Gender Issue?," *Deakin Law Review* 20, no. 1 (September 2015): 140.

2 Vanessa Fuhrmans, "What #MeToo has to do with the Workplace Gender Gap," *Wall Street Journal,* 23 October 2018, https://www.wsj.com/articles/what-metoo-has-to-do-with-the-workplace-gender-gap-1540267680.

3 Helen Chan and Julie DiMauro, "Black Lives Matter Movement Turns Up Heat for Boards to Walk the Talk of Racial Diversity," *Reuters,* 5 October 2020, https://www.reutersevents.com/sustainability/black-lives-matter-movement-turns-heat-boards-walk-talk-racial-diversity.

4 Jena McGregor, "The Lone All-Male Board in the S&P 500 Just Added a Woman to Its Ranks," *Washington Post*, 25 July 2019, https://www.washingtonpost.com/business/2019/07/25/lone-all-male-board-sp-just-added-woman-its-ranks.

5 Deloitte, "Women in the Boardroom – A Global Perspective (6th Edition)," accessed 13 August 2021, https://www2.deloitte.com/global/en/pages/risk/cyber-strategic-risk/articles/women-in-the-boardroom-global-perspective.html.

6 Morgan Ellis and Meggin Thwing Eastman, "Women on Boards – Progress Report 2018," MSCI ESG Research LLC, 9 January 2019, 24, https://www.msci.com/www/research-paper/women-on-boards-progress-report/01210712745.

7 Ibid.

8 Cynthia Soledad et al., "2018 Global Board Diversity Tracker: Who's Really on Board?," Egon Zehnder, 3 January 2019, https://www.egonzehnder.com/what-we-do/board-advisory/insights/2018-global-board-diversity-tracker-whos-really-on-board.

9 Deloitte, "Women in the Boardroom," 7.

10 The "comply-or-explain" approach originated with the Cadbury Committee in the UK as a means of monitoring corporate governance

compliance while giving room for explanations for non-compliance. See David Seidl, Paul Sanderson, and John Roberts, "Applying the 'Comply-or-Explain' Principle: Discursive Legitimacy Tactics with Regard to Codes of Corporate Governance," *Journal of Management & Governance* 17, no. 3 (2013): 791–826.

11 The "apply-and-explain" approach has its origins in South Africa's King IV Report on Corporate Governance. Mervyn King and Fabian Ajogwu. *Outcomes-Based Governance: A Modern Approach to Corporate Governance* (Cape Town: Juta and Company, 2020).

12 Many countries adopt a mixture of these approaches. In this chapter, only soft law or mandatory quotas are highlighted and discussed.

13 Ley Orgánica 3/2007, de 22 de marzo, para la igualdad efectiva de mujeres y hombres ("the 3/2007 Equality Law"). See Emanuela Lombardo, *Gender Equality Policies in Spain – Update* (Brussels: European Parliament – Policy Department for Citizen's Rights and Constitutional Affairs, 2016).

14 Ruth Mateos de Cabo et al., "Do 'Soft Law' Board Gender Quotas Work? Evidence from a Natural Experiment," *European Management Journal* 37, no. 5 (October 2019).

15 Ibid.

16 Siri Terjesen, "Why Some Board Gender Quotas Don't Work," *Catalyst*, 12 February 2019, https://www.catalyst.org/2019/02/12/why-some-board-gender-quotas-dont-work.

17 Ellis and Eastman, "Women on Boards," 22.

18 Constitution of Kenya, art. 27(8). See also International Finance Group, World Bank Group, "Women on Boards in Nigeria," 2019, 3, https://www.ifc.org/wps/wcm/connect/7f01fe3c-21e2-4653-98f6-b82e0f8833cb/Women_on_Boards_in_Nigeria.pdf?MOD=AJPERES&CVID=mLyezop.

19 International Finance Corporation, "Women on Boards in Nigeria," 3.

20 Marilyn Muthoni Kamuru, "Kenya's Gender Bill: Battling Inequality, Saving the Constitution," *Al Jazeera*, 17 March 2019, https://www.aljazeera.com/opinions/2019/3/17/kenyas-gender-bill-battling-inequality-saving-the-constitution. In 2015, the courts had mandated the Kenyan Parliament to enact the Gender Bill within sixty days, which they failed to do.

21 Geraldine J. Fraser-Moleketi and Simon Mizrahi, *Where are the Women: Inclusive Boardrooms in Africa's Top Listed Companies?* (Abidjan: African Development Bank Group, 2015), 14.

22 Ibid., 38.

23 The policy was based on memorandum titled, "A Policy on at Least 30 Per Cent Women at Decision Making Level in the Private Sector" prepared by the Ministry for Women, Family and Community Development

and subsequently approved by the Cabinet. See Daniel C.M. Low, Helen Roberts, and Rosalind H. Whiting, "Board Gender Diversity and Firm Performance: Empirical Evidence from Hong Kong, South Korea, Malaysia and Singapore," *Pacific-Basin Finance Journal* 35 (November 2015): 381.

24 Meggin Thwing Eastman, Damion Rallis, and Gaia Mazzucchelli, "The Tipping Point: Women on Boards and Financial Performance (Women on Boards Report 2016)," MSCI ESG Research Inc., 13 December 2016, 17, https://www.msci.com/www/research-paper/the-tipping-point-women-on/0538947986.

25 Hwok-Aun Lee, "The Lessons of Malaysia's Push for Gender Equality," *Nikkei Asian Review*, 7 September 2017, https://asia.nikkei.com/Politics/Hwok-Aun-Lee-The-lessons-of-Malaysia-s-push-for-gender-equality.

26 Ellis and Eastman, "Women on Boards," 21.

27 Sonja A. Kruisinga and Linda Senden, "Gender Diversity on Corporate Boards in the Netherlands: Waiting on the World to Change," in *Gender Diversity in the Boardroom,* volume 1, *Use of Different Quota Regulations*, edited by Cathrine Seierstad, Patricia Gabaldon, and Heike Mensi-Klarbach (Cham: Palgrave Macmillan 2017), 177.

28 Art. 2:391 s. 7 *Dutch Civil Code*, Josephus Jitta (translation).

29 Kruisinga and Senden, "Gender Diversity on Corporate Boards," 177.

30 Ellis and Eastman, "Women on Boards," 21.

31 *The Indian Companies Act 2013* and Rules 3, Companies (Appointment & Qualification) Rules, 2014.

32 Deloitte Touche Tohmatsu Limited, "Women in the Boardroom: A Global Perspective, 3rd ed.," 2013, 6, https://www2.deloitte.com/global/en/pages/risk/cyber-strategic-risk/articles/women-in-the-boardroom-a-global-perspective.html.

33 Deloitte Touche Tohmatsu Limited, "Women in the Boardroom: A Global Perspective, 5th ed.," 2017, 4, https://www2.deloitte.com/content/dam/Deloitte/cn/Documents/risk/deloitte-cn-ra-ccg-e1-women-in-the-boardroom-a-global-perspective-fifth-edition.pdf.

34 Ellis and Eastman, "Women on Boards," 21–3.

35 Ibid., 4.

36 Ayushi Agarwal, "India's 'One Woman Quota' on Board of Directors Fails to Bring About Gender Equality," Oxford Human Rights Hub, 28 February 2018, https://ohrh.law.ox.ac.uk/indias-one-woman-quota-on-board-of-directors-fails-to-bring-about-gender-equality.

37 Ellis and Eastman, "Women on Boards," 23.

38 *Finland: Act on Equality between Women and Men*, 1 January 1987, https://www.refworld.org/docid/3ae6b51c0.html.

39 Deloitte Touche Tohmatsu Limited, "Women in the Boardroom: A Global Perspective, 6th ed.," 2019, 99, https://www2.deloitte.com/au/en/pages/risk/articles/women-boardroom-sixth-edition.html.
40 Linda-Eling Lee et al., "Women on Boards: Global Trends in Gender Diversity on Corporate Boards," MSCI ESG Research Inc, November 2015, 22, https://www.msci.com/documents/10199/04b6f646-d638-4878-9c61-4eb91748a82b.
41 Ellis and Eastman, "Women on Boards," 21.
42 Ibid., 21–3.
43 Andrew MacDougall and Michele Qu, "Gender Diversity on Boards and in Senior Management," Osler, Hoskin & Harcourt, 2014, https://www.osler.com/uploadedFiles/Gender-Diversity-on-Boards-and-in-Senior-Management.pdf.
44 Jennifer M. Piscopo and Susan Clark Muntean, "Corporate Quotas and Symbolic Politics in Advanced Democracies," *Journal of Women, Politics & Policy* 39, no. 3 (June 2018): 285.
45 Jean Du Plessis, "The Case for and against Mandatory Gender Quota Legislation for Company Boards," *Deakin Law Review* 20, no. 1 (September 2015): 5.
46 Financial Reporting Council, "The UK Corporate Governance Code," July 2018, https://www.frc.org.uk/getattachment/88bd8c45-50ea-4841-95b0-d2f4f48069a2/2018-UK-Corporate-Governance-Code-FINAL.PDF.
47 Mervyn Davies, "Women on Boards," Department for Business, Innovation & Skills, 24 February 2011, https://www.gov.uk/government/news/women-on-boards.
48 Sarah Gordon, "UK plc Behind Target for Number of Women on Boards," *Financial Times*, 27 June 2018, https://www.ft.com/content/ac1449b8-79f7-11e8-bc55-50daf11b720d.
49 Department for Business, Energy & Industrial Strategy, "The Changing Face of Business: Number of Women on FTSE Boards Up by 50% in Just Five Years," *GOV.UK*, 23 February 2021, https://www.gov.uk/government/news/the-changing-face-of-business-number-of-women-on-ftse-boards-up-by-50-in-just-5-years.
50 Financial Reporting Council, "Board Diversity Reporting," September 2018, https://30percentclub.org/assets/uploads/UK/Third_Party_Reports/Board-Diversity-Reporting-September-2018.pdf.
51 Statistics Canada, "Study: Representation of Women on Boards of Directors, 2016," 7 May 2019, https://www150.statcan.gc.ca/n1/daily-quotidien/190507/dq190507a-eng.htm.

52 *An Act to Amend the Canada Business Corporations Act*, the *Canada Cooperatives Act, the Canada Not-for-profit Corporations Act and the Competition Act* 2018, c. 8, s. 172(1).

53 Suzette Viviers, Nadia Mans-Kemp, and Rebecca Fawcett, "Mechanisms to Promote Board Gender Diversity in South Africa," *Acta Commercii* 17, no. 1 (September 2017): 1.

54 The Institute of Directors in Southern Africa NPC, "King IV Report on Corporate Governance for South Africa, 2016," 2016, principle 7, https://cdn.ymaws.com/www.iodsa.co.za/resource/collection/684B68A7-B768-465C-8214-E3A007F15A5A/IoDSA_King_IV_Report_-_WebVersion.pdf.

55 Ellis and Eastman, "Women on Boards," 22.

56 International Labour Organization, "More Women Needed at Top Management Positions in Africa," 12 January 2015, https://www.ilo.org/africa/media-centre/pr/WCMS_335704/lang--en/index.htm.

57 Deloitte, "Women in the Boardroom, 6th ed," 72.

58 Ibid. See also Hong Kong Exchanges and Clearing Limited, "Review of the Corporate Governance Code and Related Listing Rules," 27 July 2018, https://www.hkex.com.hk/News/Regulatory-Announcements/2018/180727news?sc_lang=en.

59 Ellis and Eastman, "Women on Boards," 21.

60 Deloitte, "Women in the Boardroom 6th ed.," 59. See also CCE, *Code of Best Practices of Corporate Governance* (Mexico: Consejo Coordinador Empresarial, 2018), https://cce.org.mx/2021/05/10/codigo-de-mejores-practicas-de-gobierno-corporativo.

61 Ellis and Eastman, "Women on Boards," 21.

62 Ibid, 23.

63 Øyvind Bøhren and Siv Staubo, "Does Mandatory Gender Balance Work? Changing Organizational Form to Avoid Board Upheaval," *Journal of Corporate Finance* 28 (October 2014): 152.

64 Mingzhu Wang and Elisabeth Kelan, "The Gender Quota and Female Leadership: Effects of the Norwegian Gender Quota on Board Chairs and CEOs," *Journal of Business Ethics* 117, no. 3 (14 December 2012): 449.

65 Aagoth Storvik and Mari Teigen, "Women on Board: The Norwegian Experience," International Policy Analysis, Friedrich Ebert Stiftung, June 2010, 8, https://library.fes.de/pdf-files/id/ipa/07309.pdf.

66 Ellis and Eastman, "Women on Boards," 21.

67 Kenneth R. Ahern and Amy K. Dittmar, "The Changing of the Boards: The Impact on Firm Valuation of Mandated Female Board Representation," *Quarterly Journal of Economics* 127, no. 1 (2012): 137.

68 David A. Matsa and Amalia R. Miller, "A Female Style in Corporate Leadership? Evidence from Quotas," *American Economic Journal: Applied Economics* 5, no. 3 (July 2013): 136.
69 Abigail Levrau, "Belgium: Male/Female United in the Boardroom," in *Gender Diversity in the Boardroom,* volume 1, *Use of Different Quota Regulations*, edited by Cathrine Seierstad, Patricia Gabaldon, and Heike Mensi-Klarbach (Cham: Palgrave Macmillan 2017), 164. See also Deloitte, "Women in the Boardroom 6th ed.," 54.
70 Levrau, "Belgium: Male/Female," 164.
71 Ellis and Eastman, "Women on Boards," 21.
72 Ibid.
73 *TVL.BE,* "Economy has not Collapsed Because There are Now Women on Boards of Directors," 26 February 2016, https://www.tvl.be/nieuws/hannelore-roos-25302.
74 Emmanuel Zenou, Isabelle Allemand, and Bénédicte Brullebaut, "Gender Diversity on French Boards: Example of a Success from a Hard Law," in *Gender Diversity in the Boardroom,* volume 1, *Use of Different Quota Regulations*, edited by Cathrine Seierstad, Patricia Gabaldon, and Heike Mensi-Klarbach (Cham: Palgrave Macmillan 2017), 103.
75 Ibid., 114.
76 Lee et al., "Women on Boards: Global Trends," 22.
77 Ellis and Eastman, "Women on Boards," 21.
78 Patrizia Pastore and Silvia Tommaso, "Women on Corporate Boards. The Case of 'Gender Quotas' in Italy," *Corporate Ownership and Control* 13, no. 4 (2016).
79 Ibid.
80 Ibid.
81 Deloitte, "Women in the Boardroom, 6th ed.," 121.
82 Ellis and Eastman, "Women on Boards," 21.
83 Lee et al., "Women on Boards: Global Trends," 22.
84 Bill 826, *An act to add Sections 301.3 and 2115.5 to the Corporations Code, relating to corporations,* c. 954, California Legislative Information. https://leginfo.legislature.ca.gov/faces/billTextClient.xhtml?bill_id=201720180SB826.
85 Patrick McGreevy, "Gov. Jerry Brown Signs Bill Requiring California Corporate Boards to Include Women," *Los Angeles Times*, 30 September 2018, https://www.latimes.com/politics/la-pol-ca-governor-women-corporate-boards-20180930-story.html.
86 Gabriella Okafor, "California's Gender Board Quota Legislation is Likely Unconstitutional," *Columbia Business Law Review*, 13 August 2019,

https://journals.library.columbia.edu/index.php/CBLR/announcement/view/191.

87 Ellis and Eastman, "Women on Boards," 14.

88 Cathrine Seierstad, "Beyond the Business Case: The Need for Both Utility and Justice Rationales for Increasing the Share of Women on Boards," *Corporate Governance: An International Review* 24, no. 4 (July 2016): 390.

89 United Nations Human Rights Office of the High Commissioner, "Convention on the Elimination of All Forms of Discrimination against Women," accessed 17 August 2021, https://www.ohchr.org/en/professionalinterest/pages/cedaw.aspx.

90 Güler Turan, "Why Quotas Work for Gender Equality," OECD, 2015, https://www.oecd.org/social/quotas-gender-equality.htm.

91 Mari Teigen, "The Affirmative Action Controversy," *NORA: Nordic Journal of Feminist and Gender Research* 8, no. 2 (2000): 65.

92 Ibid.

93 Beate Sjåfjell, "Gender Diversity in the Boardroom and Its Impact: Is the Example of Norway a Way Forward?," *Deakin Law Review* 20, no. 1 (September 2015): 25.

94 See par 2.3nn 61–2.

95 See par 2.3nn67–8.

96 See par 2.3nn73–4.

97 See par 2.3nn77–8.

98 2020 Women on Boards, "Gender Diversity Index," October 2019, 6, https://2020wob.com/wp-content/uploads/2019/10/2020WOB_Gender_Diversity_Index_Report_Oct2019.pdf.

99 Lynda Gratton and Lamia Walker, "Gender Equality: A Solid Business Case at Last," *Financial Times*, 28 October 2007, https://www.ft.com/content/79238 4e4-8591-11dc-8170-0000779fd2ac. See also Sjåfjell, "Gender Diversity," 39.

100 Bøhren and Staubo, "Does Mandatory Gender Balance Work?" India is an exception as previously highlighted; see Agarwal, "India."

101 Aaron A. Dhir, *Challenging Boardroom Homogeneity: Corporate Law, Governance, and Diversity* (New York: Cambridge University Press 2015).

102 Rey Dang and Linh-Chi Vo, "Women on Corporate Boards of Directors: Theories, Facts and Analysis," in *Board Directors and Corporate Social Responsibility*, edited by Sabri Boubaker and Duc Khuong Nguyen (London: Palgrave Macmillan 2012), 3.

103 The Canadian Press, "Navdeep Bains on Board Diversity: 'We Want to Send a Clear Signal,'" *Maclean's*, 26 October 2016, https://www.macleans.ca/politics/ottawa/navdeep-bains-on-board-diversity-we-want-to-send-a-clear-signal.

104 Ibid.

105 Jorge L. Ortiz, "California's 'Giant Step Forward': Gender-Quotas Law Requires Women on Corporate Boards," *USA TODAY*, 30 September 2018, https://www.usatoday.com/story/news/2018/09/30/california-law-sets-gender-quotas-corporate-boardrooms/1482883002.

106 Ibid.

107 Katz and McIntosh, "Gender Diversity."

108 Raphael Koch, "Board Gender Quotas in Germany and the EU: An Appropriate Way of Equalising Participation of Men and Women?," *Deakin Law Review* 20, no. 1 (2015): 69.

109 Maria Aluchna and Güler Aras, eds., *Women on Corporate Boards: An International Perspective* (New York: Routledge 2018), 75.

110 Margarethe Wiersema and Marie Louise Mors, "What Board Directors Really Think of Gender Quotas," *Harvard Business Review*, 14 November 2016, https://hbr.org/2016/11/what-board-directors-really-think-of-gender-quotas.

111 Agarwal, "India."

112 Ferdinand A. Gul, Marion Hutchinson, and Karen Lai, "Gender-Diverse Boards and Properties of Analyst Earnings Forecasts," *Accounting Horizons* 27, no. 3 (September 2013): 511.

113 Ahern and Dittmar, "The Changing."

114 See generally Mary Jane Lenard et al., "Impact of Board Gender Diversity on Firm Risk," *Managerial Finance* 40, no. 8 (July 2014): 787.

115 Vathunyoo Sila, Angelica Gonzalez, and Jens Hagendorff, "Women on Boards: Does Boardroom Gender Diversity Affect Firm Risk?," *Journal of Corporate Finance* 36 (2016): 26.

116 David Katz and Laura McIntosh, "Gender Diversity and Board Quotas," *Harvard Law School Forum on Corporate Governance and Financial Regulation*, 27 July 2018, https://corpgov.law.harvard.edu/2018/07/27/gender-diversity-and-board-quotas.

117 Ibid.

118 Nina Smith, "Gender Quotas on Boards of Directors," IZA World of Labor, December 2018, 3, https://wol.iza.org/uploads/articles/461/pdfs/gender-quotas-on-boards-of-directors.pdf.

119 Marianne Bertrand et al., "Breaking the Glass Ceiling? The Effect of Board Quotas on Female Labour Market Outcomes in Norway," *The Review of Economic Studies* 86, no. 1 (January 2019): 191.

120 Smith, "Gender Quotas," 9.

121 Deloitte Touche Tohmatsu Limited, "On the Board's Agenda: Independent Board Members Can Be a Valuable Resource for Private Companies,"

February 2016, https://www2.deloitte.com/content/dam/Deloitte/global/Documents/Risk/gx-ccg-on-boards-agenda-feb-2016.pdf.

122 Donald C. Clarke, "Three Concepts of the Independent Director," *Delaware Journal of Corporate Law* 32, no. 1 (March 2007): 73–5.

123 Katz and McIntosh, "Gender Diversity."

124 Ibid.

125 Clare McDonald, "Focus on Diversity, Not Gender, Says Most Influential Woman in UK IT 2016," *ComputerWeekly.Com*, 23 June 2016, https://www.computerweekly.com/news/450298802/Focus-on-diversity-not-gender-says-most-influential-woman-in-UK-IT-2016.

126 Pippa Stevens, "Companies are Making Bold Promises about Greater Diversity, But There's a Long Way to Go," *CNBC*, 11 June 2020, https://www.cnbc.com/2020/06/11/companies-are-making-bold-promises-about-greater-diversity-theres-a-long-way-to-go.html.

127 Alliance for Board Diversity, Deloitte Touche Tohmatsu Limited, "Missing Pieces Report: The 2018 Board Diversity Census of Women and Minorities on Fortune 500 Boards," 16 January 2019, https://www.catalyst.org/wp-content/uploads/2019/01/missing_pieces_report_01152019_final.pdf.

128 Erika Watson, "Quotas Aren't the Best Way to Get More Women into Boardrooms," *The Guardian*, 18 March 2012, https://www.theguardian.com/commentisfree/2012/mar/18/quotas-women-boardroom-equality.

129 Ellis and Eastman, "Women on Boards," 21.

130 Ibid.

131 Mateos de Cabo et al., "Soft Law," 133.

132 Rainbow Murray, "Merit vs Equality? The Argument That Gender Quotas Violate Meritocracy is Based on Fallacies," *British Politics and Policy at LSE*, 7 December 2015, https://blogs.lse.ac.uk/politicsandpolicy/merit-vs-equality-argument.

133 Wiersema and Mors, "What Board."

134 Ibid.

135 Piscopo and Muntean, "Corporate Quotas," 285.

136 MacDougall and Qu, "Gender Diversity." See also LOPRESPUB, "Women's Representation on Corporate Boards in Canada," *HillNotes,* 5 March 2015, https://hillnotes.ca/2015/03/05/womens-representation-on-corporate-boards-in-canada.

137 Ellis and Eastman, "Women on Boards," 6.

138 Seierstad, "Beyond," 399.

139 Jean du Plessis, James O'Sullivan, and Ruth Rentschler, "Multiple Layers of Gender Diversity on Corporate Boards: To Force or Not to Force?," *Deakin Law Review* 19, no. 1 (August 2014): 46.

140 Ibid.

141 Smith, "Gender Quotas," 8.

142 Sjåfjell, "Gender Diversity," 49.

143 United Nations Global Compact, "Endorse the Women's Empowerment Principles," accessed 17 August 2021, https://www.unglobalcompact.org/take-action/action/womens-principles. Although businesses sign on to the principles, it seems very few go on to implement actions that promote, monitor, and report on gender equality. See United Nations Global Compact, Business for Social Responsibility, "Women's Empowerment and Business: 2020 Trends and Opportunities," 12 March 2020, https://www.bsr.org/en/our-insights/report-view/womens-empowerment-and-business-2020-trends-and-opportunities-weps.

144 Ibid.

4

Crowdfunding for Social Impact Bonds: A Theoretical Solution to Difficulties in Practice

Saul Wang

In recent years, investors have begun looking beyond financial profits and towards social impacts when considering investment opportunities; as a result, demand is growing for social impact bonds (SIBs)[1] in the US and social benefit bonds (SBB) in Australia, with increasing interest in Canada. SIBs belong to a particular class of impact investing that uses a relatively new form of public-private partnership to provide social services and interventions. Unlike the traditional social intervention project model, which depends on the government to provide upfront capital, SIB funds are raised from private investors.[2] These investors are rewarded by the outcome funder – typically the government – only when defined metrics reach certain thresholds.[3]

Although SIBs have garnered interest from both researchers and policymakers, they have failed to attract significant private capital.[4] The shortage of capital commitment has created a power imbalance in favour of investors, which allows them to demand "compromises" that run counter to key qualities of the SIB model, such as the freedom to explore more innovative service delivery methods and insulation from project failure for the outcome funder.[5] In practice, the difficulty of attracting and retaining investors often means that SIB intermediaries (who play the integral role of raising capital and coordinating with and paying the service providers) and outcome funders are required to utilize proven service delivery methods[6] and are pressured to bear significant financial risks associated with the project.[7] I propose a potential solution to the lack of capital commitment in the SIB market, which in theory should alleviate some of the pressure on SIB parties to make such compromises. Namely, I argue that crowdfunding can be a viable source of funds for SIB projects. While crowdfunding may not create substantial monetary savings in upfront capital, the injection of new capital into the market could eliminate the need for compromises and thereby allow for increased usage of more innovative service delivery methods as well as a reduction of the risk borne by intermediaries and outcome funders. Financing by SIB intermediaries prior to obtaining a project contract (that determines payout terms) can be facilitated using a Simple Agreement for Future Equity (SAFE) contract, which is an agreement between the company and an investor that enables the company to raise funds from the investor, while in return giving the investor the right to acquire equity in the company at a future triggering event (discussed in detail in the section below titled "Fundraising Before Securing Contract").[8] SAFE contracts are widely used to generate seed capital for start-up companies. Projects with predetermined payout terms can be crowdfunded based on equity-like contractual terms.

This chapter is organized as follows: the first section describes the essential characteristics of an SIB project; the second section canvasses some of the criticisms levied against SIBs in existing literature and continued challenges; the third section elaborates on the problems created by a lack of private capital commitment in the SIB market; the fourth section discusses crowdfunding and its applicability to raising investor funds; and the fifth section concludes. Throughout this chapter, the Massachusetts Juvenile Justice Pay for Success Initiative (Massachusetts SIB)[9] is used as a case study to illustrate the conceptual framework underlying SIBs as well as to project the potential savings that could be generated by crowdfunding.

PROJECT REQUIREMENTS AND ESSENTIAL ACTORS

This section outlines the main characteristics of SIB projects, including essential criteria and actors, capital and payout structures, and project development process. SIBs are performance-based contractual arrangements in which private investors put up capital to fund a social intervention and government outcome funders repay the investor only if an agreed upon social outcome is achieved.[10] If the services provided fail to achieve these outcomes, the investors will lose their money.

Investors' returns are generally capped by a maximum contract value determined in advance by the outcome funder. Appropriate outcomes and success metrics are negotiated and agreed upon between the outcome funder and the SIB intermediaries who are responsible for delivering these outcomes. Contract lengths can vary from twenty months up to 120 months and each SIB project should satisfy four basic criteria:

1 *There must be at least one well-defined social outcome that is meaningful and measurable in an intervention area* (e.g., rate of criminal reoffending among youth; education, employment, or training of young people). The outcome metric should be a meaningful proxy for long-term economic outcomes or be aligned with a broader political agenda of the outcome funders to attract their interest.
2 *It must be possible to achieve outcomes within a reasonable time horizon*, which requires substantial evidence from previous evaluations supporting that the specified outcomes will occur within the desired time frame. Investors and outcome funders must also be willing and able to make and receive payments within this time horizon.
3 *SIBs require evidence of success in achieving outcomes, which should come from evaluations of interventions that closely mirror the services offered by the proposed SIB*. The risk appetite of the investors and the requirements of the outcome funders will determine the rigorousness of the evidence required.
4 *There must be appropriate legal and political conditions that support the services to be delivered by relevant stakeholders.* Such support may come from policy frameworks, strategy documents, or funding allocated to similar services; these conditions will enable the government to pay for outcomes beyond the fiscal year in which the contract is made (this is necessary since most public expenditure is committed on a yearly basis while time horizons of SIBs are longer than one year), facilitate transactions in such a way that investors have contract protections and are incentivized to provide capital for the SIB, and allow the government to direct funds to an intermediary to disburse payouts to investors when the intervention achieves success.[11]

The Massachusetts SIB meets each of these four criteria. The goal of the project is to reduce recidivism (rate of reoffending) and improve employment outcomes for young men who are at risk of reoffending in Massachusetts,[12] which can be measured by: (1) comparing the number of days of incarceration between the treated group and the control group that was not receiving treatment, and (2) comparing the number of calendar quarters between the treated group and the control group in which the young men had employment earnings over US$1,000.[13] Given the high cost of incarceration (US$55,000 per year per person), a 40 per cent reduction in incarceration would generate US$21.8 million in savings, while a 65 per cent reduction in incarceration would generate US$41.5 million in savings.[14] Criteria 2 and 3 are also fulfilled since the intervention is delivered over a four-year period and the results are readily observable by following treated individuals' record of incarceration and employment. Finally, the political and legal conditions allow for the Commonwealth of Massachusetts to commit to the payout terms of a contract executed among the government outcome funder, the service provider, and the SIB intermediary.

The essential actors in an SIB are: (1) the investors, (2) the intermediary, (3) the outcome funder, (4) the service providers, and (5) the evaluators. The *investors* (commercial investors and non-profit organizations) provide capital to the intermediary rather than directly to the service provider.[15] Using a special purpose vehicle, the SIB *intermediary* raises capital, brings stakeholders (i.e., investors, outcome funders, service providers) together to determine and agree upon transactional details, and disburses funds to service providers. The intermediary also monitors the progress of the social intervention and determines whether any outcome payments should be made to the investors.[16] The intermediary is often paid a closing fee or a success fee out of the program budget as well as fees for performance management during implementation. The *outcome funder* (again, typically the government) determines the terms for payouts at the initial stage of the project and makes payments to investors (usually through the intermediary) only if the intervention creates sufficient, documented cost savings for the public (e.g., reduced public costs associated with recidivism).[17] The *service providers* (non-profit organizations, social enterprises, for-profit businesses) deliver social services to the population in need as part of the intervention.[18] Finally, the *evaluators* provide the ultimate validation of the results achieved by the intervention for the purpose of determining repayment.[19]

Table 4.1
Massachusetts SIB payout structure*

Reduction in bed days of incarceration (per cent)	*Performance payment (US$)*	*Projected cost savings (US$)*
70	27 million	45 million
55	26 million	33 million
40	22 million	22 million
25	11 million	11 million
10	2 million	2 million
5	0 million	0.9 million
0	–	–

* Retrieved from Third Sector, "Pay for Success Contract Among the Commonwealth of Massachusetts, Roca, Inc. and Youth Services Inc.," 7 January 2014, http://www.thirdsectorcap.org/wp-content/uploads/2015/03/final-pay-for-success-contract-executed-1-7-2013.pdf.

For the Massachusetts SIB, the essential actors are as follows. Upfront capital is provided by a combination of for-profit (Goldman Sachs), non-profit (Kresge Foundation and Living Cities), and philanthropic entities.[20] The intermediaries that established the project are Third Sector Capital Partners and its subsidiary Youth Services Inc.[21] The outcome funders are the Commonwealth of Massachusetts and the US Department of Labor.[22] The intervention services are delivered by Roca Inc., a non-profit social service provider that aims to help disengaged, disenfranchised youth escape violence and poverty.[23] The project results are evaluated by Urban Institute and validated by Public Consulting Group.[24] Table 4.1 illustrates the payout structure. The target success rate is a 40 per cent reduction in bed days of incarceration, at which point all upfront capital committed would be paid off.[25] SIB investors may invest in a layered capital structure, which includes senior investments and a combination of subordinate investments, recoverable grants, non-recoverable grants, and investment guarantees.[26] Subordinate (junior) investments are often structured as equity investments, as they are not repaid until senior investments (structured more like debt) are paid out first.[27] Non-recoverable grants, generally contributed by philanthropic foundations, are not repaid. Investment guarantees are triggered only if the program is unsuccessful.

In the Massachusetts SIB, Goldman Sachs holds US$9 million in senior loans with an annual interest rate of 5 per cent, while the Kresge Foundation and Living Cities each hold US$1.5 million in junior loans with an annual interest rate of 2 per cent.[28] Any payouts made by the project must be allocated in the following priority: (1) interest on senior loans, (2) interest on junior loans, (3) senior loan principal, and (4) junior loan principal.[29] This layered structure increases the share of risk borne by the non-profit organizations holding junior loans because their loans only break even when the project success rate reaches 40 per cent (US$22 million in total payout), while the break-even success rate for Goldman Sachs' senior loans is a mere 25 per cent (US$11 million in total payout).[30] The investors and service provider would also receive additional payouts from any leftover success fees once the outstanding project fees, interest and principal of loans, service provider fees, and intermediary fees are paid out.[31] Three philanthropic foundations (Laura and John Arnold Foundation, New Profit, and The Boston Foundation) also contributed US$6 million in non-recoverable grants. While their contributions are not repaid, up to US$6 million in outcome payments (leftover payments after investors and the service provider are paid out[32]) may be disbursed to these foundations to assist future SIB initiatives and support the scaling of Roca Inc.

Regarding the project development process, the development process for an SIB transaction is unique to each deal, but there are four major stages that are fairly common across all deals: (1) feasibility study, (2) structuring the deal, (3) implementation, and (4) evaluation and repayment.[33] Each stage consists of tasks to be completed. For example, at the second stage of structuring the deal, an SIB intermediary must raise capital, determine outcome metrics, procure service providers, and finalize contracts; however, these tasks need not take place in that order.[34]

SIGNIFICANT CHALLENGE FACING SIBS: LACK OF FUNDING

As noted at the start of this chapter, while SIBs have garnered interest from researchers and policymakers, they have failed to attract significant private capital.[35] To date, only US$370 million has been invested in SIBs over an eight-year period, compared to US$228 billion invested in impact assets,[36] which is less than 1 per cent of the US$22.89 trillion of assets professionally managed under socially responsible investment strategies.[37] Commercial investors attribute their absence in the market with SIBs' inappropriate risk-return profile.[38] Large institutional investors such as pension funds, endowments, or insurers are bound by their fiduciary duties and must apply conventional portfolio allocation frameworks that are not easily reconciled with the social risks that are at play in impact investing. The lack of capital commitment has created an imbalance of power favouring investors,[39] which allows them to select only projects with proven service delivery methods and greater guarantees on investments. As a result, outcome funders and SIB intermediaries have had to adjust their behaviour, and SIBs are thereby deprived of two theoretical advantages: (1) the ability to commission more innovative – and, therefore, riskier – service delivery programs; and (2) the ability to shift risks onto private investors.[40]

Failure to Deliver Innovation

In theory, SIB intermediaries should be able to use SIB projects as experimental playgrounds by employing service providers with innovative service delivery methods.[41] In practice, proven service delivery methods and proven service providers are strongly preferred because investors make their choices based on risk-to-return ratios; between projects with similar expected returns, investors will invest in the safer project.[42] In the SIB context, investors are wary of risks from highly innovative service delivery ideas and risks from unproven service providers.[43]

Even if a more innovative program has the potential to deliver greater cost savings to the public, "safer" project ideas delivered by proven service delivery programs are preferred by investors.[44] This was the case in the London Homeless SIB, where St Mungo's, a charitable organization with a long history of traditional program funding from government sources, was chosen as a service provider over others with more innovative ideas, in part because of its proven track record.[45]

Failure to Shift Risks

A crucial design feature of the SIB model is that financial risks are passed onto private investors; however, investors' preferences for safer projects with guaranteed investment returns has prevented SIBs from utilizing this feature.[46] To maintain investor interest in both the SIB program and the service providers themselves, non-profit service providers and the government are forced to bear financial risks.[47] Service providers fear the flight of capital because the reputational damage from the failure of one project may preclude them from future projects.[48] This fear can drive even the most established service providers to restructure the delivery of programs, cut costs elsewhere, or make other changes in order to achieve the outcomes that they have been contracted to achieve.[49]

Government guarantees have also been essential to attracting investors and launching SIBs.[50] Government outcome funders have made compromises by: (1) guaranteeing principal or interest payments; (2) capping reversals of targeted outcomes (meaning that investors will receive some payout even when the underlying metrics that triggered the payout have reversed)[51]; and (3) making an upfront standing charge.[52] For the Newpin SBB, the Government of New South Wales guaranteed an interest rate of 5 per cent per annum for the first three years of the project and gave partial guarantees on investors' principal payments in the event of early termination of the project.[53] These guarantees were central to the launching of the Newpin SBB,[54] yet they directly contradicted the state's dominant rationale for using the SIB model in the first place, which was to pass on risks to private investors.[55] So not only do SIBs fail to fund more innovative/riskier social interventions, they also fail to pass the risk of project failure on to private investors. Thus, the lack of capital commitment to the SIB market has prevented the SIB model from realizing two of its key strengths.

PROPOSED SOLUTION: CAPITAL INFUSION FROM CROWDFUNDING

This section describes how a capital infusion in the SIB market may resolve the issues identified in the previous section, as well as how crowdfunding may bring about this infusion. Basic supply and demand theory states that all things being equal, an increase in the supply of capital will lower the cost of capital.[56] Consequently, a capital infusion from more risk-tolerant investors may shift the balance of power away from investors and towards government and service providers, which should relieve the financial risks borne by these parties in the event of project failure. Additionally, since projects utilizing established service delivery methods are already being funded, newly infused capital can flow into projects using more innovative ideas.

Risk-averse institutional investors currently participating in the SIB market may leave once more risk-tolerant investors trickle in, which could offset some of the inflow of capital. However, this concern can be resolved (partially or completely) using a layered capital structure, such as employed by the Australian Benevolent Society SBB.[57] Under the dual-class structure, SIB intermediaries can first raise capital for junior class bonds that are exposed to the full costs of project failure. The risk-averse institutional investors can still participate by investing in senior class bonds that will bridge the gap between total capital required and capital raised by the junior class. This capital structure accommodates the infusion of new capital because it allows SIBs to substitute the expensive institutional investor capital with the cheaper new capital until there is enough new capital (that does not require government guarantees) to fully finance SIB projects, at which point institutional investors must either reduce the cost of their capital or exit the market entirely. This arrangement also accommodates institutional investors' preference for debt-like (over equity-like) investments.[58]

Crowdfunding as a Viable Alternative

While some authors posit that the proliferation of SIBs can only be guaranteed by their ability to attract institutional investors who can provide significant amounts of capital,[59] I argue that crowdfunding is a viable alternative method to increase funding for SIBs. Crowdfunding refers to a financing model, often utilized by entrepreneurs to fund their ventures, that draws on relatively small contributions from a large number of individuals (the "crowd") using the internet and without standard financial intermediaries.[60] Using crowdfunding platforms,[61] the crowd (as opposed to sophisticated investors) can invest their money in return for financial compensations (revenue, equity, profit-sharing scheme) or non-financial benefits (the acquisition of some new product).[62] Crowdfunding can be a viable source of funds for the SIB market for the following three reasons.

First, crowdfunding can help SIBs access more risk-tolerant investors from around the world. Many entrepreneurs have employed this new source of financing to raise capital when they are denied access to traditional sources, such as bank loans or equity capital.[63] Crowdfunded start-ups and SIBs both face difficulties in securing traditional financing due to their risk profiles. In the case of start-ups, this is due to their lack of credit, operating history, cash flow, collateral, and proven track record.[64] Similarly, SIBs' troubles stem from being perceived as too risky relative to their returns (see previous section). Crowdfunding investors are, in theory, more risk-tolerant,[65] as evidenced by their willingness to invest in ventures that are rejected by traditional lenders. The combination of higher risk tolerance, lower investment threshold, and greater pool of investors in crowdfunding should allow SIB intermediaries to attract financers that do not focus solely on financial returns.[66]

Second, crowdfunding may be integrated into a layered capital model for financing SIBs, such as the dual-class capital structure, whereby crowdfunders and institutional investors fund the junior and senior classes, respectively.[67] According to Armin Schwienbacher, crowdfunding and other sources of entrepreneurial finance are complementary because the optimal funding structure is determined to be a co-investment by the crowd and a deep-pocketed investor.[68] The first group ensures better knowledge of the market potential, while the deep-pocketed professional investors (such as venture capital funds, angel investors, and institutional investors) secure follow-up funding where crowdfunding fails to generate sufficient capital.[69]

Third, there is a large source of capital in the global market for crowdfunding, and this market continues to grow.[70] Globally, crowdfunding generated US$3.82 billion in transaction value in 2018.[71] The market for crowdfunding has grown rapidly in recent years, and it is projected to grow further as the transaction value of crowdfunding is projected to be US$4.79 billion in 2019 and US$8.01 billion by 2023.[72] SIB intermediaries should test the waters of this growing market, and attempt to capture a stake in investor interest as the market projects to double in size over the next five years.

Crowdfunding Framework for SIBs

Morteza Farajian and Brian Ross discuss crowdfunding public-private partnership (P3) infrastructure projects in the US based on the framework set by the commercial real estate industry for crowdfunding investment in real estate development projects.[73] This framework centers on:

1. the P3 developer setting up a special purpose vehicle (SPV) to undertake a defined project;
2. investors purchasing debt or equity shares in the SPV on a crowdfunding platform to fund the project; and
3. the SPV then making debt service payments or equity returns, depending on the success of the project.[74]

SIBs are a form of P3,[75] and SIB intermediaries can apply the above framework to raise upfront capital for SIB projects by soliciting funds on crowdfunding platforms. Note that the process of crowdfunding an SIB may differ slightly from Farajian and Ross's framework, as SIB investments are debt instruments (albeit with some equity-like qualities) and Farajian and Ross focus their discussions on equity crowdfunded P3 infrastructure projects.

To introduce crowdfunding into the SIB model, the outcome funder, who typically commissions projects by selecting bids submitted by partnerships consisting of service providers and SIB intermediaries, can require or indicate a preference for capital to be raised through crowdfunding in its request for bids. The outcome funder can then place a ceiling and a floor on the amount of capital solicited from crowdfunding. Prior to undertaking a project idea, the SIB intermediary or the outcome funder can test the waters by providing preliminary information on a crowdfunding platform to solicit non-binding indications of investment interest from the public; a strong indication of interest reflects the feasibility of a project's idea and its financial viability. However, Farajian and Ross caution that these "testing the waters campaigns" must adhere to applicable securities regulations to avoid allegations of market tampering.[76]

As discussed earlier, while several components must be satisfied during the project development process of an SIB, the order in which these components are completed may vary. Since capital can be raised either before or after securing an outcome funder,[77] I will outline how SIB intermediaries can initiate crowdfunding campaigns at different times to accommodate for either scenario.

FUNDRAISING AFTER SECURING CONTRACT

If an SIB intermediary chooses to raise capital after securing the SIB contract, the crowdfunding campaign can begin once the SIB project is awarded and the terms are agreed. The SIB intermediary can then post teaser summaries of the project on a crowdfunding platform, publish offering documents on the platform, and contact any parties interested in the project from the "testing the waters campaign" (if such campaign has been conducted). Investor traffic can be directed to the crowdfunding platform using "public agency outreach, social media, traditional media, search engine optimization, Google AdWords, and complementary sites, such as investment crowdfunding sites that target other industries."[78]

If the crowdfunding platform hosts multiple SIB financing campaigns, investors may compare characteristics such as project length, rate of return, and time horizon across SIB projects. Once investors review the offering documents and decide to commit capital, they can make a pledge to invest upon successful completion of the campaign at its financial close. Even though crowdfunding SIBs would be a crowdfunding of debt rather than equity, we can nevertheless utilize the deal structure discussed by Farajian and Ross, which involves holding investors' funds in a limited liability company (LLC) formed by the crowdfunding platform (or an equivalent legal entity depending on the applicable corporate statute and jurisdiction).[79] Upon the successful completion of the crowdfunding campaign, the LLC would enter into debt contracts with the SIB intermediary (in an equity sale, the LLC would purchase the securities issued by intermediary via a private placement), which would outline capital commitment, payment schedule, evaluation parameters, and other key contractual rights. This structure should assist the SIB intermediary with investor management as it would be working with only one party – the LLC – as opposed to the numerous crowdfunders who have committed capital.

When capital is raised after securing the SIB contract, Farajian and Ross caution against structuring the financing plan such that it depends solely on the crowdfunding campaign so that the project's financial close is not jeopardized by an unsuccessful campaign.[80] In other words, the financing plan should account for the possibility that no capital is raised from crowdfunding. Where the crowdfunded amount falls short of the target, the SIB intermediary can either choose to increase the rate of return on the crowdfunded portion of debt to attract more investors or raise the additional amount through senior class bonds marketed to institutional investors.

Once fundraising closes, the crowdfunding platform can act as an ongoing engagement tool for investors. The platform can distribute all financial statements as well as disclosures of progress made by social interventions. Platform permitting, investors who are entitled to periodic payments can also receive their payments through the crowdfunding platform. Having a readily accessible platform to disseminate project information may assist towards making SIBs more transparent.[81]

FUNDRAISING BEFORE SECURING CONTRACT

Alternatively, SIB intermediaries can initiate crowdfunding campaigns even before they secure the winning bid from the outcome funder. In such cases, the crowdfunding campaign can theoretically begin at any time, and I argue that the SIB can be crowdfunded using SAFE contracts.

SAFE contracts were introduced by Y Combinator in 2013 and have been commonly utilized by angel investors in funding start-up companies.[82] SAFE contracts are simple contracts between a young company and investors that enable the company to raise money quickly without predetermining the company's valuation at the time of investment.[83] This simplicity and the lack of need to determine valuation in advance can enable more cost-effective fundraising as fewer negotiations means fewer legal fees.[84] SAFE contracts can serve as an advantageous tool for fundraising prior to the awarding of SIB contracts because the investment horizon and key events in this crowd-funding scenario mirror an angel investor's investment horizon for early-stage companies.

Under SAFE contracts, investors make cash investments in a company and in exchange they receive the right to purchase equity in the company at some triggering event (such as a future equity round, the acquisition of the company, or an initial public offering) that determines the company's value.[85] The number of shares the investors would receive depends on the amount of cash committed by the investor and the value of the company as determined by the event.[86] Where the company is sold in a private transaction or an initial public offering, SAFE investors would receive cash compensation in return for their shares; this exit event may coincide with the triggering event if applicable, or may occur at a much later date after a future equity round.[87]

Raising capital for an SIB project prior to securing the SIB contract is analogous to investing in a company that has not yet been priced because the value of the project is determined only when the contractual terms are finalized. When SAFE contracts are used in SIBs, the rate of return for SAFE investors are crystalized once the payment outcomes are determined by the contract. The termination of the project (either from completing its intended course or premature termination) mirrors the exit event as crowdfunders will receive their payment along with the termination of their contractual interest in the project. If a campaign fails due to either failing to procure the contract or failing to secure sufficient capital, the investors' money would be returned to them through the crowdfunding platform. In addition to the aforementioned simplicity and flexibility in capital structure, SAFE contracts also help minimize and possibly eliminate the fundraising period that takes place after the SIB contract is awarded because a substantial or entire portion of the upfront capital is raised via crowdfunding by the time the contract is awarded.

Table 4.2
Projected savings from crowdfunding

Crowdfunded capital (US$)	*Senior lender amount (US$)*	*Savings (at 4 per cent interest) (US$)*	*Savings (at 3 per cent interest) (US$)*	*Savings (at 2 per cent interest) (US$)*	*Senior loans total value after six years (US$)*
0	9,000,000	0	0	0	12,060,861
3,000,000	6,000,000	224,330	438,130	641,800	8,040,574
6,000,000	3,000,000	448,660	876,260	1,283,600	4,020,287
9,000,000	0	672,990	1,314,390	1,925,399	0

As described in the first section, the Massachusetts SIB has incurred US$9 million in senior loans with an annual interest rate of 5 per cent, and US$3 million in junior loans with an annual interest rate of 2 per cent.[88] Table 4.2 illustrates potential monetary savings generated by crowdfunding (some or the entire portion of) the US$9 million in senior loans. Savings from crowdfunding are presented based on lower interest rates of 4 per cent, 3 per cent, and 2 per cent. Based on Table 4.2 above, crowdfunding does not lead to significant monetary savings, as even crowdfunding the entire senior loan amount at the low rate of 2 per cent would yield just under US$2 million in savings (less than 25 per cent of the US$9 million principal). Rather, the true value of crowdfunding lies in its potential to fund more innovative projects without placing the cost of failure on the government and intermediaries. Empirical evidence from actual crowdfunding campaigns is required to determine whether crowdfunding can truly deliver this potential value.

CONCLUSION

The SIB financing structure is intended for outcome funders, intermediaries, and service providers to test new service delivery methods on a trial basis while passing some of the financial risks off to private investors. In reality, this goal has fallen short of expectations due to the lack of funding in the SIB market. At its core, the motivation for using SIBS comes from the belief that there may be some solution in the unknown that is better than the status quo at solving existing problems and the benefit from finding this solution justifies the cost of trying. In the same vein, outcome funders and SIB intermediaries should try crowdfunding for SIBS to solve SIB's funding problem.

Crowdfunding for SIBS is a theoretical idea that is ultimately untested and requires confirmation using empirical studies and trials to determine its feasibility. Similarly, new service delivery methods need to be tested through SIB projects, and SIB as a concept needs to be tested as a way for governments to promote innovation without incurring greater risk. Further research is required to address the following concerns. First, it is unclear whether crowdfunding platforms will want to host campaigns for SIB fundraising, and whether crowdfunders have the appetite to invest in SIBS at all. Second, it is unknown whether an injection of crowdfunded capital into the market would in fact reduce investors' bargaining power and improve innovation in service delivery methods. These concerns can be addressed by conducting market studies and test runs for crowdfunding using the crowdfunding framework described above.

Ultimately, there is no guarantee that crowdfunding will produce better results for SIBs than existing financing options. However, in the same spirit of employing the SIB structure, outcome funders and SIB intermediaries should try something outside of the box, especially if the alternative is to allow the cost of capital to prevent SIBs from achieving their intended goals.

NOTES

1 Also known as Pay for Success Bonds (PFS).

2 Sheela Pandey et al., "Use of Social Impact Bonds to Address Social Problems: Understanding Contractual Risks and Transaction Costs," *Nonprofit Management and Leadership* 28, no. 4 (Summer 2018): 515.

3 The government is often the outcome funder for SIB projects and for the purpose of this chapter, the two terms shall be used interchangeably.

4 Alfonso Del Giudice and Milena Migliavacca, "Social Impact Bonds and Institutional Investors: An Empirical Analysis of a Complicated Relationship," *Nonprofit and Voluntary Sector Quarterly* 48, no. 1 (2019): 50–70.

5 Christine Cooper, Cameron Graham, and Darlene Himick, "Social Impact Bonds: The Securitization of the Homeless," *Accounting, Organizations and Society* 55 (November 2016): 63–82.

6 Ibid., 76, 80.

7 John Loxley, *Social Impact Bonds and the Financing of Child Welfare* (Manitoba: Canadian Centre for Policy Alternatives, 2017), 20.

8 Daniel Kariv, "SAFE (Simple Agreement for Future Equity)," *JumpStart*, 15 October 2018, https://shibolet-jumpstart.com/safe-simple-agreement-for-future-equity.

9 Commonwealth Massachusetts, "Fact Sheet: The Massachusetts Juvenile Justice Pay for Success Initiative," last modified 16 December 2014, https://govlab.hks.harvard.edu/files/govlabs/files/massachusetts_roca_pfs_project_fact_sheet.pdf.

10 Emily Gustafsson-Wright, Sophie Gardiner, and Vidya Putcha, *The Potential and Limitations of Impact Bonds: Lessons from the First Five Years of Experience Worldwide* (Washington, DC: Global Economy and Development at Brookings, 2015), 4, https://www.brookings.edu/wp-content/uploads/2016/07/impact-bondsweb.pdf.

11 Gustafsson-Wright, Gardiner, and Putcha, *Potential*, 4–5.
12 Commonwealth Massachusetts, "Fact Sheet," 1.
13 Third Sector, "Second Amended and Restated Pay for Success Contract Among the Commonwealth of Massachusetts, Roca, Inc. and Youth Services Inc.," 2016, https://www.thirdsectorcap.org/wp-content/uploads/2016/12/Second-Amended-PFS-Contract-EXECUTION-COPY-11-01-16.pdf.
14 Lili Elkins and Yotam Zeira, "Pay for Success," Roca, Inc., Spring 2017, https://rocainc.org/wp-content/uploads/2017/04/a-pay-for-success-opportunity-to-prove-outcomes-with-the-highest-risk-young-people.pdf.
15 Gustafsson-Wright, Gardiner, and Putcha, *Potential*, 6.
16 Ibid., 7; Pandey et al., "Use of Social Impact Bonds," 516.
17 Gustafsson-Wright, Gardiner, and Putcha, *Potential*, 6; Pandey et al., "Use of Social Impact Bonds," 512.
18 Gustafsson-Wright, Gardiner, and Putcha, *Potential*, 6.
19 Ibid., 6. Pandey et al., "Use of Social Impact Bonds," 516.
20 Pandey et al., "Use of Social Impact Bonds," 518.
21 Commonwealth Massachusetts, "Frequently Asked Questions: The Massachusetts Juvenile Justice Pay for Success Initiative," last modified 16 December 2014, 6, https://www.thirdsectorcap.org/wp-content/uploads/2015/03/MA-JJ-PFS-Frequently-Asked-Questions-Revised-Final.pdf.
22 Ibid., 6–7.
23 Pandey et al., "Use of Social Impact Bonds," 517.
24 Commonwealth Massachusetts, "Frequently Asked Questions," 4, 8.
25 Commonwealth Massachusetts, "Fact Sheet," 3.
26 Emily Gustafsson-Wright and Sophie Gardiner, *Policy Recommendations for the Applications of Impact Bonds: A Summary of Lessons Learned from the First Five Years of Experience Worldwide* (Washington, DC: Global Economy and Development at Brookings, 2015), 8, https://www.brookings.edu/wp-content/uploads/2016/07/SIB20Policy20Brief201web-1.pdf.
27 Ibid., 8.
28 Pandey et al., "Use of Social Impact Bonds," 518; Commonwealth Massachusetts, "Fact Sheet," 2–3.
29 Third Sector, *Second Amended*, 111–13.
30 Pandey et al., "Use of Social Impact Bonds," 523–5.
31 Commonwealth Massachusetts, "Fact Sheet," 3. Goldman Sachs may receive up to US$1 million in success fees, the non-profit investors

may receive up to US$300,000, the service provider Roca Inc. may receive up to US$1 million.

32 Ibid., 1. Service provider Roca Inc. agreed to defer US$3.26 million in fees.

33 Gustafsson-Wright, Gardiner, and Putcha, *Potential*, 7.

34 Ibid., 7.

35 Del Giudice and Migliavacca, "Social Impact Bonds," 65.

36 Izzy Boggild-Jones and Emily Gustafsson-Wright, "A Global Snapshot: Impact Bonds in 2018," *Brookings*, 2 January 2019, https://www.brookings.edu/blog/education-plus-development/2019/01/02/a-global-snapshot-impact-bonds-in-2018.

37 Del Giudice and Migliavacca, "Social Impact Bonds," 52.

38 Christian Berndt and Manuel Wirth, "Market, Metrics, Morals: The Social Impact Bond as an Emerging Social Policy Instrument," *Geoforum* 90 (March 2018): 31.

39 Gustafsson-Wright, Gardiner, and Putcha, *Potential*, 19. In the Massachusetts SIB and Newpin SBB, senior investors have the right to terminate the project prior to the completion date.

40 Cooper, Graham, and Himick, "Social Impact Bonds," 80.

41 Berndt and Wirth, "Market, Metrics, Morals," 33.

42 Cooper, Graham, and Himick, "Social Impact Bonds," 80.

43 Ibid.

44 Cooper, Graham, and Himick, "Social Impact Bonds," 76, 80. The innovative ideas are deemed "too risky" relative to their expected returns.

45 Ibid., 80.

46 Ibid., 80; Pandey et al., "Use of Social Impact Bonds," 523.

47 Loxley, *Social Impact Bonds*, 20; Berndt and Wirth, "Market, Metrics, Morals," 33.

48 Cooper, Graham, and Himick, "Social Impact Bonds," 80; Loxley, *Social Impact Bonds*, 12.

49 Ibid., 80, citing David MacDonald, "Social Impact Bonds: Profiting From Human Suffering," *Alberta Views – Magazine for Engaged Citizens*, 1 December 2013, https://albertaviews.ca/social-impact-bonds.

50 Loxley, *Social Impact Bonds*, 20.

51 Ibid., 8, 11.

52 Ibid., 14, 18; KPMG, *Evaluation of the Joint Development Phase of the NSW Social Benefit Bonds Trial* (Sydney: Office of Social Impact Investment, 2014), https://www.osii.nsw.gov.au/assets/office-of-social-impact-investment/files/Evaluation-of-the-Joint-Development-Phase.pdf.

53 Loxley, *Social Impact Bonds*, 7.

54 Ibid., 20.
55 Cooper, Graham, and Himick, "Social Impact Bonds," 75.
56 Gregory Mankiw, Ronald Kneebone, and Kenneth McKenzie, *Principles of Microeconomics*, 5th Canadian ed. (Toronto: Nelson Education 2011), 88–9.
57 Loxley, *Social Impact Bonds*, 14.
58 Del Giudice and Migliavacca, "Social Impact Bonds," 61, 63, 65.
59 Ibid., 52.
60 Ethan Mollick, "The Dynamics of Crowdfunding: An Exploratory Study," *Journal of Business Venturing* 29, no. 1 (January 2014): 2.
61 European Commission, "Crowdfunding Explained," last modified 30 August 2017, https://ec.europa.eu/growth/tools-databases/crowdfunding-guide/what-is/explained_en. Crowdfunding platforms are websites that allow fundraisers to solicit and collect funds from the crowd. Many platforms will return all money pledged if the fundraising campaign fails to reach its target.
62 Nuno Bento, Gianfranco Gianfrate, and Sara Virginia Groppo, "Do Crowdfunding Returns Reward Risk? Evidences from Clean-Tech Projects," *Technological Forecasting and Social Change* 141 (April 2019): 107.
63 Paul Belleflamme, Thomas Lambert, and Armin Schwienbacher, "Crowdfunding: Tapping the Right Crowd," *Journal of Business Venturing* 29, no. 5 (September 2014): 586.
64 Abbey R. Stemler, "The JOBS Act and Crowdfunding: Harnessing the Power – and Money – of the Masses," *Business Horizons* 56, no. 3 (Summer 2013): 8.
65 Bento, Gianfrate, and Groppo, "Do Crowdfunding Returns Reward Risk?," 107; Silvio Vismara, "Information Cascades among Investors in Equity Crowdfunding," *Entrepreneurship Theory and Practice* 42, no. 3 (2018): 489; Lee Fleming and Olav Sorenson, "Financing by and for the Masses: An Introduction to the Special Issue on Crowdfunding," *California Management Review* 58, no. 2 (2016): 11.
66 Morteza Farajian and Brian Ross, "Crowd Financing for Public-Private Partnerships in the United States: How Would It Work?," *Transportation Research Record: Journal of the Transportation Research Board* 2597, no. 1 (2016): 46.
67 Loxley, *Social Impact Bonds*, 14.
68 Armin Schwienbacher and Benjamin Larralde, "Crowdfunding of Small Entrepreneurial Ventures," *The Oxford Handbook of Entrepreneurial Finance* (September 2010): 856.
69 Ibid., 856.

70 PwC, "Global Fintech Report 2019," 4, accessed 17 August 2021, https://www.pwc.com/gx/en/industries/financial-services/assets/pwc-global-fintech-report-2019.pdf.

71 Statistica Market Forecast, "Crowdinvesting – Worldwide," accessed 17 August 2021, https://www.statista.com/outlook/dmo/fintech/alternative-financing/crowdinvesting/worldwide.

72 Ibid.

73 Farajian and Ross, "Crowd Financing," 45.

74 Ibid.

75 Del Giudice and Migliavacca, "Social Impact Bonds," 51.

76 Farajian and Ross, "Crowd Financing," 47.

77 Gustafsson-Wright, Gardiner, and Putcha, *Potential*, 7.

78 Farajian and Ross, "Crowd Financing," 49.

79 Ibid.

80 Ibid., 49.

81 Social Ventures Australia, "Newpin Social Benefit Bond," last modified 14 October 2020, https://www.socialventures.com.au/work/newpin-social-benefit-bond.

82 Carolynn Levy, "Safe Financing Documents," Y Combinator, last modified March 2021, https://www.ycombinator.com/documents.

83 Kariv, "SAFE."

84 Ibid.

85 Funders Club, "What is a SAFE?," accessed 17 August 2021, https://fundersclub.com/learn/safe-primer/safe-primer/safe.

86 Jill McKnight, "What is a Simple Agreement for Future Equity?," *LegalVision*, 15 November 2020, https://legalvision.com.au/simple-agreement-for-future-equity-a-safe-way-of-raising-capital.

87 Kariv, "SAFE," 10.

88 Pandey et al., "Use of Social Impact Bonds," 518; Commonwealth Massachusetts, "Fact Sheet," 2–3.

PART TWO

CSR as Risk Management in Industry Practice

5

Bell, Let's Talk About Reputational Risk and Opportunity

Asha Young

There is a good chance that this morning you woke up to the iPhone default alarm clock sound. Nowadays, people wake up with their phones,[1] carry them around all day,[2] feel naked when they misplace them,[3] and they are often the last thing people look at before they go to sleep.[4] In 2021, mobile phones and Wi-Fi have become essential tools used in the modern world. The advent of the internet, social media, and instant communication has changed the way our modern world functions.[5] The switch from dial-up and desktop computers to unrestricted internet access in the palm of one's hand has had profound impacts on relationships with one another, with business, and in our markets. As businesses can now reach consumers in unprecedented ways, so too can individual stakeholders hold businesses accountable for their actions in unprecedented, immediate, and very public ways. A company's reputation in the digital era is arguably its most vulnerable and valuable asset.[6] With the increased awareness surrounding climate change, gender and racial inequities, and other environmental and social crises, companies are feeling the pressure from stakeholders to engage in more responsible business practices.[7] Social media has bestowed upon the public the power to pressure companies into responding directly to consumer concerns, capable of holding even large multinational companies accountable for their actions beyond traditional legal avenues. This aspect of social media poses grave reputational risks for companies, insofar as consumers and stakeholders now have an immediate public platform to have their voices heard, meaning corporate management must be nimble in their responses.

Conversely, businesses have also been able to utilize social media as a powerful tool to grow their brand and reputation. Reputational opportunity and reputational risk have become significantly influential factors affecting how businesses operate.[8]

Social media and corporate social responsibility (CSR) have each been identified as important triggers for change in this century; however, whether or not CSR is good or bad for industries has been contested amongst scholars.[9] Despite its voluntary characteristics, CSR continues to pervade the business industry and has become widely recognized and utilized by business.[10] While there is no universal, clear definition for CSR, many scholars, policymakers, and companies themselves have attempted their own definitions.[11] This chapter focuses on those CSR-type specific initiatives that companies promote through social media, and in particular will examine one particular event, Bell's Let's Talk Day.

Bell Canada Inc. (Bell) is a Canadian telecom giant. Bell Let's Talk Day is an annual social media campaign that takes place across many social media platforms aiming to reduce stigma towards mental illness. For every social media interaction, Bell donates towards mental health initiatives.[12] Through an analysis of Bell Let's Talk Day, this chapter examines how social media can be used as a tool to bolster or hinder a company's reputation. Specifically, how social media can be utilized by companies to build brand reputation, and potentially tear it down. Social media has allowed both companies and the public to shape notions of reputational risk and reward; it is possible to flesh out the advantages and risks of social media for businesses today. The purpose of this study is twofold: first, to delineate how social media is used by companies to enhance reputation, and second, to demonstrate how consumers and stakeholders use the same platform to diminish reputation as a method of social accountability.

By performing an analysis of Bell Let's Talk Day, this chapter aims to explain how social media has created a robust platform for both companies and the public to control the reputational capital of any given company. Bell Let's Talk Day is widely recognized and endorsed by the Canadian public, and it has also been subjected to criticism from stakeholders in recent years. While many company-backed CSR initiatives are often used as virtue-signaling opportunities,[13] Bell has managed to straddle the nexus between reputational growth and reputation risk in an impressive way. As time passes, it is increasingly clear that social media has placed renewed significance on a company's reputation as its most prized asset, which can either be enhanced or tarnished through channels such as Facebook, Twitter, and Instagram.

This analysis comprises of four sections. The first section emphasizes the importance of a company's reputation, drawing on various scholars who have written about reputation in different forms, such as reputation as a bankable commodity, as a form of accountability, and as part of CSR. The second section analyzes how companies have employed social media to build their brand and reputation, and in particular how Bell uses Bell Let's Talk Day as a way to deploy CSR initiatives to further its brand and reputation. The third section examines how social media poses a threat of reputational risk for companies, focusing on consumers and stakeholders and how they use social media as a tool to hold companies accountable for their actions. This section also dives into the consequential effects Bell Let's Talk Day has had on Bell's reputation. The final section reflects on this nexus between reputational risk and reward and identifies how lawyers must increasingly consider these new realities in risk when executing their fiduciary duties and providing legal advice to their clients. CSR initiatives like Bell Let's Talk Day straddle a fine line between using social media to build a brand while being increasingly vulnerable to criticism by the Canadian stakeholders.

THE IMPORTANCE OF A COMPANY'S REPUTATION

Corporate reputation can be understood as "the process of building, over the long term, a corporate perception or good name through feedback or general comments from stakeholders."[14] While publicly traded companies may not have to disclose their reputation to a securities regulator or jot it down in the company's minute books, in the age of social media, it has become one of the most valuable assets a company can have.[15] With social media platforms such as Facebook and Twitter, there is free flowing information available to anyone who has an internet connection and, undoubtedly, poses an increase in reputational risk for companies.[16] These risks can impact company performance in more ways than just decreased revenue and loss of brand value.[17] Negative reputational events can increase consumer suspicion about future CSR initiatives, making it difficult for companies to regain their previous good reputation.[18] Reputational damage can also lead to the inability to attract and retain high quality staff and can decrease current employee morale.[19] As a result, the internet and social media have become a means for fostering relationships between companies and the public, and, at the same time, serves as a tool that is used to manage a company's reputation.[20]

It is not difficult to think of a company or individual who has had their reputation ruined because of inappropriate activities shared on social media. Moreover, because positive reputations are fragile and difficult to form, develop, and maintain, once a negative reputation has been earned, it is difficult to reverse.[21] In the words of Warren Buffet, "it takes 20 years to build a reputation and five minutes to ruin it."[22] With the arrival of social media and the CSR movement, companies have to adapt; instead of focusing solely on black letter legal accountability, they have to consider both their legal and reputational obligations.[23] Reputational accountability can be described as a concept "understood in terms of the rule of reputation, which is upheld by market participants that evaluate business conduct within several forums; in other words, reputational capital is generated from CSR backed by genuine intention."[24]

Scholar Asha Kaul posits that the adoption of social media tools is essential to ensure a positive image or reputation as a "bankable commodity" for the company.[25] While this rings true for most companies, it is crucial to note that not all business sectors are affected equally by the shift toward social media. For instance, many junior mining companies continue to exist and succeed without a significant social media presence despite carrying on business in an area that is directly linked with CSR initiatives such as environmental sustainability.[26] Given that consumer-based companies are at the forefront of consumer interface, they are under more pressure to be aware of their actions on social media and are particularly concerned about keeping their reputational accountability in check.

Social media can play a prominent role in a company's reputation; "there have been umpteen horror stories where stakeholders have tarnished [a] company['s] reputation, and stories where smart organizations have used the medium to build credibility and trust."[27] To quote an IBM report, "social media is no longer the adorable baby everyone wants to hold, but the angst-filled adolescent – still immature yet no longer cute – who inspires mixed feelings."[28] Despite the attitude of weariness surrounding social media some might hold, most companies looking to uphold and enhance their reputation will have to utilize social media in a way that is advantageous for their brand while effectively addressing any reputational risk that is posed by stakeholders.

REPUTATIONAL OPPORTUNITY: HOW COMPANIES UTILIZE SOCIAL MEDIA TO GROW THEIR REPUTATION

Social media has changed the way that companies interact with their stakeholders; communication is more direct, company decisions are more transparent, and the methods by which a company can increase their visibility has increased manifold.[29] While a company may be exposed to additional reputational risk by using social platforms, many businesses are cognizant of the power that social media wields and are adapting in order to take advantage of it.[30] As a platform, social media allows companies to generate increased visibility, which they often use for the betterment of their reputation. Concerning CSR specifically, companies use social media as a medium for increasing positive reputability by creating shared goals with the public through ongoing conversations.[31] In Canada, there is no better example than Bell implementing Bell Let's Talk Day in 2010.[32]

Social Media as a Tool for Companies

With the dawn of social media, business operations for companies have undergone a major shift. Companies can advertise in new and innovative ways, they can connect with their consumer base instantaneously, and they can receive feedback from stakeholders in a way that was not possible before. Craig Carroll suggests that social media allows organizations to gain five types of feedback about their reputation, namely regarding prominence, public esteem, properties, and positioning. [33] This feedback allows a company to understand how consumers feel about them, which then allows the company to respond accordingly. In a sense, social media acts as an equalizing platform, which creates a back-and-forth communication between consumers and companies with reputation being the common denominator. Some scholars even argue that social media can also be utilized by companies with bad CSR reputations to counteract their prior reputation by engaging in more CSR activities and placing more emphasis on brand image development.[34] While the internet has allowed for significant progress in how information about a company is disseminated to the public, the saturated use of social media has changed the landscape for how companies can control their branding and reputation.[35]

In the past, information regarding a company was delivered to the public based on one-way communication, with the introduction of social media, conversations around companies have become increasingly interactive, which is forcing companies to involve stakeholders in the conversation.[36] Sun Young Lee posits that companies can convey their CSR messages through two different channels: controlled and uncontrolled.[37] Controlled CSR messages are those that are disseminated through company-channels, whereas uncontrolled messages are those that are received through third-party endorsement, which she suggests "[have] more credibility than controlled media."[38] Social media channels lay in between these controlled and uncontrolled channels because companies can choose to utilize these mediums and control the message that is distributed. However, Lee advocates that "the more controllable the channels are, the more likely the public is to think they are self-serving and biased towards the corporation."[39] Companies today must strike a balance between building a reputation through initiatives that the public supports and not appearing self-serving while doing it.

Bell Let's Talk Day as a Method for Building Brand and Reputation

Bell created Bell Let's Talk Day in September 2010.[40] The campaign is built around stakeholder involvement; Bell says that for every social media interaction using the hashtag #BellLetsTalk or text message sent by a Bell Mobile Canada user, the company will donate five cents to mental health initiatives in Canada.[41] The funds that are raised go to a variety of organizations through either major or community grants, which must be applied for. Some of the organizations include Kids Help Phone and the Centre for Addiction and Mental Health.[42] This initiative has arguably been one of the most successful Canadian CSR initiatives to date; it is widely recognized by the Canadian public, it is endorsed by celebrities, and the cause – mental health awareness – is embraced by individuals. While there has been some backlash in recent years (discussed in the next section), the campaign is a successful one and Bell reports that since the introduction of Bell Let's Talk Day, "four out of five Canadians reported [that] they're more aware of mental health issues."[43]

Mary Deacon, as a representative of Bell, states that they "had a debate about whether to call it Bell Let's Talk or simply Let's Talk, but decided to use the Bell brand to combat the stigma around mental health issues. [Additionally], the 'let's talk' aspect fit the company's core business of telephone, wireless and internet connections."[44] CSR initiatives are usually self-serving, whether that is to boost reputation or gain favourable terms with a certain demographic.[45] It seems highly improbable that the Bell name had enough notoriety to combat the stigma of talking about mental illness on its own and, rather, it was a smart marketing strategy. Despite this, Bell has been successful in using social media as a tool for building brand and reputation. It has created a CSR campaign that has lasted over a decade, which has proffered impactful results, all the while retaining its credibility from most of the public.

In 2019, nine years after its pilot year, Bell Let's Talk Day had 1,013,915,275 social media interactions, 1,208,040 individuals were supported with access to mental health care, and CA$100,695,763.75 was donated to mental health initiatives across Canada.[46] There is no standard method companies can use to implement CSR initiatives across social media with the purpose of building brand,[47] but Bell has undoubtedly used the platform in a way that is unprecedented in this country.

One theory on CSR communication strategies suggests that companies deliver CSR messages to stakeholders either through information, response, or involvement.[48] Applied to Bell Let's Talk Day, Bell has chosen to implement the involvement method of delivering its message, opting to base the success of its campaign on consumer participation. Moonhee Cho, Lauren Furey, and Tiffany Mohr note the significance of including external stakeholders in CSR communications, pointing out that the public tend to trust CSR information more when it comes from activist consumers or independent organizations and not a corporate spokesperson.[49] Public engagement is one of the underlying reasons why Bell Let's Talk Day has become so successful. When people see their friends, celebrities, or trusted mentors participating in this campaign, they are more willing to participate and get on board with the message.[50] Lee purports how, "[o]nce someone shares a post or likes a page on Facebook, it will appear on the Facebook newsfeed of that person's friends, which will increase that person's visibility and make him or her appear altruistic or conscientious while simultaneously increasing the visibility of the company involved."[51] Despite being coupled with an obvious marketing strategy,[52] Bell Let's Talk Day has been widely successful in its reach.

By utilizing new technology and grabbing hold of the CSR movement, Bell has created a pseudo-national "day" that is dedicated to both mental health awareness and Bell's brand awareness. Bell's success can be measured by the fact that Bell Let's Talk Day is more well-known by the Canadian public than World Mental Health Day, which is held on 10 October each year.[53] By choosing to make this campaign interactive, the public continues to participate each year and since its inception there have been increased numbers of involvement, despite the occasional backlash.[54] Social media allows companies to utilize their platforms to disseminate CSR messages to the public to any degree. While some argue that companies are not taking full advantage of social media as a channel,[55] Bell certainly proved that it can take full advantage of social media platforms to grow their reputation as a company that cares about important social causes such as mental health.

REPUTATIONAL RISK: HOW STAKEHOLDERS USE SOCIAL MEDIA TO KEEP COMPANIES ACCOUNTABLE FOR THEIR ACTIONS

Despite Bell's success, consumers are not ignorant; Ryerson University Professor Ida Berger states that consumers "can see through things that are simply marketing ploys."[56] Moreover, some of the Canadian public have chimed in to say that there may be a risk in thinking that Bell Let's Talk Day is enough on its own.[57] They posit that it is a good starting point and as more people discuss mental health on a daily basis, more pressure can be put on the system to provide for individuals in need.[58]

Social media has been regarded as the "unfettered voice of [the] citizens."[59] Stakeholders have gained a new method for holding companies accountable for their actions as social media has allowed the public to engage, connect, and influence other members of the online community with a mutual interest.[60] In the age of social media, consumers have taken on "the role of a journalist, a watchdog, and opinion influencers."[61] Through social media platforms such as Facebook and Twitter, people now have free rein to express their opinions on everyone and everything, including companies and their practices.[62] Consumers find themselves with the power to hold companies accountable for their actions because companies care about their good reputation. In the words of Kaul, a company's online reputation is their reputation and the public's ability to undermine that is of substantial significance.[63]

Social Media as a Tool of Reputational Accountability

While it took radio thirty-eight years and television thirteen years to reach an audience of fifty million, it only took AOL two and a half years.[64] This time difference demonstrates just how pervasive the internet and social media can be and it shows the massive audiences that the internet can reach. The internet has made it easier for individuals to access and distribute information about companies, which allows for a more informed public. Data from the United States and the United Kingdom show a trend in consumers shifting towards social media and moving away from traditional company-controlled channels of mass communication.[65] Social media is a powerful tool that can have devastating consequences for both individuals and companies.[66] This form of public shaming is seen repeatedly as viral social media has publicly dragged countless companies and people – such as United Airlines and Starbucks[67] – through the mud, damaging their reputation for breaching the social contract.

Lawyers advising their corporate clients need to be cognizant of the shift in how businesses and consumers interact, and some argue that the relationship between companies and the public now "hinge[s] on conversation and connectedness with stakeholders."[68] Transparency and globalization have empowered external stakeholders to detect wrongdoing and publicize their concerns with companies or businesspeople. The conversation has surpassed being between a company and its customers and moved into the framework of a company and global stakeholders. Adam Spence argues that "when almost everyone has a telephone and almost every telephone is also a camera, there is an increasing probability that business wrongdoing will not only be reported by media outlets but will be posted for all to see on YouTube or some other website."[69] It is more important than ever for companies to stay true to the messages that they are delivering to the public, and, for the sake of reputational accountability, it is important that companies only "talk the talk" if they can "walk the walk."

Bell Let's Talk Day and Reputational Risks

Since its inaugural implementation in January 2011, Bell Let's Talk Day occurs every January like clockwork; however, in recent years, the Canadian public has begun to criticize the telecommunications giant for incongruencies in their messaging.[70] In January 2019, reporter

Elizabeth Keith wrote, "currently, on various social media platforms, there are multiple trending posts from Canadians claiming that this day is a giant marketing campaign for Bell, claiming that Bell should be doing more than just talk, and even saying that Bell is a national disgrace."[71] While these accusations vary – and are refuted by Bell – there is no doubt that this type of online journalism coverage is a reputational hazard for Bell.[72] While Bell Let's Talk Day has continued to be successful despite growing skepticism, there is a real cause for concern regarding the increasing reputational risk that this campaign may pose for Bell in future years.

Social media allows individuals to share their stories with the world and this has been both vital and problematic for the Bell Let's Talk campaign. Individuals sharing their stories and using the hashtag #BellLetsTalk is the pinnacle of Bell's campaign. However, unsolicited feedback about the company and horror stories of mistreatment concerning the mental health of Bell employees cast doubts on the company's reputation.[73] In the past couple of years, employees of Bell – past and present – have come forward to report that working at Bell has harmed their mental health, often criticizing the company's policies and methods of responding to individual grievances.[74] The two most common criticisms Bell faces are (1) that they are not putting their money where their mouth is, and (2) that the company is not addressing that it is a part of the mental health crisis.[75] These criticisms are highlighted in turn.

The public's most significant complaint about Bell and Bell Let's Talk Day is that the company holds itself out to be a leader in caring about mental health while treating its employees in a manner that is harmful to their mental health.[76] The public have also aired concerns about where the money raised is actually going and the corporatization of mental health,[77] suggesting that "capitalism has laid the foundations for Bell to now dominate the conversation around mental health – a position which the telecommunications provider, while unqualified, is happy to fill" and how Bell is doing nothing more than paying lip service to the issue of mental health.[78]

Maria McLean, a former Bell employee, publicly shared how she was fired from Bell after presenting a doctor's note to her boss, which recommended a ten-day leave from work, and asking for the time off.[79] She emphasized that she was fired for reasons unknown to her.[80] This story garnered a lot of attention on social media, with a lot of public support for abandoning Bell Let's Talk Day because of the company's hypocrisy.[81] In 2017, more than six hundred Bell employees reached out to the Canadian Broadcasting Corporation about their treatment as employees working at Bell, where "in email after email, employees describe panic attacks in the workplace, stress-induced vomiting and diarrhea. Some reported crying before starting call-centre shifts and said taking stress leave is common."[82] While Bell has refuted all of these accusations, saying that only two per cent of the Bell workforce is on a mental health disability leave,[83] the reputational damage that has occurred has not gone unnoticed by the Canadian public.

A second common criticism that Bell has been facing in recent years is the fact that it sells products that may be harmful to mental health, according to research on cell phone addiction.[84] One Canadian went so far as to say that the products Bell sells is "making people's mental health worse" and wrote an article stating "Bell, you have great intentions, but this is like a cigarette company donating to cancer charities; or like Kylie Jenner's recent fundraising campaign for Smile Train, which treats kids with cleft palates."[85]

It is abundantly clear that companies like Bell and their advisors, should be cognizant of the fact that the public can use social media to hold companies accountable for their actions and that it is pertinent that companies practice what they preach to minimize reputational risk.[86] Social platforms, such as Twitter and Facebook, have allowed consumers to effectively participate in conversations with companies, often allowing the public to help dictate the actions of any given company. Public influence on corporate behaviour was effectively demonstrated when Starbucks closed all its American stores for mandatory training following public outcry regarding a viral video where a barista called the cops on two Black customers.[87] Generally, the shift towards social media has given stakeholders the power to fight back and use reputational accountability against corporations to keep them in check.

CONCLUSION: STRIKING A BALANCE BETWEEN REPUTATIONAL OPPORTUNITY AND RISK

Social media has changed the business landscape dramatically. Both stakeholders and companies have equal power in using social media. A variety of stakeholders now "have the power to question and provide feedback to companies, [while simultaneously,] they can use these messages as a weapon against businesses to serve their own agenda."[88]

The collective voice that is created because of social media has dramatically reduced a company's ability to control communication.[89] It is a new era where social media presents an abundance of risk alongside tremendous opportunity. While Bell has been successful in establishing itself as a leader in creating change for mental health in Canada, it has not been without backlash. Bell has managed to reap great rewards with their campaign-based CSR initiative, despite opening themselves to reputational risk. It is important to be cognizant of the fact that this may not always be the case and that not all companies are as fortunate.

In 2020, how companies interact with their consumers and stakeholders differs vastly from how it was a decade ago.[90] Lawyers advising their clients on whether to pursue certain avenues need to be very cognizant of this new reality. Reputation has become a key component in how successful a company is and from a risk perspective is increasingly a top priority for companies. Social media channels are used as tools to control a company's reputation as there is a push-and-pull between what companies and stakeholders want. Returning to the notion that "social media is no longer a cute, adorable baby and is now an angst-filled teenager," it is true that it is often difficult to anticipate what will go viral and how stakeholders will react on the internet. More so than ever, it is necessary for companies and their lawyers to consider how their actions will be viewed in the eyes of the public. Social media opens companies up to a large degree of risk, but this is matched equally with opportunities for businesses to grow and expand their reputation in positive ways.

Corporate lawyers delivering advice on director fiduciary duties to the corporation and holding a narrow reading of the board's legal obligations are at risk of providing outdated information. With the advent of the internet and in the age of social media, it is difficult to predict what will happen next or how stakeholders may use these platforms against companies, but the consideration of stakeholder interests and broader social and environmental risks must be integrated into corporate decision-making. While Bell, thus far, has been quite successful in rebutting accusations of hypocrisy, it would be prudent for the company to implement strategies that mitigate this moving forward, as social media signifies a prominent risk to any given company's reputation. The best way to ensure corporations do not fall into a reputational tailspin is for them and their advisors to always ensure these companies "walk the walk."

NOTES

1 Mary Gorges, "90 Percent of Young People Wake up with Their Smartphones," *Ragan Communications*, 21 December 2012, https://www.ragan.com/90-percent-of-young-people-wake-up-with-their-smartphones.

2 Pew Research Center: Internet, Science & Tech, "Demographics of Mobile Device Ownership and Adoption in the United States," 7 April 2021, https://www.pewresearch.org/internet/fact-sheet/mobile.

3 James A. Roberts, Chris Pullig, and Chris Manolis, "I Need My Smartphone: A Hierarchical Model of Personality and Cell-Phone Addiction," *Personality and Individual Differences* 79 (June 2015).

4 *Asurion*, "The Goodnight Kiss is Dead," 25 July 2018, https://www.asurion.com/about/press-releases/the-goodnight-kiss-is-dead.

5 Clay Shirky, "The Political Power of Social Media: Technology, the Public Sphere, and Political Change," *Foreign Affairs* 90, no. 1 (Winter 2011): 28–41. Social media can be defined as "the production, consumption and exchange of information across platforms for social interaction."

6 Alexander F. Brigham and Stefan Linssen, "Your Brand Reputational Value Is Irreplaceable. Protect It!," *Forbes*, 1 February 2010, https://www.forbes.com/2010/02/01/brand-reputation-value-leadership-managing-ethisphere.html?sh=358cddbf3790.

7 Sandra A. Waddock, Charles Bodwell, and Samuel B. Graves, "Responsibility: The New Business Imperative," *The Academy of Management Executive (1993–2005)* 16, no. 2 (May 2002): 132–48.

8 KPMG International, "Expect the Unexpected: Building Business Value in a Changing World," in *Managing Sustainable Business*, edited by Gilbert G. Lenssen and N. Craig Smith (Dordrecht: Springer 2019), 107–31.

9 Namrata Rana and Utkarsh Majmudar, "The Need to Do More," in Asha Kaul et al., "Social Media: The New Mantra for Managing Reputation," *Vikalpa* 40, no. 4 (2015): 455–91, 479.

10 Asha Kaul et al., "Social Media: The New Mantra for Managing Reputation," *Vikalpa* 40, no. 4 (2015): 459.

11 See for example, Moonhee Cho, Lauren Furey, and Tiffany Mohr, "Communicating Corporate Social Responsibility on Social Media: Strategies, Stakeholders, and Public Engagement on Corporate Facebook," *Business and Professional Communication Quarterly* 80, no. 1 (2017): 52–69, 53–4.

12 Bell Canada, "Our Initiatives," *Bell Let's Talk*, accessed 18 August 2021, https://letstalk.bell.ca/en/our-initiatives.

13 David B. Spence, "Corporate Social Responsibility in the Oil and Gas Industry: The Importance of Reputational Risk," *Chicago-Kent Law Review* 86, no. 1 (2011).

14 Vincent Dutot, Eva Lacalle Galvez, and David W. Versailles, "CSR Communications Strategies through Social Media and Influence on E-Reputation: An Exploratory Study," *Management Decision; London* 54, no. 2 (March 2016): 363–89, 367.

15 Brigham and Linssen, "Your Brand Reputational Value."

16 Kaul et al., "Social Media," 458.

17 Deloitte, "2014 Global Survey on Reputation Risk," October 2014, https://www2.deloitte.com/content/dam/Deloitte/pl/Documents/Reports/pl_Reputation_Risk_survey_EN.pdf.

18 KyuJin Shim and Sung-Un Yang, "The Effect of Bad Reputation: The Occurrence of Crisis, Corporate Social Responsibility, and Perceptions of Hypocrisy and Attitudes toward a Company," *Public Relations Review* 42, no. 1 (March 2016): 75.

19 *CareerBuilder*, "71 Percent of U.S. Workers Would Not Apply to a Company Experiencing Negative Publicity, According to a Recent CareerBuilder Survey," 20 July 2017, https://press.careerbuilder.com/2017-07-20-71-Percent-of-U-S-Workers-Would-Not-Apply-to-a-Company-Experiencing-Negative-Publicity-According-to-a-Recent-CareerBuilder-Survey.

20 Dutot et al., "CSR Communications," 364.

21 Kaul et al., "Social Media," 459.

22 Ibid.

23 Robert G. Eccles, Scott C. Newquist, and Roland Schatz, "Reputation and Its Risks," *Harvard Business Review*, 1 February 2007, https://hbr.org/2007/02/reputation-and-its-risks.

24 Kevin Jackson, "Global Corporate Governance: Soft Law and Reputational Accountability," *Brooklyn Journal of International Law* 35, no. 1 (2010): 92, 105.

25 Kaul et al., "Social Media," 456.

26 Michelle Hohn, *Investing in Community: Canadian Junior Mining Companies, Corporate Social Responsibility, and the Communication Gap* (Victoria: Royal Roads University, 2009), 14–15.

27 Kaul et al., "Social Media," 458.

28 IBM Unica, *11 Key Marketing Trends for 2011* (New York: IBM Unica, 2011), 3.

29 Sugandha Agarwal, Ankur Kumar, and Pragya, "Social Media: Changing the Way Businesses Interact and Engage Customers," *IJLTEMAS* 5, no. 4 (April 2016): 53–60.

30 Cho, Furey, and Mohr, "Communicating," 52–3.

31 Sun Young Lee, "Can Companies Gain CSR Reputation via Social Media," in Asha Kaul et al., "Social Media: The New Mantra for Managing Reputation," *Vikalpa* 40, no. 4 (2015): 476.
32 Bell Canada, "Our Initiatives."
33 Craig Carroll, "Matching Dimensions of Reputation and Media Salience for Feedback, Alignment, and Organizational Self-awareness," in Asha Kaul et al., "Social Media: The New Mantra for Managing Reputation," *Vikalpa* 40, no. 4 (2015): 481.
34 Hyuksoo Kim, Seounmi Youn, and Doohwang Lee, "The Effect of Corporate Social Responsibility Reputation on Consumer Support for Cause-Related Marketing," *Total Quality Management & Business Excellence* 30, no. 5–6 (2019): 682–707, 682.
35 Agarwal, Kumar, and Pragya, "Social Media."
36 Cho, Furey, and Mohr, "Communicating," 64; Lee, "Can Companies Gain."
37 Lee, "Can Companies Gain," 438.
38 Ibid.
39 Ibid.
40 Emily Jackson, "How Bell Let's Talk Became a Triple Win for BCE, Consumers and the Mental Health Cause," *Financial Post*, 2 February 2018, https://financialpost.com/telecom/how-bell-lets-talk-became-a-triple-win-for-bce-consumers-and-the-mental-health-cause.
41 Bell Canada, "Our Initiatives."
42 Emily Duffy, "Let's Talk: The Hypocrisy of Bell Canada and Mental Health under Capitalism," *Fightback*, 7 February 2018, https://www.marxist.ca/article/lets-talk-the-hypocrisy-of-bell-canada-and-mental-health-under-capitalism.
43 Jackson, "How Bell Let's Talk."
44 Ibid.
45 Spence, "Corporate Social Responsibility in the Oil and Gas Industry," 68.
46 Bell Canada, "Results and Impact | Bell Let's Talk," *Bell Let's Talk*, accessed 18 August 2021, https://letstalk.bell.ca/en/results-impact.
47 Kaul et al., "Social Media," 455.
48 Cho, Furey, and Mohr, "Communicating," 55–6.
49 Ibid., 57.
50 Bell Canada, "It's Bell Let's Talk Day!," *Bell Let's Talk*, 30 January 2019, https://letstalk.bell.ca/en/news/1194/its-bell-lets-talk-day.
51 Lee, "Can Companies Gain," 476.
52 Duffy, "Let's Talk."
53 World Health Organization, "10 October is World Mental Health Day," accessed 18 August 2021, https://www.who.int/campaigns/world-mental-health-day.

54 Bell Canada, "Results and Impact."
55 Cho, Furey, and Mohr, "Communicating."
56 Jackson, "How Bell Let's Talk."
57 See e.g., Duffy, "Let's Talk."
58 Adam Miller, "Mental Health Awareness Campaign Exposes Challenges in Combatting Stigma," *CMAJ* 185, no. 6 (April 2013), 471.
59 Dilip Cherian, "How Social Media is Changing the PR Landscape," in Asha Kaul et al., "Social Media: The New Mantra for Managing Reputation," *Vikalpa* 40, no. 4 (2015): 461.
60 Kaul et al., "Social Media," 458.
61 Ibid.
62 Mark Lanterman, "Social Media and Managing Reputational Risk Law & Technology," *Bench & Bar of Minnesota* 8, no. 75 (2018), 8; Cho, Furey, and Mohr, "Communicating," 53.
63 Kaul et al., "Social Media," 456.
64 Mark Bunting and Roy Lipski, "Drowned Out? Rethinking Corporate Reputation Management for the Internet," *Journal of Communication Management* 5, no. 2 (April 2001): 170–1.
65 Kaul et al., "Social Media," 456.
66 See e.g., Jon Ronson, "How One Stupid Tweet Blew Up Justine Sacco's Life," *The New York Times*, 12 February 2015, https://www.nytimes.com/2015/02/15/magazine/how-one-stupid-tweet-ruined-justine-saccos-life.html.
67 MoneyWatch, "Starbucks Faces Brand Crisis after Arrest of 2 Black Men," *CBC News*, 17 April 2018, https://www.cbsnews.com/news/starbucks-faces-brand-crisis-after-arrest-of-two-black-men.
68 Vidhi Chaudri and Asha Kaul, "Playing for the Future: The 'Digital Roulette'!," in Asha Kaul et al., "Social Media: The New Mantra for Managing Reputation," *Vikalpa* 40, no. 4 (2015): 486.
69 Ibid., 487.
70 Meagan Campbell, "Boycotting Bell Let's Talk Day," *The Signal*, 30 January 2019, https://signalhfx.ca/boycotting-bell-lets-talk-day; Jasmine Vido, "A Critical Investigation of Bell Let's Talk," *Major Papers* 74, 11 February 2019, https://scholar.uwindsor.ca/major-papers/74.
71 Elizabeth Keith, "Canadians Are Using Bell Let's Talk Day to Criticize Bell Despite Their Mental Health Initiatives," *Narcity*, 30 January 2019, https://www.narcity.com/canadians-are-using-bell-lets-talk-day-to-criticize-bell-despite-their-mental-health-initiatives.
72 Erica Johnson, "Bell's 'Let's Talk' Campaign Rings Hollow for Employees Suffering Panic Attacks, Vomiting and Anxiety," *CBC News*,

25 November 2017, https://www.cbc.ca/news/health/bell-employees-stressed-by-sales-targets-1.4418876.

73 Keith, "Canadians."

74 Duffy, "Let's Talk."

75 Kate Robertson, "Dear Bell, Let's Talk about How You're Part of the Mental Health Problem," *NOW Magazine*, 25 January 2017, https://nowtoronto.com/news/bell-let-s-talk-day-part-of-the-mental-health-problem-2.

76 Keith, "Canadians."

77 Meghan Bell, "Talk is Cheap: On Capitalism, Mental Health, and Taxing the Rich," *The Tyee,* 27 January 2020, https://thetyee.ca/Analysis/2020/01/27/Talk-Cheap-Capitalism-Bell-Mental-Health.

78 Duffy, "Let's Talk."

79 Maria McLean, "Let's Talk About How Bell Fired Me After I Asked For Mental-Health Leave," *Canadaland,* 25 January 2017, https://www.canadaland.com/bell-lets-talk-mental-health-fired.

80 Ibid.

81 "Salacious Scandal for Bell Let's Talk," *The Concordian*, 2 February 2017, http://theconcordian.com/2017/02/salacious-scandal-for-bell-lets-talk.

82 Johnson, "Bell's 'Let's Talk' Campaign Rings Hollow."

83 Statista, "Bell Canada Employees 20112–018," accessed 1 May 2019.

84 Jackson, "How Bell Let's Talk."

85 Robertson, "Dear Bell, Let's Talk."

86 Jackson, "How Bell Let's Talk."

87 Jennifer Calfas, "Starbucks Is Closing All Its U.S. Stores for Diversity Training Day. Experts Say That's Not Enough," *Time*, 28 May 2018, https://time.com/5287082/corporate-diversity-training-starbucks-results.

88 Kaul et al., "Social Media," 458.

89 Ibid.

90 Blake Morgan, "The Evolution of Customer Service," *Forbes*, 18 April 2016, https://www.forbes.com/sites/blakemorgan/2016/04/18/the-evolution-of-customer-service/?sh=4a07bfdc2442.

6

Elephants Among Chickens: Responsible Lobbying and the Fossil Fuel Industry in the Transition to Net-Zero

Megan Parisotto

In January 2019, people across Canada took to the streets to show their support for members of the Wet'suwet'en Nation (the Nation). For several days, the Nation prevented Coastal GasLink pipeline workers from accessing its traditional territory near Houston, British Columbia (BC). This natural gas pipeline, operated by TransCanada, is intended to transport natural gas from northeastern BC to the coast for export to global markets.[1] An agreement was eventually reached between the Nation's hereditary chiefs and police to allow pipeline workers to access the territory. However, this result was only after the police arrested several members of the Nation to enforce a court injunction for access.[2]

TransCanada is one of many fossil fuel corporations that have been accused of using its deep pockets to secure access to the BC provincial government.[3] The issues of corporate electoral donations and lobbying were at the forefront of the 2017 provincial election,[4] particularly after *The New York Times* published an article exposing BC's lax political donation laws.[5] The election of a new provincial government did lead to changes in legislation surrounding both corporate donations to political parties[6] and corporate lobbying.[7] Nevertheless, due to their access to more financial resources compared to other stakeholders, fossil fuel corporations are still the more prominent "elephants among chickens" in the political playing field, using these resources to exert greater influence over decision-makers than other stakeholders.[8]

Despite their politically dominant role, the environment in which fossil fuel corporations operate has undergone significant change over the past two decades. The concept of political corporate social responsibility (PCSR) recognizes that emerging governance gaps require corporations to address various social, environmental, and legal issues regardless of whether this provides them with a financial benefit.[9] At the same time, society has moved towards moral legitimacy as the basis for corporate legitimacy.[10] As a result, moral legitimacy has become critical for corporations that seek to obtain social license to operate and increase their chances of long-term survival.

In the transition to a net-zero carbon economy, this chapter engages in the ongoing transition phase, recognizing that we will not get to net-zero overnight. Thus, this chapter addresses that uncomfortable yet necessary discussion on when something is not the best but is better than other alternatives, and how certain industries should conduct themselves within the space where there is not a perfect villain. This chapter argues that for fossil fuel corporations to increase their moral legitimacy, and thereby secure social license to operate in BC, they must abandon traditional lobbying and instead adopt *responsible* lobbying practices. These practices will help ensure that fossil fuel corporations are engaging in the deliberative discourse processes necessary for cultivating moral legitimacy. This chapter first examines the political donation and lobbying activities of BC's fossil fuel industry, as well as the changes made to the province's electoral finance and lobbying laws in 2017. The second section presents an overview of the history of corporate lobbying and current corporate lobbying practices across Canada. The third section analyzes how fossil fuel corporations could draw upon their internal resources to implement responsible lobbying practices in BC through the application of Theresa Bauer's multidimensional framework for responsible lobbying.[11] The fourth section discusses a responsible lobbying framework for BC's fossil fuel industry.

CORPORATE LOBBYING IN BC

Pre-2017: BC as the "Wild West" of Corporate Donations

On 13 January 2017, *The New York Times* published an article by Dan Levin entitled "British Columbia: The 'Wild West' of Canadian Political Cash."[12] In the article, the founder of Democracy Watch branded BC as the Canadian province of lawlessness regarding corporate political donations.[13] Unlike most provinces in Canada, BC had no limit on political donations, allowing corporations to give large amounts to political parties.[14] Big donors to the BC Liberal Party (BC Liberals), the governing party at the time, were perceived to benefit financially from their political contributions. For example, the article noted that the BC Liberal government approved the Kinder Morgan Trans Mountain Pipeline project after opposing the project at hearings just one year earlier. Despite this indication in the article, it is actually the federal government that green-lit the project first, with the pipeline falling under the federal jurisdiction of the National Energy Board.[15] However, regardless of the fact that it was the federal government that approved the pipeline, the BC Liberal government still indicated political and environmental support of the project, with Kinder Morgan satisfying all five conditions the BC Liberal government required for its support.[16] This switch in perspective came after Kinder Morgan and other supporters of the project donated over CA$700,000 to the BC Liberals in the months following the hearings.[17]

Two months after *The New York Times* article was released, a study by Nicolas Graham, Shannon Daub, and Bill Carroll revealed the extent of the fossil fuel industry's influence on BC politics. The study detailed how forty-eight fossil fuel corporations and industry groups donated CA$5.2 million to the BC Liberals and the BC New Democratic Party (NDP) between 2008–15.[18] These contributions were largely concentrated among a small number of corporations – Teck Resources Ltd and Encana Corporation alone accounted for approximately half of the donations during this period.[19] Ninety-two per cent of political contributions made by fossil fuel corporations between 2008–15 were to the governing BC Liberals.[20] However, donations to the BC NDP spiked in the year leading up to the 2013 provincial election, as "firms were 'hedging' donations in advance of the 2013 election, in which fossil fuel development ... became a central election issue, and which the NDP was widely predicted to win."[21]

Contributions made by these fossil fuel corporations aligned with trends in lobbying and access to key political decision-makers in the provincial government.[22] The study identified forty-three fossil fuel corporations that conducted lobbying activities in BC between 2010 (the year information on lobbying activities in the province became publicly available through the Lobbyist Registry) and 2016. Seven of the top ten political donors were among the top ten most active lobbyists in the province.[23] The primary lobbying targets for fossil fuel corporations during this period were ministers and their ministries; the most sought-after minister was Rich Coleman, Minister of Natural Gas Development, with an average of three contacts per week from fossil fuel corporations between 2010–16.[24] Again, fossil fuel corporations used a hedging approach leading up to the 2013 provincial election by attempting to build strategic relations with the leader of the BC NDP, who was (mistakenly) predicted to lead the party to victory in the election.[25]

Post-2017: Changes to BC's Donation and Lobbying Legislation

The BC Liberals suffered politically by not acting to strengthen donation and lobbying laws in the province after *The New York Times* article was published. As Rob Shaw and Richard Zussman describe, in the months leading up to the 2017 provincial election, BC's lax donation and lobbying laws became "inextricably linked" to the issue of the BC Liberal leader's integrity.[26] Recognizing its opponent's weakness, the BC NDP ran on a platform of "taking big money out of politics,"[27] which proved to be popular with voters.

The BC NDP was called upon to form government after the 2017 provincial election and quickly passed the *Election Amendment Act, 2017*[28] and the *Lobbyists Registration Amendment Act, 2018*[29] to fulfill its campaign promise. Among other things, the *Election Amendment Act, 2017* ended corporate and union donations to political parties, limited individual contributions to CA$1,200 per year, banned out-of-province donations, and provided transitional public funding for political parties over a period of five years.[30] The *Lobbyists Registration Amendment Act, 2018* introduced a series of changes that were primarily intended to increase transparency in lobbying. The definition of "former public office holder" in the *Lobbyists Registration Act* (now called the *Lobbying Act*[31]) was amended to include anyone who has previously worked in a minister's office.[32] Other amendments built a new Lobbyists Registry by requiring monthly reporting of actual lobbying activities; broadening the range of public office holders who must be named when lobbied; requiring reporting on whether a lobbyist follows a particular code of conduct; and providing stronger compliance and enforcement powers to the Office of the Registrar of Lobbyists, the independent office that oversees lobbying activities.[33] As corporate donations to political parties are now banned in BC, the remainder of this chapter will focus on lobbying as the primary activity through which fossil fuel corporations attempt to influence decision-makers in the province.

UNDERSTANDING CORPORATE LOBBYING

This chapter conceives of corporate lobbying as a process of communication between corporations and those who are responsible for enacting policy and legislation in BC, with an intention on the part of the corporation to influence policy and legislation. This understanding is based on the following definition of "lobby" in the *Lobbyists Registration Act*:

> "lobby" … means,
> (a) in relation to a lobbyist, to communicate with a public office holder in an attempt to influence
> (i) the development of any legislative proposal by the government of British Columbia, a Provincial entity or a member of the Legislative Assembly,
> (ii) the introduction, amendment, passage or defeat of any Bill or resolution in or before the Legislative Assembly,
> (iii) the development or enactment of any regulation …
> (iv) the development, establishment, amendment or termination of any program, policy, directive or guideline of the government of British Columbia or a Provincial entity.[34]

This understanding is further based on Bauer's definition of lobbying as "any communication process between individuals representing the firm interest and policymakers, stimulated by the firm representative with the intent to influence policy-making."[35] Bauer's definition characterizes lobbying as a two-way process in which corporations and policymakers engage in dialogue during various stages in the policymaking process.

The Evolution of Corporate Lobbying in Canada

Lobbying has been a part of Canadian politics since the country's inception; however, the practice became more important for corporations following the Second World War when they began dealing with growing government bureaucracies.[36] Lobbying remained a largely unregulated activity in Canada until 1989, when the federal government implemented legislation in response to growing concerns about the influence of lobbyists on policymaking.[37] The federal *Lobbyists Registration Act*[38] was based on the following key principles: lobbying is a legitimate activity; influence by lobbyists must be made transparent; and public access and open government are fundamental and must not be hindered by regulation.[39] Provinces such as Ontario and BC followed suit in enacting their own lobbying legislation in 1999 and 2001, respectively, using the federal legislation as a template.[40]

While lobbying regulations developed across the country, corporations transformed lobbying into a sophisticated practice.[41] Corporations now pour large amounts of money into their lobbying activities, recognizing that "[d]ollar for dollar, lobbying is a better investment than campaign contributions."[42] The primary objective of corporate lobbying is generally to improve the corporation's competitive position in the market.[43] This objective represents a pragmatic rather than an ideological pursuit of interests as corporations seek to build relationships with politicians that could result in beneficial policy decisions.[44] Indeed, the fossil fuel industry in BC lobbies to "promote policies that increase the potential for making profit while blocking policies and regulations that impede its interests."[45] In Canada's parliamentary system of government, corporate lobbyists typically target the executive branch due to its important role in setting the direction for policy and legislation.[46] While some corporations lobby using internal resources, others retain external consulting firms to lobby on their behalf.[47] This chapter largely focuses on how fossil fuel corporations could apply their internal resources to practice responsible lobbying in BC.

The Benefits and Harms of Corporate Lobbying

There are consequentialist arguments for and against corporate lobbying in democratic societies. These arguments are generally "concerned with the direct effects of the action on the quality and degree of representation in the system."[48] Like lobbyists from non-governmental organizations and other interest groups, corporate lobbyists have an important informational role to play in Canadian democracy. As Anthony Nownes describes:

> Lobbyists provide three types of information to government actors: (1) political information about the status and prospect of a proposed or potential government decision; (2) career-relevant information about the implications of a particular course of action for a government official's prospects of keeping and/or advancing in his or her job; and (3) policy-analytic information about the potential economic, social, or environmental consequences of a particular course of action.[49]

Corporations are well positioned to provide governments with information about the potential economic consequences of different policy options. Fossil fuel corporations undoubtedly have valuable insight about how to improve the performance of BC's fossil fuel industry, and it is prudent for policymakers to take this insight into consideration when making policy decisions.

However, serious problems arise when corporations exert greater influence on policymakers than other groups and individuals. As Elisabeth Gidengil and Heather Bastedo observe, "[h]ealthy democracies are inclusive ... if certain groups in society are systematically underrepresented in politics, then that society can hardly be considered fully democratic."[50] Due to their vast financial resources, corporations are the "elephants among chickens" [51] in the political playing field, as they are better positioned to influence government policy relative to other stakeholders. For example, fossil fuel corporations operating in BC have been able to use their ample financial resources to gain greater access to policymakers than environmental and Indigenous groups.[52]

Significantly, this political inequality can impede the effectiveness of government decisions. Brisman identifies that public participation in decision-making "helps to improve the quality of decisions by bringing more information, views, and expertise to the table."[53] Therefore, the involvement of environmental non-governmental organizations, Indigenous groups, and others in the formation of laws and policies regarding BC's fossil fuel industry could improve the quality of these laws and policies. Furthermore, the economic development of a society may be hindered when wealthy corporations have a disproportionate amount of political influence. This influence may lead to the implementation of laws and policies that allow wealthy corporations to monopolize economic activities and prevent others from prospering.[54] For example, the fossil fuel industry may lobby the BC government to direct resources away from the development of renewable energy projects and towards the development of oil and gas projects, which may be harmful to the province's long-term economic development.

To combat the detrimental effects of corporate lobbying, British Columbian society will need to determine how to "maintain a reasonably level playing field on which both elephants and chickens can compete."[55] By adopting responsible lobbying practices, fossil fuel corporations could do their part in helping to level the political playing field, while also benefiting themselves in the process.

POLITICAL CSR, RESPONSIBLE POLITICAL CSR, RESPONSIBLE LOBBYING, AND MORAL LEGITIMACY FOR THE BC FOSSIL FUEL INDUSTRY

From Corporate Political Activity to Political CSR

Over the past two decades, there has been a "shift in the steering mechanism" underlying the political engagement of corporations, from corporate political activity (CPA) to PCSR.[56] CPA views corporations as engaging in political activities in an attempt to control their external environment and improve their financial performance.[57] It adopts a rather limited view of corporate political engagement by focusing primarily on the interactions between corporations and governments. Lobbying is included in a corporation's CPA, as well as lawsuits to challenge executive action and contributions to political campaigns.[58]

PCSR rejects this limited view of corporate political engagement. Instead, it recognizes that governance gaps have required corporations to take on a new political role in society.[59] In this role, corporations work alongside governments and civil society actors to address various social, environmental, and legal issues, regardless of whether this will benefit them financially. As Andreas Rasche describes, PCSR "sharpens our attention to the fact that many firms have assumed state-like functions ... and the fact that state and non-state actors are working together in the attempt to find solutions to governance challenges."[60] For example, more corporations are now partaking in public deliberations, collective decision-making, and the provision of public goods to address issues such as public health and education; the enforcement of social and environmental standards; and the fight against climate change, inequality, and corruption.[61]

Due to this new state-like role, a fundamental concern of PCSR is the legitimacy of the political activities in which corporations are engaged.[62] As Florian Wettstein and Dorothea Baur indicate, "legitimacy is understood to result from undistorted communicative processes involving all relevant stakeholders ... [t]hus, corporations as legitimate political actors are asked to openly participate in such public processes of political will formation."[63] PCSR, therefore, requires a deliberative discourse process amongst stakeholders that is (1) ethical, using truth, sincerity, appropriateness, and understandability to reach a consensus between stakeholders; (2) transparent, so that stakeholders can ascertain which issues are relevant for them; and (3) accountable, so that stakeholders are responsible for their statements and subsequent actions.[64] It is possible for corporations to align their CPA activities, such as lobbying, with their PCSR activities, such as partaking in ethical and transparent public deliberations with stakeholders.[65] Indeed, it may be imperative for corporations to do so in order to retain their legitimacy with the public.

The Importance of Moral Legitimacy for BC's Fossil Fuel Industry

Along with the shift from CPA to PCSR, there has been a shift in the nature of corporate legitimacy, which examines the appropriate role of corporations in society.[66] Mark Suchman distinguishes between three types of corporate legitimacy: (1) cognitive; (2) pragmatic; and (3) moral.[67] Cognitive legitimacy is based on public acceptance that a corporation is necessary or inevitable, and operates primarily at the subconscious level.[68] Pragmatic legitimacy is the result of self-interested calculations by individuals who perceive that a corporation will bring them some benefit, whether it is a specific favourable exchange or the protection of their general interests.[69] Finally, moral legitimacy is based on a positive normative evaluation of a corporation and its activities by society.[70] As Guido Palazzo and Andreas Georg Scherer indicate, "in the ... transition from stable industrial society to a globalized postindustrial society, cognitive legitimacy is eroding ... while pragmatic legitimacy provokes growing resistance ... [t]herefore, moral legitimacy has become the core source of societal acceptance."[71]

As the basis for corporate legitimacy in a globalized society, moral legitimacy is important for corporations seeking to obtain social license to operate and benefit their long-term survival. Social license to operate is a concept that relates to obtaining the approval of groups that may be affected by certain activities of the corporation.[72] Moral legitimacy can help a corporation obtain social license to operate in two ways. First, moral legitimacy can provide an objective and higher reference point beyond the divergent interests of groups from which a corporation seeks to obtain social license to operate.[73] This objective reference point is particularly important when the interests of groups are influenced by a lack of reliable information or fear.[74] Second, moral legitimacy can provide strong arguments for corporations negotiating with groups from which they hope to obtain social license to operate, particularly when those groups are adopting a "not in my backyard" stance against corporate activities.[75] In addition to helping a corporation obtain social license to operate, moral legitimacy can promote a corporation's chances of long-term survival. Accumulating moral legitimacy can assist a corporation in attracting customers and acquiring both financial and human capital.[76] In doing so, a corporation is more likely to enhance its economic performance and overcome performance crises that may otherwise threaten its long-term survival.[77]

Lobbying jeopardizes a corporation's moral legitimacy due to its strategic character, which can cause moral outrage and reduce public acceptance of the corporation's activities.[78] While the lobbying activities of fossil fuel corporations in BC have traditionally occurred out of the public eye, more public attention has been drawn to these activities since *The New York Times* article was published in January 2017. The BC NDP's campaign promise to "take big money out of politics"[79] in the 2017 provincial election clearly resonated with voters who were dissatisfied with BC Liberal ties to fossil fuel corporations. Scrutiny of the lobbying activities of fossil fuel corporations in Canada is by no means isolated to BC; in May 2019, environment advocates accused Canadian senators of submitting to pressure from fossil fuel lobbyists in relation to proposed environmental assessment legislation.[80] More than 130 amendments to the legislation were being considered by a Senate committee, many of which were asked word-for-word by fossil fuel lobbyists.[81] The environment advocates noted that, although they also reached out to Canadian senators in support of the legislation, very few of the suggestions they made were being considered by the Senate committee.[82]

Due to increased public scrutiny, fossil fuel corporations should be concerned with how their lobbying practices are being perceived by the public, as this could be impacting their ability to achieve social license to operate, enhance their economic performance, and overcome performance crises. These impacts are particularly important due to the nature of the market in which fossil fuel corporations currently operate. As David Spence explains:

> Today's oil and gas companies work within an ever-broader and more complex set of social institutions – norms and expectations that exist alongside market forces, but which are created and shaped in other ways. Some of these expectations take the form of legal requirements, but only some of them; others reflect ethical norms that may turn out to be every bit as important to companies in the long run as laws and regulations.[83]

The last decade has been difficult for fossil fuel corporations in Canada, particularly those in the oil sector. Fierce opposition from Indigenous and environmental groups has "attack[ed] the oil sector's heart by choking its arteries – pipelines."[84] As noted in the introduction of this chapter, opposition to pipeline projects continues to cause disruptions for fossil fuel corporations in BC. There is a clear need for these corporations to increase their moral legitimacy in the province, which includes reforming their lobbying practices.

It is worthwhile to question whether fossil fuel corporations should undertake this exercise at all, given the federal government's commitment to reduce Canada's carbon emissions to "net-zero" by 2050.[85] This commitment has been adopted by a number of countries, cities, and businesses[86] after a 2018 Intergovernmental Panel on Climate Change special report indicated that global carbon emissions need to hit net-zero by 2050 in order to prevent global warming from exceeding 1.5 degrees Celsius of pre-industrial levels.[87] The commitment to achieve net-zero emissions does not mean that current fossil fuel corporations will cease to exist by 2050. However, these corporations will need to make significant changes to their operations to reduce their emissions, which inevitably means a transition away from oil and gas production.[88] For example, in April 2020, Royal Dutch Shell plc (Shell) committed to become a net-zero emissions energy business by 2050 or sooner. Shell plans to meet this target by (1) becoming net-zero on all emissions from the manufacturing of its products; (2) reducing the net carbon footprint of its products by selling more products that have a lower carbon intensity, including renewable power, biofuels, and hydrogen; and (3) helping customers decarbonize by working with businesses, governments, and other parties to promote decarbonization.[89] Fossil fuel production will undoubtedly be slashed as countries, cities, and businesses such as Shell attempt to reach their net-zero targets; however, fossil fuel production is not likely to be ceased altogether. Shell itself acknowledges that it will continue to sell energy products that create emissions, as society will still require these energy products for the foreseeable future. Nevertheless, Shell states that this will not stop it from becoming a net-zero emissions energy business because it will work with its customers to mitigate emissions.[90] Thus this discussion on the need for responsible lobbying practices within the fossil fuel industry is not a discussion that can be ignored any time soon.

A RESPONSIBLE LOBBYING FRAMEWORK FOR BC'S FOSSIL FUEL INDUSTRY

While *traditional* lobbying jeopardizes a corporation's moral legitimacy, *responsible* lobbying is compatible with it.[91] Responsible lobbying can be understood as lobbying that is congruent with a corporation's overall responsibilities to society.[92] This type of lobbying helps to prevent criticism of the corporation's political influence,[93] and thereby promotes a more positive normative evaluation of the corporation by the public.

Through extensive quantitative and qualitative studies, Bauer has crafted a multidimensional model of responsible lobbying that identifies how a corporation can align both the content and process of its lobbying activities with its overall responsibilities to society. In Bauer's model, three pillars form the content of responsible lobbying: (1) a commitment to corporate social responsibility (CSR) and coherence between the corporation's stated CSR policies and its lobbying activities; (2) a consideration of the perspectives and needs of the corporation's stakeholders; and (3) an alignment of the corporation's policy positions with the long-term objectives and values of broader society.[94] At the base of Bauer's model is a process that establishes an ethical and democratic dialogue among all participants.[95] These four components of Bauer's model – the three pillars and base – are discussed in turn, along with suggestions about how fossil fuel corporations could adopt responsible lobbying practices in BC. These suggestions integrate sources from government and industry bodies in both BC and Canada, to craft a regional approach to responsible lobbying.

Pillar 1: Commitment to CSR and Coherence with Lobbying

The first pillar of Bauer's model of responsible lobbying focuses on the coherence of the corporation's lobbying activities with its CSR policies. Bauer observes that a growing number of corporations have developed clearly articulated CSR policies that "ensure that not only economic success is achieved, but that social and environmental impacts are managed and morally sound decisions and actions are ensured."[96] However, while some corporations build their CSR policies directly into their business models and organizational cultures, others choose to keep them separate.[97] Bauer finds that corporations that take the less integrated approach face challenges in achieving consistency between their CSR policies and their lobbying activities, leaving them vulnerable to public criticism.[98] To prevent this inconsistency, Bauer suggests that a corporation should (1) recognize the importance of CSR, which involves a commitment to serve society, manage environmental impacts, and act in a morally sound manner; (2) make CSR an integral element of the corporation's business model and organizational culture; (3) make the corporation's lobbyists aware of clearly articulated CSR policies; and (4) encourage collaboration between the corporation's CSR and lobbying departments.[99]

To move towards responsible lobbying, fossil fuel corporations in BC should have well-crafted CSR policies that are integrated into all aspects of their business model, including their lobbying activities. In 2014, Industry Canada (now known as Innovation, Science, and Economic Development Canada) released the *Corporate Social Responsibility Implementation Guide for Canadian Business* (the Guide).[100] The Guide offers a five-step CSR implementation framework, which can be applied to corporations of various sizes across different industries. This framework can be used by corporations that do not have a CSR policy, as well as those that have a CSR policy that needs to be improved:

1 Assess the corporation's current CSR practice, which involves forming a CSR team, coming up with a working definition of CSR, and identifying the corporation's key stakeholders.
2 Develop a CSR policy and initiatives, by researching what competitors are doing, coming up with CSR initiatives, identifying CSR performance measures, getting feedback from major stakeholders, and publishing a CSR policy.

3 Implement the CSR policy and initiatives, by forming an integrated CSR decision-making structure, holding CSR training, and developing ways to address problematic behaviours.
4 Communicate about the CSR policy and initiatives, which involves identifying a target audience, selecting a message, and determining how to communicate that message to the target audience.
5 Evaluate and scale-up the corporation's CSR policy and initiatives.[101]

The Guide recognizes that for CSR initiatives to be effective, they must be integrated throughout the corporation's operations.[102] Fossil fuel corporations must ensure that their CSR and lobbying departments are cohesive so that their lobbying activities are aligned with their articulated CSR policies.

Pillar 2: Consideration of Stakeholders' Perspectives and Needs

The second pillar of Bauer's model of responsible lobbying considers a corporation's responsiveness to the perspectives and needs of its stakeholders. A corporation must first identify the stakeholders whose perspectives and needs it should consider. Bauer notes that "[t]he identification and categorization of stakeholders is ideally a firm-specific, continuous process that includes further specifying stakeholders touched by lobbying issues."[103] These stakeholders will undoubtedly include policymakers; however, the second pillar primarily focuses on stakeholders whose perspectives and needs are not automatically included in the corporation's lobbying activities. These "non-political" stakeholders include shareholders, employees, consumers, and non-governmental organizations.[104] In addition to considering the perspectives and needs of these stakeholders, a corporation should engage them in a genuine dialogue regarding policy issues. This genuine dialogue will help the corporation develop a lobbying strategy that promotes the interests of both the corporation and non-political stakeholders, thereby reducing the risk of public criticism of the corporation's lobbying activities.[105]

To practice responsible lobbying, fossil fuel corporations should have processes in place to identify their stakeholders and engage in a genuine dialogue with them. In 2018, the Corporate Oversight and Governance Board of the Chartered Professional Accountants of

Canada released a briefing on stakeholder engagement.[106] The briefing provides a straightforward checklist for managing an effective stakeholder engagement program, which fossil fuel corporations may find instructive:

1 Prepare for successful stakeholder engagement by assigning this activity to a committee comprised of individuals who will be able to enhance shareholder relationships.[107] Fossil fuel corporations could benefit by having members of BC's Indigenous and environmental science communities on their stakeholder engagement committees.
2 Decide on which stakeholders it will engage, by identifying the stakeholders who are most impacted by the corporation's activities and who can exert the greatest influence on the corporation's long-term success.[108] For fossil fuel corporations, this will undoubtedly include shareholders, employees, Indigenous groups, environmental non-governmental organizations, and communities in which the corporation plans to operate.
3 Decide on the best method for engaging with its selected stakeholders; providing written disclosure, soliciting passive feedback, handing out surveys, using email and social media, and holding in-person meetings are all ways in which a corporation could engage with its stakeholders.[109] In the interest of facilitating a genuine dialogue with stakeholders, fossil fuel corporations should strive to hold in-person meetings when feasible.
4 Continually assess the effectiveness of its stakeholder engagement activities and be prepared to make changes to these activities when necessary.[110]
5 Disclose its engagement activities, so that stakeholders can better understand what feedback the corporation received and how this feedback was used by the corporation in its decision-making processes.[111]

Ultimately, each fossil fuel corporation will have to devise an individualized stakeholder engagement process that accounts for factors such as its operating location and stakeholder demographics. Understandably, there will inevitably be certain stakeholders concerned about climate change that may not want to engage in this ongoing discussion about more responsible lobbying practices, as they will not want to be promoting fossil fuels. Fossil fuel corporations will have to do as much as they can to be open with these reluctant stakeholders, advising them that their feedback is important and following through on engaging in thoughtful and careful dialogue. These actions will show stakeholders that fossil fuel corporations want to improve their practices and engage in lobbying that will have stakeholders' interests in mind. What is ultimately most important is that each fossil fuel corporation engages in a genuine dialogue with impacted stakeholders that directly informs its decision-making processes.

Pillar 3: Alignment of Lobbying Practices with Long-Term Societal Objectives and Values

The third pillar of Bauer's model of responsible lobbying looks at how the corporation's lobbying activities align with the long-term objectives and values of society. Bauer recognizes that defining these objectives and values is difficult because they are socially constructed and can change over time.[112] However, she provides some "widely accepted points of reference" that corporations should seek to align with their lobbying practices: (1) prosperity, which includes economic growth and social well-being; (2) justice, which involves the equal allocation of resources across society; (3) sustainability, which involves environmental quality and intergenerational justice; and (4) human rights, which include moral rights recognized by international covenants, such as the Universal Declaration of Human Rights.[113] Where these objectives and values conflict, a corporation should ascertain which course of action best serves the interests of both society and the corporation by engaging in public dialogue.[114]

To move towards responsible lobbying, fossil fuel corporations should strive to align their lobbying activities with the long-term objectives and values of society, considering what will be most beneficial to society's future. It is understandable that due to the nature of what a fossil fuel corporation does, this may be difficult, as fossil fuel companies will have to especially draw their attention to the environmental and human rights impacts their lobbying will have not just in their own jurisdiction, but around the world as well.

One such objective could be that fossil fuel corporations align their lobbying activities with the development of BC's renewable energy sector. Fossil fuel corporations contribute directly to climate change, which is a worldwide crisis; according to the United Nations, climate change will have unprecedented impacts not only on human rights all around the world, concerning access to water, food, and shelter, but also to democracy and the rule of law.[115] The impacts of climate change will lead to hundreds of millions of people around the world facing food insecurity, droughts, displacement, and even death.[116] Despite the fact that fossil fuel corporations are generally aware of this problem, the industry is not doing enough to address it, although there have been some positive first steps. As the cost of technology for harvesting wind and solar energy has dropped, some of the largest oil companies in the world – including Shell and BP plc – have made significant investments in renewable energy projects.[117] Fossil fuel corporations in BC could bolster their support for the development of renewable energy projects in the province. By doing so, they would be promoting environmental sustainability and the creation of well-paying jobs.[118]

Furthermore, fossil fuel corporations could advocate for these renewable energy projects to be built in partnership with Indigenous communities, thereby offering "a promising path forward for [BC's] transition to a sustainable, just and climate-friendly energy system."[119] In 2015, the Truth and Reconciliation Commission of Canada released its 94 Calls to Action, which aim to "redress the legacy of residential schools and advance the process of Canadian reconciliation."[120] Call to Action 92 is particularly relevant for fossil fuel corporations:

> We call upon the corporate sector in Canada to adopt the United Nations Declaration on the Rights of Indigenous Peoples as a reconciliation framework and to apply its principles, norms, and standards to corporate policy and core operational activities involving Indigenous peoples and their lands and resources. This would include, but not be limited to, the following:
> (i) Commit to meaningful consultation, building respectful relationships, and obtaining the free, prior, and informed consent of Indigenous peoples before proceeding with economic development projects.
> (ii) Ensure that Aboriginal peoples have equitable access to jobs, training, and education opportunities in the corporate sector, and that Aboriginal communities gain long-term sustainable benefits from economic development projects.
> (iii) Provide education for management and staff on the history of Aboriginal peoples, including the history and legacy of residential schools, the United Nations Declaration on the

> Rights of Indigenous Peoples, Treaties and Aboriginal rights, Indigenous law, and Aboriginal–Crown relations. This will require skills-based training in intercultural competency, conflict resolution, human rights, and anti-racism.[121]

Fossil fuel corporations should strive to carry out their lobbying activities in accordance with the Calls to Action to facilitate reconciliation with BC's Indigenous Peoples, whose traditional lands are often impacted by oil and gas developments in the province.

If fossil fuel corporations genuinely want to increase moral legitimacy, they must do as much as they can to counter the environmental damage they cause and promote reconciliation with BC's Indigenous Peoples, even if it is sometimes to their detriment. For example, this could involve a fossil fuel corporation not moving forward with a specific project if it does not receive consent from an Indigenous community whose land it would be using to build the project; although this decision could arguably harm the corporation's bottom line, it would contribute to reconciliation efforts and in turn increase the corporation's moral legitimacy.

Base: Commitment to Ethical and Democratic Dialogue

At the base of Bauer's model of responsible lobbying is a corporation's commitment to lobbying in a manner that fosters an ethical and democratic dialogue with policymakers and other stakeholders. A corporation should not only follow the relevant lobbying legislation in its jurisdiction; it should go a step further by providing policymakers with balanced, reliable information.[122] In addition, a corporation should strive to engage in a power-free dialogue with stakeholders, resisting the opportunity to use its financial resources to amplify its voice to the detriment of others.[123] It is also essential that lobbying activities be as transparent as possible, so that stakeholders have enough information to participate in a free dialogue. However, Bauer notes that a corporation should "balance the necessity to involve affected parties and to keep specific information private on a case-by-case basis."[124] Finally, a corporation should engage in discussions with policymakers with the goal of achieving mutual understanding. These discussions require a corporation to accept policymakers as legitimate actors, listen and consider alternative positions, and aim for broadly accepted decisions rather than private ends.[125]

As previously discussed, the *Lobbyists Registration Amendment Act, 2018* introduced a series of changes that have increased lobbying transparency in BC. However, to practice responsible lobbying, fossil fuel corporations need to do more than merely comply with the new laws. Democracy Watch has identified several loopholes that the *Lobbyists Registration Amendment Act, 2018* failed to close. These loopholes include the fact that secret lobbying will continue to be legal if: (1) the lobbyist is not paid for their lobbying, or is only paid expenses; (2) the lobbyist is asked by a public official to lobby; (3) the lobbying activities are regarding the interpretation, application, or enforcement of legislation; and (4) the lobbyist is an in-house lobbyist at an organization who lobbies for less than one hundred hours annually.[126] Fossil fuel corporations should consider making these activities more transparent to the public in order to facilitate responsible lobbying.

Perhaps more importantly, fossil fuel corporations should ensure they are using their informational and financial resources to promote an ethical, democratic dialogue with policymakers and other stakeholders. Regardless of whether the provincial government continues to strengthen transparency in lobbying by closing loopholes in lobbying legislation, fossil fuel corporations will maintain their informational and financial advantage over policymakers and other stakeholders. Fossil fuel corporations should, therefore, seek to provide policymakers in BC with balanced, reliable information about the benefits and drawbacks of proposed natural resource projects in the province. Further, fossil fuel corporations should resist the temptation to use their vast resources to drown out the voices of other stakeholders, including environmental non-governmental organizations and Indigenous groups. Indeed, as the elephants in BC's political playing field, it is up to the fossil fuel corporations not to step on any chickens.

CONCLUSION

While new legislation has increased the transparency of lobbying activities in BC, this legislation has not addressed the inequality of resources that allows fossil fuel corporations to exert greater influence over government decision-makers than other stakeholders, such as environmental non-governmental organizations and Indigenous groups. Fossil fuel corporations must take a different approach to their lobbying activities in the province. As demonstrated by the climate strikes held across BC (and around the world) in September 2019, young people are dissatisfied with the current business as usual approach to climate action.[127] Fossil fuel corporations must recognize that these engaged young people – who are the next generation of voters, consumers, employees, directors, and government decision-makers – will be heavily scrutinizing corporate practices, including corporate lobbying activities. Forward-thinking fossil fuel corporations should, therefore, implement Bauer's model of responsible lobbying, considering their unique business models, stakeholders, and the long-term objectives and values of society to maintain their moral legitimacy into the future.

NOTES

1 "Protestors across Canada Support Wet'suwet'en Anti-Pipeline Camps," *CBC News*, 8 January 2019, https://www.cbc.ca/news/indigenous/wet-suwet-en-camp-anti-pipeline-rallies-1.4969916.

2 Chantelle Bellrichard, "Wet'suwet'en Hereditary Leaders, Supporters Call for Stop Work Order on Coastal GasLink Pipeline," *CBC News*, 3 February 2019, https://www.cbc.ca/news/indigenous/wet-suwet-en-stop-work-coastal-gaslink-pipeline-1.5003495.

3 Nicolas Graham, Shannon Daub, and Bill Carroll, *Mapping Political Influence: Political Donations and Lobbying by the Fossil Fuel Industry in BC* (Vancouver: Canadian Centre for Policy Alternatives 2017), 17, https://www.policyalternatives.ca/sites/default/files/uploads/publications/BC%20Office/2017/03/ccpa-bc_mapping_influence_final.pdf.

4 Rob Shaw and Richard Zussman, *A Matter of Confidence: Inside Story of the Political Battle for BC* (Toronto: Heritage House 2018), 162.

5 Dan Levin, "British Columbia: The 'Wild West' of Canadian Political Cash," *The New York Times*, 13 January 2017, https://www.nytimes.com/2017/01/13/world/canada/british-columbia-christy-clark.html.

6 Bill 3, *Election Amendment Act, 2017*, 2d sess., 41st Parliament, 2017, RSBC 1996.

7 Bill 54, *Lobbyists Registration Amendment Act, 2018*, 3d sess., 41st Parliament, 2018, SBC 2001.

8 William D. Oberman, "A Framework for the Ethical Analysis of Corporate Political Activity," *Business and Social Review* 109, no. 2 (June 2004): 251.

9 Andreas Rasche, "The Corporation as a Political Actor – European and North American Perspectives," *European Management Journal* 33, no. 1 (February 2015): 6.

10 Guido Palazzo and Andreas Georg Scherer, "Corporate Legitimacy as Deliberation: A Communicative Framework," *Journal of Business Ethics* 66, no. 1 (2006): 78.

11 Theresa Bauer, *Responsible Lobbying: Conceptual Foundations and Empirical Findings in the EU* (Weisbaden: Springer Gabler, 2017).

12 Levin, "Wild West."

13 Ibid. Democracy Watch is a Canadian non-governmental organization that advocates for greater government accountability. See Democracy Watch, "About Democracy Watch," accessed 18 August 2021, https://democracywatch.ca/about.

14 Ibid.

15 Rob Shaw, Gordon Hoekstra, and Stephanie Ip, "All Five Conditions Met for BC Approval of Kinder Morgan pipeline: Christy Clark," *Vancouver Sun*, 12 January 2017, https://vancouversun.com/news/local-news/b-c-government-grants-environmental-approval-for-kinder-morgan-pipeline/wcm/8854ed8e-5d57-4b43-9710-d62c8880ba1a.

16 Ibid.

17 Levin, "Wild West."

18 Graham, Daub, and Carroll, *Mapping Political Influence*, 16.

19 Ibid., 15.

20 Ibid., 17.

21 Ibid.

22 Nicolas Graham, Shannon Daub, and Bill Carroll, "5.2 Million Reasons the Fossil Fuel Industry has the BC Government's Ear," *Policy Note*, 8 March 2017, https://www.policynote.ca/5-2-million-reasons-the-fossil-fuel-industry-has-the-bc-governments-ear.

23 Ibid.

24 Graham, Daub, and Carroll, *Mapping Political Influence,* 21.

25 Ibid., 24.

26 Shaw and Zussman, *Matter of Confidence,* 160–1.

27 BC New Democratic Party (BC NDP) Platform, *Working for You: Our Commitments to Build a Better BC* (Ottawa: New Democratic Party of Canada 2017), 86.

28 Bill 3, *Election Amendment Act, 2017*, 2d sess., 41st Parliament, 2017, RSBC 1996.

29 Bill 54, *Lobbyists Registration Amendment Act, 2018*, 3d sess., 41st Parliament, 2018, SBC 2001.

30 Office of the Premier, "New Government Ends Era of 'Big Money' in Politics," *BC Gov News*, 18 September 2017, https://news.gov.bc.ca/releases/2017PREM0084-001592.

31 *Lobbying Act*, RSC 1985, c. 44 (4th Supp.).
32 "Upcoming Changes to the *Lobbyists Registration Act*," Office of the Registrar of Lobbyists for British Columbia, published November 28, 2018, https://www.lobbyistsregistrar.bc.ca/handlers/DocumentHandler.ashx?DocumentID=303.
33 Ibid.
34 *Lobbyists Registration Act*, SBC. 2001, c. 42, s. 1(1), https://www.canlii.org/en/bc/laws/stat/sbc-2001-c-42/latest/sbc-2001-c-42.html.
35 Bauer, *Responsible Lobbying*, 38.
36 A. Paul Pross and Robert P. Shepherd, "Innovation Diffusion and Networking: Canada's Evolving Approach to Lobbying Regulation," *Canadian Public Administration* 60, no. 2 (June 2017): 153.
37 Ibid., 153–4.
38 *Lobbying Act*, RSC 1985, c. 44 (4th Supp.), https://laws-lois.justice.gc.ca/eng/acts/l-12.4.
39 Pross and Shepherd, "Innovation Diffusion," 167.
40 Ibid.
41 Nikos Passas and Neva Goodwin, *It's Legal but It Ain't Right: Harmful Social Consequences of Legal Industries* (Ann Arbor: University of Michigan Press, 2004), 264.
42 Ibid.
43 Florian Wettstein and Dorothea Baur, "'Why Should We Care About Marriage Equality?': Political Advocacy as a Part of Corporate Responsibility," *Journal of Business Ethics* 138, no. 2 (2016): 201.
44 Iain McMenamin, *If Money Talks, What Does it Say?: Corruption and Business Financing of Political Parties* (Oxford University Press 2013), 59.
45 Graham, Daub, and Carroll, *Mapping Political Influence*, 25.
46 Theresa Bauer, "Responsible Lobbying: The Impact of the Institutional Context," *Journal of Global Responsibility* 6, no. 2 (September 2015): 151.
47 Madina Rival and Richard Major, "What Lobbying Ethics and What for? The Case of French Lobbying Consulting Firms," *Journal of Business Ethics* 150, no. 1 (2018): 99.
48 Oberman, "Ethical Analysis," 253.
49 Anthony J. Nownes, *Total Lobbying: What Lobbyists Want (and How They Try to Get It)* (New York: Cambridge University Press, 2006), 28.
50 Elisabeth Gidengil and Heather Bastedo, eds., *Canadian Democracy from the Ground Up: Perceptions and Performance* (Vancouver: UBC Press 2014), 5.
51 Oberman, "Ethical Analysis," 251.
52 Graham, Daub, and Carroll, "5.2 Million Reasons."

53 Avi Brisman, "The Violence of Silence: Some Reflections on Access to Information, Public Participation in Decision-making, and Access to Justice in Matters Concerning the Environment," *Crime, Law and Social Change* 59, no. 3 (January 2013): 300.
54 Christian Houle, "Does Economic Inequality Breed Political Inequality?" *Democratization* 25, no. 8 (Summer 2018): 1501.
55 Oberman, "Ethical Analysis," 251.
56 Rasche, "Corporation," 6.
57 Ibid.
58 Stephenos Anastasiadis, Jeremy Moon, and Michael Humphreys, "Lobbying and the Responsible Firm: Agenda-Setting for Freshly Conceptualized Field," *Business Ethics: European Review* 27, no. 3 (July 2018): 208.
59 Rasche, "Corporation," 6.
60 Ibid.
61 Andreas Georg Scherer et al., "Managing for Political Corporate Social Responsibility: New Challenges and Directions for PCSR 2.0," *Journal of Management Studies* 53, no. 3 (May 2016): 276.
62 Wettstein and Baur, "Marriage Equality," 205.
63 Ibid.
64 Irina Lock and Peter Seele, "Deliberative Lobbying? Toward a Non-contradiction of Corporate Political Activities and Corporate Social Responsibility," *Journal of Management Inquiry* 25, no. 4 (Spring 2016): 418.
65 Ibid., 419.
66 Palazzo and Scherer, "Corporate Legitimacy," 72.
67 Mark C. Suchman, "Managing Legitimacy: Strategic and Institutional Approaches," *Academy of Management Review* 20, no. 3 (July 1995): 572.
68 Ibid., 582.
69 Ibid., 578.
70 Ibid., 579.
71 Palazzo and Scherer, "Corporate Legitimacy," 78.
72 Domènec Melé and Jaume Armengou, "Moral Legitimacy in Controversial Projects and its Relationship with Social License to Operate: A Case Study," *Journal of Business Ethics* 136, no. 4 (July 2016): 730.
73 Ibid., 733.
74 Ibid., 740.
75 Ibid., 733.
76 Se-Yeon Ahn and Dong-Jun Park, "Corporate Social Responsibility and Corporate Longevity: The Mediating Role of Social Capital and Moral Legitimacy in Korea," *Journal of Business Ethics* 150, no. 1 (2018): 130.

77 Ibid., 131.
78 Bauer, *Responsible Lobbying*, 38.
79 BC NDP Platform, *Working for You*, 86.
80 Mia Rabson, "Senators Bowing to Oil Industry Pressure to Gut Assessment Bill, Environmentalists Say," *CBC News*, 14 May 2019, https://www.cbc.ca/news/canada/calgary/environment-oil-and-gas-c69-1.5135332.
81 Ibid.
82 Ibid.
83 Spence, "Corporate Social Responsibility in the Oil and Gas Industry," 60–1.
84 Rod Nickel and Julie Gordon, "'A Made-in-Canada Crisis': How Political Stumbles, Savvy Activists Brought the Oilpatch to its Knees," *Financial Post*, 24 December 2018, https://financialpost.com/commodities/energy/rpt-political-stumbles-savvy-activists-knock-canadas-oil-sector-to-its-knees.
85 Jonathan Arnold and Nancy Olewiler, "Getting to Zero: Canada Plans to hit Net-Zero Emissions by 2050. What's Next?," *Canadian Institute for Climate Choices*, 21 January 2020, https://climatechoices.ca/getting-to-zero-canada-plans-to-hit-net-zero-emissions-by-2050-whats-next.
86 Isabelle Turcotte, "How Companies Can Get Net-Zero Right," *Pembina Institute*, 30 June 2020, https://www.pembina.org/op-ed/how-companies-can-get-net-zero-right.
87 Myles Allen et al., "Summary for Policymakers," IPCC, 2018, https://www.ipcc.ch/sr15/chapter/spm.
88 Turcotte, "How Companies."
89 Shell Group, "Our Climate Target," accessed 18 August 2021, https://www.shell.com/energy-and-innovation/the-energy-future/our-climate-target.html.
90 Ibid.
91 Bauer, *Responsible Lobbying*, 107.
92 Bauer, "Institutional Context," 148.
93 Ibid.
94 Bauer, *Responsible Lobbying*, 108.
95 Ibid.
96 Ibid., 110.
97 Ibid.
98 Ibid., 111.
99 Ibid., 112.
100 Industry Canada, "Corporate Social Responsibility, An Implementation Guide for Canadian Business," 2014, https://www.ic.gc.ca/eic/site/csr-rse.nsf/eng/h_rs00599.html.
101 Ibid.
102 Ibid., 18.

103 Bauer, *Responsible Lobbying*, 112.
104 Ibid.
105 Ibid., 113.
106 Andrew J. MacDougall and Josh Pekarsky, *Director Briefing – Stakeholder Engagement* (Toronto: Chartered Professional Accountants of Canada 2018).
107 Ibid., 12.
108 Ibid., 13.
109 Ibid., 14.
110 Ibid.
111 Ibid., 15.
112 Bauer, *Responsible Lobbying*, 116.
113 Ibid., 116–7.
114 Ibid., 118.
115 Dana Drugmand, "UN Human Rights Expert Condemns Fossil Fuel Companies for Being Main Drivers Behind Climate Crisis," Business and Human Rights Resource Centre, 4 July 2019, https://www.business-humanrights.org/en/latest-news/un-human-rights-expert-condemns-fossil-fuel-companies-for-being-main-drivers-behind-climate-crisis.
116 Ibid.
117 Tony Seskus, "As Renewable Energy Grows, So Does Interest from Big Oil," *CBC News*, 10 May 2018, https://www.cbc.ca/news/business/renewable-energy-oil-1.4656106.
118 Dan McGarvey, "Renewable Energy Jobs Provide New Opportunities for Alberta Workers," *CBC News*, 3 November 2017, https://www.cbc.ca/news/canada/calgary/alberta-renewables-wind-solar-jobs-energy-1.4385124.
119 Karena Shaw et al., "BC First Nations are Poised to Lead the Renewable Energy Transition," *Policy Note*, 12 October 2017, https://www.policynote.ca/bc-first-nations-are-poised-to-lead-the-renewable-energy-transition.
120 Truth and Reconciliation Commission of Canada, *Honouring the Truth, Reconciling for the Future: Summary of the Final Report of the Truth and Reconciliation Commission of Canada* (Government of Canada 2015), 319, https://publications.gc.ca/collections/collection_2015/trc/IR4-7-2015-eng.pdf.
121 Ibid., 306.
122 Bauer, *Responsible Lobbying*, 118.
123 Ibid., 119–20.
124 Ibid., 120.
125 Ibid., 119.

126 "BC NDP Lobbying Bill Leaves Huge Secret, Unethical Lobbying Loopholes," *Democracy Watch*, 4 October 2017, https://democracywatch.ca/b-c-ndp-lobbying-bill-leaves-huge-secret-unethical-lobbying-loopholes.

127 Eva Uguen-Csenge, "Here's Why Vancouver Teens are Staging a Climate Strike," *CBC News*, 26 September 2019, https://www.cbc.ca/news/canada/british-columbia/vancouver-climate-strike-global-thunberg-protest-1.5297743.

7

Reparations or Reputation: The Paradox of CSR and the Alcohol Industry

Catherine L.H. Lee

Corporate social responsibility (CSR) has a strong presence in modern economics and business activities. CSR is particularly relevant for firms whose business is the production of harmful products, such as those in the tobacco, alcohol, gambling, or firearms industries – labelled "SIN firms."[1] These firms differ in terms of specific products and services provided, but are all categorized as controversial industries because they are perceived to be in violation of social norms.[2] This perceived violation stems from the fact that the goods and services in question have higher social and/or public health costs and often operate in areas of society where there is no consensus on morality.[3] Engagement by firms in controversial industries thus presents an interesting paradox. Can a firm be socially responsible while producing controversial products that are harmful to human beings, society, and/or the environment?

This chapter looks at that question in the context of the alcohol industry with an emphasis on large spirit producers, considering the particular social and public health dimensions within that sector. This chapter starts with a synthesis of the empirical studies on CSR practices by firms within the alcohol industry, exploring the reasons these firms engage in CSR and the impact these CSR practices have on the firms and the general public. The findings show that, in general, alcohol firms engage in CSR activity and publish their CSR efforts that are undertaken deliberately and with a strategic purpose of legitimizing the business, enhancing the firm's reputation, and preventing regulatory measures. There are mixed findings as to the benefits of CSR on the firm, but with respect to its impact beyond the business, most studies agree that CSR activity in the alcohol industry has been largely superficial, ineffective, and potentially even detrimental as it has done more to market the firm and its products than to redress the social and public harms of the business. Policy recommendations encouraging CSR in the alcohol industry and partnerships between corporate and non-corporate actors are problematic considering research findings.

This chapter then proposes the adoption of "implicit" rather than "explicit" CSR within the alcohol industry under Dirk Matten and Jeremy Moon's 2008 implicit-explicit CSR conceptual framework.[4] Various studies and public health policymakers advocate for stronger regulation of the alcohol industry, without recognizing such actions as implicit CSR.[5] In light of policy recommendations, a change to CSR practices is proposed in the alcohol industry from a voluntary and publicized approach to a mandatory, compliance-based approach by setting collective values and expectations of social responsibility in the alcohol industry and implementing mandatory requirements through government. Policy suggestions for change to Canada's current regulatory framework include the removal of discretion from firms operating in the alcohol industry around marketing standards, imposing higher levels of national regulation on alcohol marketing and advertising activities, and health warning labels on alcohol products.

CSR PRACTICES IN THE ALCOHOL INDUSTRY AND THE INHERENT CONFLICT OF INTEREST

There was dramatic growth in CSR activities in the alcohol industry beginning in the early 2000s. Leading global spirit producers demonstrated CSR initiatives on a range of environmental, social, and governance issues. Alcohol firms expressed growing commitment to water conservation and reducing greenhouse gas emissions by improving energy efficiency and shifting to fuels with lower carbon emissions.[6] Social issues engagement could be broadly categorized into five types: alcohol information and education provision, prevention of drinking and driving, research involvement, policy involvement, and the creation of social aspects organizations.[7] The main CSR initiative undertaken by major companies in the alcohol industry by and large has been the promotion of responsible drinking.[8] The International Alliance for Responsible Drinking (IARD), a non-profit organization sponsored by global spirit producers with the goal of reducing harmful drinking and promoting responsible drinking, adopts five commitments: reducing underage drinking, strengthening and expanding marketing codes of practice, providing consumer information and responsible product innovation, reducing drinking and driving, and working with retailers to reduce harmful drinking.[9] The IARD publishes a database of industry actions that have been taken by their members, which are eleven global spirit producers, to achieve these five commitments. The implementation and promotion of responsible drinking programs are generally through mass communication, including social media.[10]

Leading spirit producers have also emphasized the importance of responsible sourcing, contribution to their local communities, and to charitable donations and the sponsorship of education or sporting events unrelated to the industry.[11] Research involvement of large alcohol firms included hosting scientific conferences, formulation of principles on industry-researcher collaborations, publication and dissemination of scientific documents, and funding researchers and support of research centres.[12] They have pledged to value employee relationships including with respect to wages, working conditions, workplace safety and anti-harassment, and diversity and anti-discrimination policies.[13] These firms have also publicly committed to reporting on and measuring CSR performance, benchmarking their performance against competitors.

Reporting and measuring CSR performance should be an important aspect of CSR in the alcohol industry as it is a form of stakeholder engagement and controversial industries are likely to pay more attention to stakeholder engagement than non-controversial industries. Although many of the leading spirit producers produced CSR reports, a study by Peter Jones, David Hillier, and Daphne Comfort found that the majority did not commission or publish external audits as part of their CSR report, and for the one company that did – Diageo plc – the report was not very comprehensive as it focused mainly on environmental issues and only offered limited assurance.[14] As for stakeholders, Agostino Vollero et al. found that stakeholder engagement in the alcohol industry does not truly engage stakeholders' participation in business decisions or CSR initiatives.[15] Controversial industries adopt a "command-and control" approach in stakeholder engagement, characterized by one-way communication and defining the CSR agenda internally by publishing CSR information on corporate websites.[16] In such an approach, a stakeholder understanding of the company's CSR initiatives are dependent on the information published by the companies, with passive stakeholder involvement.[17] This is problematic in light of Jones, Hillier, and Comfort's findings that much of the CSR reporting is unaudited or only partial information is provided even when audited.[18]

The issue faced by stakeholders and researchers is that much of the information on CSR initiatives is largely in the form of publicly available information displayed on corporate websites or based on interviews with company managers.[19] Jones, Hillier, and Comfort's study of CSR activities by ten of the world's largest spirit companies found that, because the information collected is disseminated by the corporations, CSR initiatives and commitments may be interpreted as merely aspirational.[20] By pursuing their commitments, alcohol firms encounter a conflicting commitment to generate more revenue, which requires greater consumption of their products.[21] The conflict of interest within the alcohol industry is that the volume of consumption is directly related to the sales of alcohol beverages and profits of the alcohol industry. Increased profit of the industry is likely to be associated with increased harm to the population, as studies have shown that effective public health policies require a reduction of alcohol use across the population as a whole, yet a non-negligible proportion of revenues come from addicts, and a larger share of revenues comes from non-addicted drinkers who face similar health and social harms.[22]

Corporate Reasons for Engaging in CSR and its Effect on the Business

Reasons for why firms in controversial industries engage in CSR have been considered through three hypotheses: window dressing hypothesis, value-enhancing hypothesis, and value-irrelevance hypothesis.[23] The window dressing hypothesis suggests that firms engage in CSR as window dressing to legitimize a questionable business and deceive stakeholders. This hypothesis is based on the immoral manager seeking private benefits of reputation-building at the cost of stakeholder wealth. As such, it will reduce firm value because investors will eventually realize the manager's intentions and penalize the firm on the stock market.[24] The value-enhancing hypothesis suggests that moral managers utilize CSR as a means to improve transparency, strategies, and philanthropy and to eventually enhance firm value.[25] Under this hypothesis, moral managers strategically engage in CSR as a business strategy, integrated with core business objectives to enhance firm value and social or environmental value.[26] The value-irrelevance hypothesis suggests that firms simply follow the current trend of CSR engagement as socially neutral activities without intention to deceive stakeholders or value generation.[27] This hypothesis found little support in studies, as most studies showed that CSR engagement was a deliberate, strategic business decision, and firms do not engage in CSR merely to follow current trends.

Studies showed that, in general, firms in the global alcohol industry engaged in CSR for reasons falling within one or both window dressing and value-enhancing hypotheses, though neither hypothesis was supported in full. Thus, the reason for CSR engagement in the alcohol industry is perhaps an intersection of the window dressing and value-enhancing hypotheses. Firms in the global alcohol industry primarily engage in CSR for a strategic business purpose and risk management, and to achieve that purpose, CSR engagement may be utilized as a form of window dressing or it may be that it has become a necessity of doing business in a controversial sector.[28]

CSR engagement of large industry players within the alcohol industry generally increases firm value, legitimizes the business, and neutralizes negative stigma, which supports the hypothesis that alcohol firms engage in CSR for a strategic business purpose.[29] However, the value-enhancing hypothesis, as framed in Ye Cai, Hoje Jo, and Carrie Pan's study is problematic because it assumes that CSR engagement is supported by an underlying desire of the firm to be altruistic, moral, and socially responsible.[30] Many studies support the general hypothesis that CSR enhances firm value, yet few studies offer support for altruism behind the strategic business decision. Cai, Jo, and Pan's study found that the majority of managers in controversial industries engage in CSR to enhance firm value, and thus concluded that US firms in controversial industries that generally "behave morally and strategically" are capable of being socially responsible despite their products being detrimental to the environment, humans, or society.[31] However, a later study based on global CSR data found that while CSR does enhance firm value, value enhancement does not represent support for the hypothesis that CSR is motivated by corporate morality or altruism. Firms do not engage in CSR to be socially responsible or philanthropic, but rather because it gives them a competitive advantage compared to their peers, hence offering support for the value-enhancing hypothesis but not the underlying assumptions of altruistic motivations.[32] A recent study based on a global data sample also found that less than 2 per cent of CSR actions undertaken by multinational alcohol firms, as reported by IARD, could be categorized as altruistic.[33] Zenu Sharma and Liang Song's international study suggests that any moral incentive to pursue CSR would be in the form of moral rebalancing, as firms in controversial industries suffer a "negative shock to firm value" and, therefore, CSR is an ideal mechanism to improve public perception and potentially mitigate the financial consequences of negative screening by investors.[34] The findings as a whole indicate that CSR within the global alcohol industry is driven by risk management, business efficiency, and the search for competitive advantage.

The instrumental value of CSR in enhancing business value invites ulterior motives of shaping public policy, deterring alcohol control regulation, and indirect brand and product marketing through CSR initiatives. The window dressing hypothesis, as framed in Cai, Jo, and Pan's study is only partially supported by research findings. Many studies found that CSR engagement in the alcohol industry was window dressing for other corporate intents, but there were mixed findings as to the effect of window dressing on firm value. The proposition that ingenuine motives behind CSR will be perceived negatively by stakeholders and decrease firm value has limited support from empirical studies, as most studies show that CSR engagement generally increases firm value, even within controversial industries.

In an exploratory study, Gert-Jan Steltenpool and Piet Verhoeven found that outside the alcohol industry, dissemination of CSR messages led to a more favourable attitude toward the organization, increased intention to buy, a more favourable reputation, and less skepticism; however, within the alcohol industry, CSR frames had the opposite effect of leading to a negative attitude toward the organization, less intention to buy, and more consumer skepticism.[35] In a subsequent study based on CSR data from US publicly traded companies, Hannah Oh, John Bae, and Sang-Joon Kim found that due to the inherently negative stigma of controversial industries, such as the alcohol industry, CSR frames had the effect of neutralizing the firm's negative reputation, but where messages focused on or emphasized CSR, it led to an increase of idiosyncratic risk as they were met with more consumer and investor skepticism.[36] Hoje Jo and Haejung Na's US-based study also confirmed that CSR engagement had the effect of enhancing firm value: since firms in controversial sectors face risks such as reputational risks and stakeholder skepticism, CSR engagement by firms in controversial industries can reduce firm risk and enhance corporate image.[37] Oh, Bae, and Kim's finding that perceived ingenuine engagement in CSR increased stakeholder ambivalence toward the firm because CSR activities generated "a misaligned fit between their good deeds and their stigmatized negative image."[38] However, in Yeonsoo Kim and Sun-Young Park's US-based study, they found that perceived motives, including consumer skepticism, did not have a direct effect on participants' attitudes toward the sponsor (alcohol industry or non-profit organization), the campaign message, or alcohol consumption,[39] which suggests that though engaging in CSR or marketing CSR engagement may be met with consumer skepticism, skepticism over the company's motives had little influence over overall perception of the company or alcohol consumption.

CSR tactics employed by alcohol firms are often closely tied with the industry's underlying corporate intents.[40] The alcohol industry uses social initiatives and stakeholder engagement to frame issues, define problems, and guide policy debates, which has the effect of deflecting and shifting the blame from manufacturers and promoters to consumers.[41] Thomas Babor and Katherine Robaina criticized research funding and scientific conferences supported by the global alcohol industry as being instrumental in nature, designed to maximize the industry's long-term profits by shaping the research agenda, which in turn shapes public policy.[42] CSR initiatives are also used as a means to reframe or deny conflicts of interest. Firms resort to defining "problematic drinking" narrowly and focus on the personal choices people make. Addiction is viewed as a "failure of the self rather than of the addictive goods or services."[43] Thus, the role of the "responsible corporate actor" is to help the small proportion of consumers engaged in problematic drinking in a process of self-management.[44]

The global alcohol industry also engages in and promotes CSR initiatives on voluntary regulation to delay and offset alcohol control legislation, specifically with regards to marketing and advertisement.[45] One Belgian multinational alcohol firm publicly stated on its website that the adherence to its external code was a mechanism to protect the business from future regulatory restrictions to its current marketing and advertising freedom.[46] In Babor and Robaina's study of the growth of international CSR activities over the past twenty-five years, most of the increased activity occurred around the time the World Health Assembly was preparing its Global Strategy on the Harmful Use of Alcohol, indicating that CSR activity is related to corporate intent to delay or prevent alcohol control.[47]

CSR engagement in the alcohol industry may have the stronger undercurrent of profit-making compared to other industries. Alcohol corporations undertake philanthropic sponsorships as a means of indirect brand marketing and gaining preferential access to emerging alcohol markets.[48] Daniela Pantani et al.'s study conducted on CSR practices of the alcohol industry in Latin America and the Caribbean found that while the alcohol industry claimed to undertake CSR strategies aligned with the WHO global strategy, a majority of its CSR actions also had the potential of product marketing and brand promotion.[49] The mass promotion of responsible drinking programs is a "double-edged sword," as while it promulgates messages to drink responsibly to decrease social harms, the same messages nonetheless promote drinking with little or no arguments to not drink.[50]

Effects of CSR Engagement in the Alcohol Industry on the Public

While CSR engagement is strategically beneficial for the alcohol industry, studies have found that it has a potentially adverse effect on the public. Strategic motivations for engaging in CSR do not necessarily detract from the value of CSR engagement, but CSR engagement with a strategic purpose of deterring regulation and implementation of effective public health policies does have an adverse effect on society. Adverse effects from social CSR initiatives include reframing the issue to minimize the risk of harm to consumers and marketing the product through CSR reporting, thereby enabling the industry to increase sales and revenue at the expense of public health. CSR engagement provides legitimacy to alcohol firms by allowing them to continue manufacturing and advertising their products with little government oversight.

Research has shown that CSR initiatives by the alcohol industry are largely ineffective. A study comparing IARD strategies with the WHO Global strategy to reduce the harmful use of alcohol found that the majority (72.9 per cent) of global alcohol industry actions did not conform with evidence-based policy options propounded by the WHO Global strategy, and an overwhelming majority (96.8 per cent) of CSR actions by the alcohol industry lacked scientific support of their effectiveness in reducing harmful drinking.[51] A few actions (11 per cent) even had the potential for doing harm.[52] Such findings have been affirmed in other studies on the effects of CSR in the alcohol industry.[53]

Besides being ineffective, a dangerous effect of CSR initiatives is that they reframe the issues, which can have the effect of misdirecting consumers and public policymaking. CSR initiatives targeting responsible drinking and alcohol addiction ignore a larger group of consumers – the non-addicted heavy consumers – who contribute far more to the industry's profits and contribute significantly to harms such as impaired driving, workplace intoxication, and unsafe sex.[54] Through issue-framing and CSR practices in response to self-identified issues, alcohol firms redirect public and government attention away from a far larger group of consumers to a smaller group of consumers, thereby appearing to fulfill their responsibility to society by preventing harm yet maintaining high consumption and high profits. As Hein de Vries commented, CSR actions undertaken in the global alcohol industry are aimed to ensure the government and other institutions view the industry as good corporate citizens and thus divert attention from reducing the supply of alcohol to focusing on the responsibility of "self-regulating individual drinkers."[55] By labelling and targeting addicted individuals, alcohol firms simultaneously convey the message that those individuals who do not fall under this label can freely consume their products without harm.

Organizations dedicated to the prevention of harms associated with alcohol that are funded by the alcohol industry also have a detrimental impact on health awareness by providing the alcohol industry with a platform to redirect public attention away from real health issues.[56] In a study of Twitter messages by UK, Ireland, and Australian alcohol industry-funded organizations dedicated towards promotion of responsible drinking, Nason Maani Hessari et al. found that the organizations were selective in the issues they tweeted about. Social organizations funded by the alcohol industry were significantly less likely to tweet about chronic health problems associated with alcohol consumption, especially cancer, but were more likely to tweet about education and individual responsibility.[57] Organizations also misrepresented evidence on the risks of alcohol consumption associated with pregnancy and fertility, and were less likely to place clear, visible warnings on wine bottles (a more popular choice among women).[58]

As well, the alcohol industry engages in CSR and adopts self-regulatory codes of conduct to prevent the implementation of effective liquor control policies that might be harmful to profits. The global alcohol industry's support of seemingly independent organizations and scientific research is used to support its lobbying positions in public policy processes and as evidence of its social responsibility as a good corporate citizen.[59] Research supported by the alcohol industry is often biased and can mislead policymakers.[60] The alcohol industry's self-regulation of marketing messages and introduction of voluntary labels that are ambiguous and low-impact serves to prevent the introduction of mandatory, direct labels such as warnings on cigarette packages required of the tobacco industry.[61]

Another dangerous effect of CSR engagement by the alcohol industry is the potential for CSR to be used as another marketing platform to encourage alcohol consumption. When CSR is used to market products and promote the brand, there is a danger that it is not regulated under legislation and that consumers may not perceive it as advertising and may be more susceptible to its influence.[62] In support of previous findings that CSR efforts to promote responsible drinking contained ambiguous messages that simultaneously encouraged consumption of alcohol, one US-based study has found that exposure to responsible drinking campaigns sponsored by alcohol firms actually led to stronger intention to consume alcohol amongst university students.[63] Students tended to view responsible drinking campaigns by alcohol companies as an indicator of the company's "sensitivity and concern about the well-being of its customers," thereby increasing the company's credibility in their eyes, which increased the positivity of students' attitudes toward the campaign message and drinking.[64] As Kim and Park criticized in their article, industry-sponsored responsible drinking campaigns are superficial in addressing the issue of alcohol consumption amongst students.[65]

POLICY RECOMMENDATIONS

Research findings demonstrate that CSR engagement in the global alcohol industry is prevalent and strategic, with potentially adverse effects on the public and public health policymaking due to the inherent conflict of interest between the alcohol industry and public health objectives. Self-regulation and self-imposed marketing codes and social responsibility objectives are ineffective and inconsistent with policies based on scientific evidence. It would appear that CSR engagement by the alcohol industry does more harm than good, so the question remains: is the alcohol industry antithetical to CSR?

Despite potential harms caused by CSR engagement, there is a policy argument in favour of maintaining CSR practices within the alcohol industry grounded on the recognition of the social value of harm minimization in that "any action that creates social good by a legally operating firm, whether in a controversial or non-controversial sector, should be seen as preferable to the absence of any such actions by that firm."[66] Margaret Lindorff, Elizabeth Prior Jonson, and Linda McGuire argue that from a utilitarian perspective, the "legal but regulated provision" of controversial products and services (i.e., harmful or immoral products and services) may be better than the alternative where such products or services are procurable via a black market.[67] Given that a blanket prohibition of the product may also produce more harm than good, studies have recommended CSR as a post-political form of regulation involving partnerships between regulatory bodies and firms instead of traditional forms of regulation where interests of corporate actors were opposed to those of society and constrained by legislation.[68] In this sense, the firm is viewed as a corporate citizen and a participant in solving global public issues as a part of their CSR practices.[69]

Michael Porter and Mark Kramer's shared value theory argues that firms can engage in CSR by selecting a social issue that intersects with a particular business interest and creates a "shared value" that is beneficial for society and is also valuable for the business, especially for firms in controversial industries.[70] Porter and Kramer's shared value theory may be adequate to deal with environmental and governance issues within CSR; however, due to the conflict of interest between the industry and social objectives, it would be difficult to find a "shared value" that is beneficial for society and valuable for the business without heavy compromise on either part. Current partnerships between the alcohol industry and public policymakers have been criticized as "politicized CSR" rather than "political CSR," and are an example of companies' misuse of CSR for their lobbying efforts, motivated not out of responsibility toward stakeholders but from a strategic standpoint of preventing further regulation.[71] Effective public health policy changes are hindered by pro-consumption influences of the alcohol industry.[72] The trend towards partnerships of alcohol firms with governments in public health-making has led to incremental public health policy steps such as minimum unit of alcohol pricing, but marketing largely remains unregulated.[73] The existence and denial of conflicts of interest within the alcohol industry makes it difficult to envision a successful partnership. Considering the ulterior motives behind the global alcohol industry's CSR engagement and the detrimental impacts that comparative studies have observed, it is likely that political CSR will merely increase access to policymakers to reframe issues and advance public policy in the interest of the industry's profits.[74]

The negative implications of CSR engagement in the alcohol industry and the challenges of implementing a post-political partnership between the industry and policymakers appears to paint a pessimistic future for CSR in controversial industries. However, it remains possible for firms within the alcohol industry to be socially responsible if the industry shifts to implicit CSR practices rather than explicit CSR. Implicit CSR provides a framework to limit the potential for abuse of CSR engagement within the alcohol industry and strikes a balance between the industry's need to be profitable and the protection of society and public health.

Matten and Moon's Conceptual Framework of Explicit-Implicit CSR

Matten and Moon describe explicit CSR as "corporate policies that assume and articulate responsibility for some societal interests."[75] Under their explicit framework, CSR is based on corporate discretion rather than governmental or institutional mandate.[76] Explicit CSR has been associated with signaling theory, which posits that firms' communication of CSR practices is strategically employed to "signal" superior CSR to stakeholders rather than truly engage stakeholders.[77] Most CSR activities undertaken by the alcohol industry tend to fall within the category of explicit CSR. Under the implicit CSR framework, proper obligations of a corporation are defined by collective values, norms, and rules, often implemented through codified and mandatory or customary requirements imposed by government and broader formal and informal institutions.[78] Implicit CSR is characterized by higher levels of regulation, stronger labour and employment unions, and collective decision-making.[79] Implicit CSR is associated with greater stakeholder engagement, including government institutions.[80] Engagement of implicit CSR may be similar to explicit CSR in terms of practices, but the intention differs; whereas explicit CSR is often undertaken for strategic purposes, there is less discretion with implicit CSR, which is enacted through mandatory or customary practices and is meant to reflect collective business values.[81]

The inherent conflict of interest between profitability and reduction of social and public health harms within the alcohol industry requires external control mechanisms to ensure that corporate social responsibility is adopted and exercised in a way that not only benefits firm value but also society. Explicit CSR has the demonstrated benefit of legitimizing sinful industries, such as the alcohol industry, and enhancing financial performance, even where CSR may result in stakeholder ambivalence toward the firm. The empirical studies canvassed in this chapter do not support the proposition of the window dressing hypothesis that market forces will penalize controversial industries for the harmful effects of their products and the ineffectiveness or even harmful effects of their CSR practices, but rather, support the view that CSR engagement had the positive impact of increasing firm reputation and profitability.[82]

Adopting implicit CSR would require a stronger emphasis on regulation of the market, government leadership, and involvement of the government in economic and social activity.[83] A step towards implicit CSR would involve increased regulations, especially around marketing, including sponsorship of community and sporting events, and labelling of alcoholic beverages. With increased regulations and raised standards for corporate behaviour, the alcohol industry's dissemination of information will be controlled as alcohol firms will no longer have the discretion to self-regulate or set marketing codes.[84] It is expected that responsible drinking will become less of an issue requiring corporate action within the alcohol industry, which will leave the issue to be addressed by truly independent, non-profit organizations that are in a better position to address the social and health harms of alcohol consumption.[85]

CSR in the alcohol industry mirrors the tobacco industry both in motivations and in actions. While the tobacco industry faces increasing levels of regulations around distribution and marketing,[86] the alcohol industry remains largely self-regulated regarding marketing.[87] Similar to CSR engagement in the alcohol industry, CSR actions are also widely used in the tobacco industry to influence policymaking and deter tobacco control. Like responsible drinking programs promoted by the alcohol industry, CSR actions in the tobacco industry were found to portray smoking as an adult choice and neglected discussing the dangers of smoking.[88] The similarities in CSR engagement in the alcohol and tobacco industries should serve as a warning to public policymakers regarding the ability of the alcohol industry to self-regulate and the supposed social benefits of its social responsibility. Tobacco marketing regulations have been found to be effective in reducing smokers' reported awareness of pro-smoking cues with the greatest reductions observed immediately following the enactment of regulations.[89] The same success can be expected if marketing regulations were imposed in the alcohol industry.

The Canadian Regulatory Framework and Recommendations for Change

The prerequisite political and organizational institutional structures for implicit CSR are present in Canada. In a comparative study of Canadian and American CSR practices, American firms appeared to engage more in explicit CSR than Canadian firms, and there is greater stakeholder pressure on firms to be socially responsible in Canada than in the US.[90] Despite greater government involvement in economic and social activity, government regulation over the marketing activities of the alcohol industry has been less than ideal.[91]

The advertising and marketing of alcohol products in Canada are federally regulated by the Code for Broadcast Advertising of Alcoholic Beverages (the Code) set in 1996 by the Canadian Radio-television Telecommunications Commission (CRTC).[92] The direct marketing and advertisement of alcohol products towards youth is restricted in Canada, but there are no further restrictions. The Code does not limit the volume of alcohol advertising or restrict the content of advertisements that may appeal to youth, nor does it apply to all types of media.[93] The Code only applies to radio and television advertising for alcoholic beverages, which only represents a small portion of modern media advertising. Beyond the CRTC guidelines, provinces and municipalities also make specific regulations limiting alcohol advertising and marketing practices.[94] Labelling of alcoholic products is regulated federally by the Canadian Food Inspection Agency. Warning labels on alcoholic beverages are currently optional in Canada, unlike the US where they are required.[95] Despite the absence of a federal requirement for warning labels, some provinces and municipalities have imposed point-of-sale warning sign requirements.[96] In a comparative study of provincial policies to reduce alcohol-related harms, the consolidated national mean was less than half of the ideal standard for effective reduction of alcohol-related harms.[97] Warning label and sign policies scored the lowest at 18 per cent of the ideal.[98]

It is expected that there will be resistance from the alcohol industry to proposed increases in regulation. In an Australian-based study of alcohol industry submissions against marketing regulation, an argument commonly advanced is regulatory redundancy.[99] The alcohol industry claims that its marketing only targets adults, and in Canada, the direct advertisement of alcohol products to youth is prohibited.[100] Australian research shows that apart from direct advertisement, youth are exposed to marketing, as the promotion of alcohol products is not limited to television advertisements but also includes sport sponsorship, outdoor media, and product placement in films and music videos.[101] The alcohol industry also submits that there is insufficient evidence to suggest that marketing influences consumption.[102] On the contrary, a comparative cross-national study of alcohol consumption found that higher levels of regulation in Europe were associated with lower alcohol consumption among adults.[103]

Within the Canadian regulatory framework, more marketing regulations are required at the federal level. The Canadian liquor control and retail system differs from province to province with full privatization in Alberta and a combination of government and private alcohol retailers in other provinces. An issue with regulation of marketing and advertisement on the provincial level instead of on the federal level is the existence of a conflict of interest in the liquor boards of most provinces, in that the same body that creates the rules for marketing and regulations for enforcement is also the same body that regulates product sales.[104] As Ashley Wettlaufer, Samantha N. Cukier, and Norman Giesbrecht hypothesized in their Canadian study, the ongoing threat of privatization in provinces may provide added pressure to generate revenue at the expense of implementing proper marketing restrictions.[105]

Based on the above findings, this chapter makes the following recommendations: (1) the CRTC should review and update the Code to consider enforcement mechanisms for violations of marketing regulations, extension of marketing regulations to media communications other than television and radio, and strategies for consistent implementation in provinces at the retail level;[106] (2) warning labels should be required on all alcoholic beverages. There is empirical support that alcohol labels raise awareness of label topics, especially among frequent consumers;[107] and (3) warning messages and counter-advertising be reviewed by a third party, especially if such messages may inadvertently (or advertently in the case of messages promulgated by the alcohol industry) prompt interest in consuming the product.[108]

CONCLUSION

CSR practices and motivations for CSR engagement within the alcohol industry demonstrate the instrumental value of CSR to firms operating in controversial sectors. Studies suggest a range of reasons for CSR engagement from altruistic reasons of taking moral responsibility for social issues,[109] to risk management and strategic purposes,[110] to hidden agendas such as public deception and prevention of regulatory measures.[111] CSR can have the effect of improving the firm and the industry's reputation, enhancing business value, and generating profits, especially considering the potential marketing effects of CSR practices in the alcohol industry. In considering the impact of CSR initiatives beyond the business, studies have shown that CSR has been ineffective or even detrimental in addressing public health concerns.[112] Applying Matten and Moon's implicit-explicit CSR framework, most, if not all, of the alcohol industry's CSR practices can be categorized as explicit CSR – characterized by voluntary self-regulation, corporate philanthropy, and communication of social responsibility to stakeholders. Explicit CSR has its benefits but within the alcohol industry, CSR engagement and communication of CSR activities appear to do more harm than good. Meaningful engagement of social responsibility by the alcohol industry would require a shift towards implicit CSR (adherent in the field of corporate law and sustainability), which would remove corporate discretion and "signaling" practices of CSR communication to CSR practices that genuinely foster greater stakeholder engagement and the development of effective public policies to address the social and public health harms caused by the alcohol industry. Implicit CSR calls for greater regulation of the alcohol industry's marketing activities and product labels. Implicit CSR provides a framework in which the alcohol industry can demonstrate social responsibility through compliance and in which industry profitability and sustainability are balanced with public interests. Within the implicit CSR framework, the paradox of the alcohol industry and CSR engagement unravels.

NOTES

1 Zenu Sharma and Liang Song, "Corporate Social Responsibility (CSR) Practices by SIN Firms: Evidence from CSR Activity and Disclosure," *Asian Review of Accounting* 26, no. 3 (September 2018): 359–60.
2 Agostino Vollero et al., "Corporate Social Responsibility Information and Involvement Strategies in Controversial Industries," *Corporate Social Responsibility and Environmental Management* 26, no. 1 (Winter 2019): 142.
3 Ibid.

4 Dirk Matten and Jeremy Moon, "'Implicit' and 'Explicit' CSR: A Conceptual Framework for a Comparative Understanding of Corporate Social Responsibility," *Academy of Management Review* 33, no. 2 (April 2008): 409.

5 Hein de Vries, "Invited Commentary: Corporate Social Responsibility and Public Health: An Unwanted Marriage," *Preventive Medicine* 89, (August 2016).

6 Peter Jones, David Hillier, and Daphne Comfort, "That's the Spirit: Exploring the Approach of the World's Leading Spirits' Producers to Corporate Social Responsibility," *Journal of Public Affairs* 13, no. 1 (February 2013): 6.

7 Melissa Mialon and Jim McCambridge, "Alcohol Industry Corporate Social Responsibility Initiatives and Harmful Drinking: A Systematic Review," *European Journal of Public Health* 28, no. 4 (August 2018): 665.

8 Jones, Hillier, and Comfort, "That's the Spirit," 7; Daniela Pantani et al., "'Responsible Drinking' Programs and the Alcohol Industry in Brazil: Killing Two Birds with One Stone?" *Journal of Social Science and Medicine* 75, no. 8 (October 2012): 1387.

9 International Alliance for Responsible Drinking, "Take a Look at Our Producers' Commitments," accessed 18 August 2021, https://iard.org/actions/producers-commitments.

10 Pantani et al., "Responsible Drinking," 1390; Nason Maani Hessari et al., "Alcohol Industry CSR Organisations: What Can Their Twitter Activity Tell Us About Their Independence and Their Priorities? A Comparative Analysis," *International Journal of Environmental Research and Public Health* 16, no. 5 (March 2019): 9.

11 Jones, Hillier, and Comfort, "That's the Spirit," 6; Peter J. Adams, "Addiction Industry Studies: Understanding How Proconsumption Influences Block Effective Interventions," *American Journal of Public Health* 103, no. 4 (April 2013), 35.

12 Ibid.

13 Ibid.

14 Jones, Hillier, and Comfort, "That's the Spirit," 6; Adams, "Addiction Industry Studies," 35.

15 Vollero et al., "Corporate Social Responsibility," 147.

16 Ibid.

17 Ibid.

18 Jones et al., "That's the Spirit," 9.

19 Ibid., 1; Ben Baumberg Geiger and Valentina Cuzzocrea, "Corporate Social Responsibility and Conflicts of Interest in the Alcohol and

Gambling Industries: A Post-Political Discourse?" *British Journal of Sociology* 68, no. 2 (June 2017): 258.

20 Jones, Hillier, and Comfort, "That's the Spirit," 8–9.

21 Ibid.

22 Geiger and Cuzzocrea, "Corporate Social Responsibility," 259.

23 Ye Cai, Hoje Jo, and Carrie Pan, "Doing Well While Doing Bad? CSR in Controversial Industry Sectors," *Journal of Business Ethics* 108, no. 4 (July 2012): 469–70.

24 Ibid., 469.

25 Ibid.

26 Ibid.

27 Ibid., 470.

28 Cai, Jo, and Pan, "Doing Well," 477; Hoje Jo and Haejung Na, "Does CSR Reduce Firm Risk? Evidence from Controversial Industry Sectors," *Journal of Business Ethics* 110, no. 4 (November 2012): 452–3.

29 Jones, Hillier, and Comfort, "That's the Spirit," 9; Sharma and Song, "Corporate Social Responsibility," 361; Jo and Na, "Does CSR Reduce Firm Risk," 452; Hannah Oh, John Bae, and Sang-Joon Kim, "Can Sinful Firms Benefit from Advertising Their CSR Efforts? Adverse Effect of Advertising Sinful Firms' CSR Engagements," *Journal of Business Ethics* 143, no. 4 (July 2017): 645.

30 Cai, Jo, and Pan, "Doing Well," 470.

31 Ibid., 477.

32 Sharma and Song, "Corporate Social Responsibility," 369.

33 Thomas F. Babor et al., "Is the Alcohol Industry Doing Well by 'Doing Good'? Findings from a Content Analysis of the Alcohol Industry's Actions to Reduce Harmful Drinking," *Business Journal of Management Open* 8, no. 10 (2018): 5.

34 Sharma and Song, "Corporate Social Responsibility," 359–60.

35 Gert-Jan Steltenpool and Piet Verhoeven, "Sector-Dependent Framing Effects of Corporate Social Responsibility Messages: An Experiment with Non-Alcoholic and Alcoholic Drinks," *Public Relations Review* 38, no. 4 (November 2012): 629.

36 Oh, Bae, and Kim, "Can Sinful Firms Benefit," 656.

37 Jo and Na, "Does CSR Reduce Firm Risk," 442, 452.

38 Oh, Bae, and Kim "Can Sinful Firms Benefit," 657.

39 Yeonsoo Kim and Sun-Young Park, "Promoting Public Health or Underlying Business Interests? The Effectiveness (or Ineffectiveness) of Responsible Drinking Social Causes by the Alcohol Industry Versus Non-Profits," *Journal of Promotion Management* 24, no. 6 (2018): 791.

40 Sungwon Yoon and Tai-Hing Lam, "The Illusion of Righteousness: Corporate Social Responsibility Practices of the Alcohol Industry," *BMC Public Health* 13, no. 630 (July 2013): 5.
41 Ibid.
42 Thomas F. Babor and Katherine Robaina, "Public Health, Academic Medicine, and the Alcohol Industry's Corporate Social Responsibility Activities," *American Journal of Public Health* 2, no. 102 (February 2013): 206–14.
43 Geiger and Cuzzocrea, "Corporate Social Responsibility," 263.
44 Ibid.
45 Yoon and Lam, "The Illusion of Righteousness," 5; de Vries, "Invited Commentary," 346.
46 Yoon and Lam, "The Illusion of Righteousness," 5; Geiger and Cuzzocrea, "Corporate Social Responsibility," 257; Babor and Robaina, "Public Health," 211.
47 Babor and Robaina, "Public Health," 209.
48 Yoon and Lam, "The Illusion of Righteousness," 5.
49 Daniela Pantani et al., "The Marketing Potential of Corporate Social Responsibility Activities: The Case of the Alcohol Industry in Latin America and the Caribbean," *Addiction* 112 (January 2017): 79.
50 Pantani et al., "Responsible Drinking," 1390.
51 Babor et al., "Is the Alcohol Industry Doing Well," 7.
52 Ibid.
53 Pantani et al., "The Marketing Potential," 79.
54 Adams, "Addiction Industry Studies," 35.
55 de Vries, "Invited Commentary," 346.
56 Ibid.
57 Hessari et al., "Alcohol Industry," 8.
58 Ibid.
59 Irina Lock and Peter Seele, "Politicized CSR: How Corporate Political Activity (Mis-)Uses Political CSR," *Journal of Public Affairs* 18, no. 3 (August 2018): 5.
60 Ibid.
61 Ibid.
62 Pantani et al., "The Marketing Potential," 79.
63 Kim and Park, "Promoting Public Health," 793.
64 Ibid.
65 Ibid., 794.
66 Margaret Lindorff, Elizabeth Prior Jonson, and Linda McGuire, "Strategic Corporate Social Responsibility in Controversial Industry Sectors: The

Social Value of Harm Minimisation," *Journal of Business Ethics* 110, no. 4 (November 2012): 464.

67 Ibid., 457.

68 Ibid., 464; Geiger and Cuzzocrea, "Corporate Social Responsibility," 256, 268.

69 Lock and Seele, "Politicized CSR," 1.

70 Michael E. Porter and Mark R. Kramer, "Creating Shared Value," *Harvard Business Review*, January 2011, https://hbr.org/2011/01/the-big-idea-creating-shared-value; see also Lindorff, Jonson, and McGuire, "Strategic Corporate Social Responsibility," 463.

71 Lock and Seele, "Politicized CSR," 6. For further discussion on CSR and lobbying in the context of the fossil fuel industry, see Megan Parisotto, "Elephants among Chickens: Increasing the Legitimacy of the Fossil Fuel Industry through Responsible Lobbying Practices," chapter 6 of this book.

72 Adams, "Addiction Industry Studies," 35.

73 Yoon and Lam, "The Illusion of Righteousness," 8.

74 Geiger and Cuzzocrea, "Corporate Social Responsibility," 268.

75 Matten and Moon, "'Implicit' and 'Explicit,'" 409.

76 Ibid.

77 Linda Thorne et al., "A Comparison of Canadian and U.S. CSR Strategic Alliances, CSR Reporting, and CSR Performance: Insights into Implicit–Explicit CSR," *Journal of Business Ethics* 143, no. 1 (June 2017): 86.

78 Matten and Moon, "'Implicit' and 'Explicit,'" 409.

79 Ibid., 407–10.

80 Ibid., 408–9; Thorne et al., "A Comparison of Canadian and U.S. CSR," 86.

81 Thorne et al., "A Comparison of Canadian and U.S. CSR," 87.

82 Cai, Jo, and Pan, "Doing Well"; Sharma and Song, "Corporate Social Responsibility"; Oh, Bae, and Kim, "Can Sinful Firms Benefit"; Kim and Park, "Promoting Public Health"; Pantani et al., "Responsible Drinking."

83 Matten and Moon, "'Implicit' and 'Explicit,'" 407, 409.

84 de Vries, "Invited Commentary," 346.

85 Kim and Park, "Promoting Public Health," 774.

86 Karin A. Kasza et al., "The Effectiveness of Tobacco Marketing Regulations on Reducing Smokers' Exposure to Advertising and Promotion: Findings from the International Tobacco Control (ITC) Four Country Survey," *International Journal of Environmental Research and Public Health* 8, no. 2 (February 2011): 322.

87 Catherine Paradis et al., "The Canadian Alcopop Tragedy Should Trigger Evidence-Informed Revisions of Federal Alcohol Regulations," *Drug and Alcohol Review* 38, no. 2 (February 2019): 199.

88 de Vries, "Invited Commentary," 345.
89 Kasza et al., "The Effectiveness of Tobacco," 336.
90 Thorne et al., "A Comparison of Canadian and U.S. CSR," 87–8.
91 Norman Giesbrecht et al., "Strategies to Reduce Alcohol-Related Harms and Costs in Canada: A Comparison of Provincial Policies," *The International Journal of Alcohol and Drug Research* 5, no. 2 (July 2016): 39.
92 Ashley Wettlaufer, Samantha N. Cukier, and Norman Giesbrecht, "Comparing Alcohol Marketing and Alcohol Warning Message Policies Across Canada," *Substance Use & Misuse* 52, no. 10 (August 2017): 1364.
93 Ibid., 1365.
94 Ibid., 1366.
95 Canadian Food Inspection Agency, "Labelling Requirements for Alcoholic Beverages: Voluntary Claims & Statements – Alcoholic Beverages," last modified 29 January 2020, https://inspection.canada.ca/food-label-requirements/labelling/industry/alcohol/eng/1392909001375/1392909133296?chap=8.
96 Wettlaufer, Cukier, and Giesbrecht, "Comparing Alcohol Marketing," 1365.
97 Giesbrecht et al., "Strategies to Reduce Alcohol-Related Harms," 39.
98 Ibid.
99 Florentine Petronella Martino et al., "Analysis of Alcohol Industry Submissions against Marketing Regulation," *PLOS ONE* 12, no. 1 (April 2017): 17.
100 Ibid.; Wettlaufer, Cukier, and Giesbrecht, "Comparing Alcohol Marketing," 1365.
101 Martino et al., "Analysis of Alcohol Industry Submissions," 1365.
102 Ibid.
103 Ibid.
104 Wettlaufer, Cukier, and Giesbrecht, "Comparing Alcohol Marketing," 1371.
105 Ibid., 1370.
106 Ibid., 1371.
107 Ibid.
108 Ibid.
109 Cai, Jo, and Pan, "Doing Well," 477.
110 Babor et al., "Is the Alcohol Industry Doing Well," 4; Sharma and Song, "Corporate Social Responsibility," 361; Jo and Na, "Does CSR Reduce Firm Risk," 452.
111 Yoon and Lam, "The Illusion of Righteousness," 1.
112 Ibid., 7; Babor et al., "Is the Alcohol Industry Doing Well," 7; Mialon and McCambridge, "Alcohol Industry," 672.

8

Behind the Veil: An Analysis of Fast Fashion Retailers' Engagement with Sustainable Supply Chain Management

Selena Chen

On 24 April 2013, during the morning rush hour, the Rana Plaza Building in Bangladesh collapsed, killing over one thousand people and injuring an additional two thousand five hundred people. Pressured by short deadlines and taking advantage of the lax labour laws in Bangladesh, the factory owners had ignored warnings to avoid using the building and ordered the garment workers to return to work to produce garments for major international brands including Zara, Mango, Loblaws, and Walmart.[1] After the collapse, thirty-eight people were charged with murder in Bangladesh,[2] and more than two hundred apparel companies, such as American Eagle Outfitters and Zara, banded together to sign on to the *Accord on Fire and Building Safety in Bangladesh* (the Accord).[3] Since 2013, the Accord has identified over one hundred and thirty thousand high-risk safety violations and terminated ninety-six factories for "failure to implement required safety renovations."[4]

As a result of globalization, fast fashion retailers have outsourced the production of their garments to developing countries with weak legal frameworks. While factory jobs provide income for thousands of people and can result in economic growth for the country, outsourcing moves the regulation of workers outside the scope of regulatory monitoring of countries with strict labour regimes, thus resulting in the exploitation of workers. Additionally, production is not just being outsourced, it is, at times, being re-sourced to even more distant facilities that the fast fashion retailers might not even be aware of.[5] In the aftermath of the Rana Plaza Building collapse, many of the involved brands were not aware that they were sourcing the products from factories located in the building. So, what exactly are fast fashion retailers doing to remedy this problem?

This chapter explores how fast fashion retailers are engaging with social sustainability within their supply chains, and how they are held accountable to initiatives directed towards their manufacturing workers. The first section examines how fast fashion retailers engage with sustainable supply chain management (SSCM) within their supply chains, and some of the difficulties in successfully implementing SSCM. The second section will then analyze how sustainability reporting is a mechanism by which fashion retailers are held accountable for their supplier's conduct and engage with the benefits and potential shortcomings of this mechanism. Through this analysis, this chapter demonstrates that while current sustainability reporting initiatives are an effective mechanism by which corporate actors are held accountable for the conduct of third-party suppliers, it is unlikely to result in real change. Instead, the third section reflects upon how the requirement for external incentives to further promote sustainability reporting, coupled with internal changes to reporting structures, is what transforms sustainability reporting into effective disclosure.

UNDERSTANDING SUSTAINABLE SUPPLY CHAIN MANAGEMENT

The fast fashion industry is made possible because of the outsourcing of production to developing countries. At the same time, it is also an industry that is "characterised by chronic downward price pressure, international sourcing, high product variety, high volatility, and low predictability."[6] With innovations in supply chain management, fast fashion retailers are able to reach their goals of producing inexpensive merchandise rapidly often with a turnaround timeline of one month as compared to the nine months to a year with traditional fashion production.[7] Between 2011–15, the lead times declined by 8.14 per cent on average and this correlates with an increase in forced overtime and work intensity.[8] The shortened lead time has led to many suppliers of the fast fashion industry ignoring ethically acceptable baselines for wages, working hours, and working conditions.

These unsafe working conditions have a human cost. Of the over one thousand people killed in the Rana Plaza collapse, half were women.[9] Some were children who were in daycare while their parents worked for as little as thirty-two cents an hour.[10] Some of the survivors were left unable to work, live healthy lives, or have children. Those who already had children lost their means of supporting them. Some found the weight of the horrific memories of the crash too heavy a burden to bear and ended their own lives. Furthermore, the Rana Plaza disaster was not an isolated event. More than five hundred workers have died because of electrical fires in Bangladeshi garment factories between 2006–12. Over one hundred more died when the Tazreen Fashions factory burned in 2012. Before Rana Plaza, only two brands agreed to take action to improve working conditions, while the rest continued to take advantage of the unsafe and exploitative working conditions that led to these tragedies.[11]

SSCM is necessary to help address this problem. In general, SSCM is understood to be an integration of corporate sustainability and supply chain management.[12] SSCM removes the single bottom line driven approach that has been historically preferred by businesses, and in its place, instills the importance of addressing "the moral, ethical, and social consequences in supplier countries of global business operations."[13] In particular, an application of SSCM to fast fashion retailers requires us to look at the specific demands of the industry.

The fast fashion industry is built upon the three core pillars of "shortened lead-times, faster inventory turnovers, and high order fulfilment rates for customer demand at its peak points."[14] To establish these three pillars, the industry needs a higher level of responsiveness and efficiency. It becomes increasingly difficult for fast fashion retailers to monitor their supply chains because of the need for low lead times. Further, high quantity of output means a tremendous number of external suppliers.[15] The sheer number of external suppliers makes it difficult for fast fashion retailers to successfully integrate these suppliers into their system and adopt the retailer's sustainability approach adequately.[16] Additionally, due to the myriad of contractors and subcontractors, the fast fashion industry's supply chains suffer from low visibility and accountability. The requirement of responsiveness, in turn, leads to the adoption of an unsustainable structure, which encompasses supply chain strategies combined with disregarding ethical, employment, and environmental issues.[17] This lack of respect for ethical, employment, and environmental issues further leads to negative social and environmental consequences, which fast fashion retailers respond to by implementing sustainable strategies and practices.[18]

In the aftermath of the Rana Plaza collapse, pressure from the media and labour activists spurred the creation of two response agreements concerning private sector regulation of building and fire safety in Bangladesh.[19] The first of these was the Accord, a five-year binding agreement that ended in 2018. The Accord required its members to disclose the subcontractor facilities they utilize, fund safety inspections of those facilities through their membership fees, and develop action plans to ameliorate current health and safety problems. The Accord also sought to empower and train workers and strengthen labour unions. However, the binding nature of the Accord, which allowed signatories to be held liable for breaches of the agreement in their country of origin, made several fashion brands unwilling to sign on to the agreement. Those who were unwilling to be legally bound launched the Alliance for Bangladesh Worker Safety (the Alliance). The Alliance was also set to expire in 2018, and while two hundred brands that signed on to the Accord came from over twenty countries, the Alliance was chiefly made up of North American brands. The Alliance largely had the same goals as the Accord, but there were no legal consequences for failure to adhere to the agreement. It was also less transparent than the Accord and did not seek to strengthen labour unions.[20]

During its five-year mandate, the Accord inspected over two thousand factories, correcting 90 per cent of the safety issues identified during the inspections. Training for workers was implemented at over one thousand factories and generated a system for health and safety complaints. The Alliance also completed over nine hundred inspections, and many Alliance affiliated factories completed their corrective plan. Fire safety training was also carried out, covering over 1.5 million workers.[21] Both agreements clearly made significant improvements to working conditions in Bangladesh and suggest a positive direction for supply chain safety. However, now that both agreements have expired, there is significant concern that the factories and companies will revert to their previous dangerous practices once regulation is back in the hands of the national government. As one Rana Plaza victim stated, "[t]he labor law in this country is pro-owner, not pro-worker … all will return to how it was when Rana Plaza happened."[22] As a result, new strategies will be necessary to ensure the fast fashion brands themselves remain accountable for the safety of their supply chains. Sustainability reporting is one mechanism that is currently employed by fast fashion retailers to help implement SSCM and may be an appropriate means to ensure continued growth in the industry.

Sustainability Reporting

Technological developments, such as the proliferation of social media, has led to an increase in information regarding the supply chains of fast fashion retailers as well as the ability for stakeholders to communicate with fast fashion retailers. The proliferation of social media has allowed an individual "to communicate instantaneously and globally to influence public opinion on a topic or a business."[23] Through this instantaneous communication, individuals are able to raise awareness of the negative social and environmental consequences of fast fashion. Fast fashion retailers are no longer just responsively reporting based on pressure from their stakeholders to provide transparency, rather, they are engaging in sustainability reporting activities to be on par with their competitors.[24] It is not just about the financial bottom line as indicated by their financial statements; rather, companies are competing with one another with regards to the triple bottom line of financial, social, and environmental performances that are documented in their sustainability reports.

Sustainability reports are published reports on a company's everyday activities and economic, environmental, and social impacts. Such reports present a company's values and governance models and demonstrate the link between the company's strategies and its commitment to sustainability.[25] The content that is reported will vary from company to company and from reporting standard to reporting standard. However, most of the sustainability reports will include a code of conduct used to evaluate the suppliers. With regards to the code of conduct for suppliers, some companies will use a pre-existing standard, while others will create their own. For example, Calida adheres to the Oeko-Text Standard 100 and BSCI's Code of Conduct, while Mango developed their own code of conduct.[26]

Sustainability reporting serves the important function of increasing transparency among fast fashion retailers' supply chains through mandatory and voluntary disclosures. Transparency is equated to traceability, which "allows products to be traced back to the whole supply chain ultimately to the raw materials used (supply chain traceability)."[27]

Through traceability, power is transferred to stakeholders who can determine whether the fast fashion retailer's supply chain is meeting expectations regarding sustainability. If they do not meet the expectations of the stakeholders, it can "trigger name and shame campaigns driven by a supplier['s] unsustainable behavior."[28] Additionally, with regards to mandatory reporting as requested by government audit authorities, if the expectations of the audit authority are not met, penalties may be levied by the agencies. Simply stated, sustainability reporting increases transparency, which allows for third parties, either government or non-government, to put pressure on the fast fashion retailers to treat foreign labourers with a minimum level of respect.

Additionally, sustainability reporting assists a company with the monitoring of their supplier's adherence to the company's code of conduct. The development and subsequent monitoring of the code of conduct for each company has become an integral part of SSCM. Currently, a problem with SSCM implementation is that for there to be successful implementation of SSCM, there must be an integration of sustainability within all aspects of management. This integration is crucial because otherwise, corporate social responsibility (CSR) in a corporation would be "rule setting with no decision power."[29] With the subsequent monitoring of adherence by suppliers, SSCM's influence is extended to the entirety of the supply chain management process. The role of SSCM is also extended to that of a decision-maker as after identifying a breach, the fast fashion retailer will need to respond to that breach, albeit in quite different ways.[30]

Sustainability Reporting in SSCM

Sustainability reporting is a mechanism by which companies generate external pressure to compel annual audits of their suppliers and thus engage in SSCM. "Reporting is … necessary to maintaining the legitimacy of the apparel brands and their social license to operate"[31] due to the heightened sense of public scrutiny that is associated with the treatment of manufacturing workers. Through exerting pressure on their suppliers, fast fashion retailers can proliferate the image of legitimacy and demonstrate engagement to achieve the triple bottom line of financial, social, and environmental performances.

Information disclosure is a way to influence business behaviour by promoting transparency and thus empowering private actors to monitor and pressure corporations to alter harmful behaviour.[32] Reporting affects behaviour change in two ways: raising awareness for opportunities for change through the measurement of environmental impacts; and facilitating benchmarking across firms through the provision of data so as to establish a universal standard.[33] However, the act of disclosure itself produces a business risk that the corporations will seek to minimize by taking steps to dissociate themselves from "sweatshop" labour practices.[34] Thus, sustainability reporting moves an internal decision into the public sphere and generates an external pressure that is used to discipline corporate actors into engaging with sustainable supply chain management.

This section divides sustainability reporting into two categories – mandatory reporting and voluntary reporting. As the name suggests, mandatory reporting consists of government legislated disclosure requirements, while voluntary reporting involves disclosures that the fast fashion retailers choose to engage in. Voluntary reporting can include initiatives or pledges that fast fashion retailers sign on to, disclosure organizations that the companies join, or an internal monitoring system developed by the companies themselves.

It should be noted that there is a growing sense that the lines between voluntary and mandatory CSR initiatives are being blurred and oftentimes both are required to achieve the desired ends. The European Commission has stated that effective CSR is achieved "through a smart mix of voluntary policy measures and, where necessary, complementary regulation."[35] The United Nations has explained how "it is certainly true that legal obligations do not encourage creative and individual speculation beyond these boundaries. On the other hand, a legal regulation can be a sensible bottom line, above which CSR can be reinvented and reassessed."[36] Even where CSR initiatives appear to be completely voluntary, they have to be considered in the social context in which they are carried out. Where social pressure demands sustainability reporting, the true "voluntariness" of corporations' action is called into question.[37] Therefore, each of the voluntary and mandatory aspects that will be discussed should not be thought of as entirely separate but potentially as one system where each requires the other for success.

MANDATORY REPORTING

There are several mandatory reporting requirements that corporations must satisfy. The specifics of these reporting requirements vary depending on the jurisdiction where the corporation is listed. For example, public companies listed in Canada have to disclose all material information, including those relating to social issues, under Canadian securities laws.[38] Additionally, with regards to more specific information about labour conditions, the *California Transparency in Supply Chains Act* (CTSCA) requires all retail and manufacturing businesses listed in California with an annual turnover of over US$100 million to publish efforts they have made to combat forced labour in their supply chain.[39] Similarly, the UK[40] and Australia[41] *Modern Slavery Acts* both require businesses with a certain amount of global annual turnover to disclose steps they are taking to ensure that there is no incident of slavery, forced labour, and human trafficking within their supply chains. France had provided a variation in that they require companies with a certain number of employees to establish due diligence safeguards to ensure that their suppliers are respecting labour laws.[42]

Nevertheless, one of the main problems with mandatory reporting is that there is often little to no penal powers attached to it. Australia's *Modern Slavery Act* does not include a government penalty for failure to lodge a statement or lodging an incomplete statement.[43] While Senate amendments allow for the minister to name and shame the companies that are in default of their filing obligations, there is a lack of a harsher penalty beyond imposing "shame."[44] This is problematic because mandatory reporting should be separated from voluntary reporting by the inclusion of an additional element of penalty. Voluntary reporting is based on a shame element and if mandatory reporting is also limited to leveraging shame, then it could potentially detract from the authority of government-mandated reporting, relegating mandatory reporting to that of a quasi-voluntary position.

VOLUNTARY REPORTING

Voluntary reporting involves information disclosure initiatives that the company chooses to engage in. One example of voluntary sustainability reporting is the sustainability or CSR reports that are prepared in accordance with the guidelines of the Global Reporting Initiative (GRI).[45] The GRI is the first and most widely adopted reporting standard for assisting an organization in understanding and communicating its impact on social, environmental, and economic issues. It is developed via a multi-stakeholder process. According to the KPMG Survey of Corporate Responsibility Reporting 2017, 93 per cent of the world's largest 250 corporations used the GRI reporting standards for reporting their sustainability performance.[46] It provides a comprehensive report and benchmark for third parties, such as academics, to use to compare different fast fashion retailers. For example, an article analyzing nine fast fashion retailers reporting under the GRI standards noted that "the main objective of SSCM was to ensure good manufacturing conditions throughout the value chain to reduce the environmental, labour, and social impacts of business operations."[47] The companies go about fulfilling this objective in different ways. Some companies attempt to accomplish the objective via mechanisms involving compliance and certification (e.g., Mango), while others emphasize long-term relationships as the vehicle for sustainability (e.g., H&M).[48]

In addition to third-party-created reporting standards, certain fast fashion retailers also have internal monitoring systems. For example, Nike debuted the SHAPE internal monitoring system in 1997, which was a basic audit intended to provide Nike with an internal assessment of whether a proposed new supplier satisfies Nike's code of conduct.[49] Then in the early 2000s, Nike introduced a regularly maintained global factory database documenting its supply chain.[50] Since 2003, Nike has also been conducting M-audits, a more comprehensive audit, of 25–33 per cent of their factories.[51] Any supplier that failed the internal audits would be required to implement a master action plan in order to remain a supplier of Nike.[52] However, even with internal monitoring methods, companies have failed to deliver good results in terms of their SSCM. Companies such as Zara, The Gap, Nike, and Mark & Spencer have been accused of unethical behaviour despite having comprehensive codes of conducts.[53] The coexistence of a comprehensive code of conduct and unethical behaviour shows that the use of only one type of voluntary reporting method is often insufficient to correct behaviour.

Companies have also signed onto pledges that promote transparency within the fast fashion retailer's supply chain. For example, the Human Rights Watch, in conjunction with eight other international labour rights groups and global unions,[54] developed the Apparel and Footwear Supply Chain Transparency Pledge in 2016 (the Transparency Pledge) in an effort to establish a minimum standard for transparency. The coalition reached out to seventy-two brands, of which seventeen leading brands in the global apparel and footwear industry committed to publishing the information required by the Transparency Pledge.[55] The companies that signed onto the Transparency Pledge are required to publish a list of all their suppliers on their website, which should be updated regularly and published in a searchable manner. The purpose of this is to promote greater knowledge of the suppliers. For example, ASOS plc, a British online fashion and cosmetics retailer, publishes a list of all their suppliers and includes a breakdown of the percentage of male and female workers.[56]

There are many different types of voluntary sustainability reporting that a fast fashion retailer can choose to engage in. The next sections of this chapter will discuss the benefits that can be derived from engaging in sustainability reporting and SSCM, and the current shortfalls of sustainability reporting.

BENEFITS AND SHORTFALLS OF SSCM AND SUSTAINABILITY REPORTING

Fast fashion retailers understand that reputation is extremely important in an industry that is highly competitive. Because of this reality, they also understand the importance of transparency within their supply chains. Sustainability reporting represents a balancing act between the costs of disclosures and the reputational benefits that can be derived from such disclosures. There is increasing concern with regards to issues such as fair labour practices and sustainable sourcing as consumers have indicated that they wish to support brands that are socially responsible.[57] In fact, 66 per cent of consumers are willing to pay more for sustainable goods.[58] Consequently, a lack of ethical sourcing will hurt the sales of fast fashion retailers and can damage their reputation, while adherence and commitment to sustainability norms can be used as a positive marketing campaign to improve a retailer's reputation through reaffirming the company's commitment to social sustainability issues.

That being said, the ultimate benefit that can be derived from engaging in sustainability reporting regarding the company's supply chain depends on factors such as the type of business the company is in, the actions of the company's competitors, and the company's costs and market structure.[59] In a 2002 report published by G&A Governance Accountability Institute, Inc., a data partner of the GRI for the US, the institute concluded after surveying all S&P 500 companies, that "companies who measure, manage, and ultimately disclose more and engage in structuring reporting on their sustainability or ESG issues enjoy considerable advantage when compared to their non-reporting peers."[60] These advantages include being more likely to be featured in leading sustainability indices and selected for key reputational lists.[61] The report also concluded that corporations who manage their sustainability issues tend to perform better in the long-term in the market, which may be due to the changing sentiments towards sustainability as a whole by investors.[62] Investors are now more inclined to support corporations who are serious about sustainability, and a sustainability report is a reflection of a corporation's commitment to the issue.[63]

As noted above, there is a trend of companies becoming more aware of the necessity of engaging in sustainability reporting, reflected in the increased number of available reporting instruments. In 2006, there were only sixty reporting instruments available (both mandatory and voluntary) covering nineteen countries and regions. In 2016, there were 383 available reporting instruments covering seventy-one countries and regions.[64] There has also been an increase from 26–34 per cent in the percentage of surveyed companies publishing a full direct supplier list according to the 2018 Ethical Fashion Report.[65] As a result of the disclosure requirements for sustainability reporting, we see that there is an increase in the percentage of companies who trace where their fabrics come from. In 2013, only about 49 per cent of companies were tracing the origins of their fabrics, but in 2018, that number increased to 78 per cent.[66] The 2018 Ethical Fashion Report further noted that more than 82 per cent of companies knew their first-tier manufacturing suppliers, whom they have the most control over.[67] All of this published information means that third parties, such as journalists, NGOs, and unions can also take on the role of an auditor and help hold these companies accountable to their claims.

In addition to the outside auditing pressure that can be exerted based upon transparency established by sustainability reporting, sustainability reporting and the promotion of SSCM also helps aid in the establishment of trust and commitment between the suppliers and the fast fashion retailers. Such a relationship between the trading parties encourages innovation and the adherence to the retailer's sustainability implementations more so than a compliance-based approach.[68] It also encourages transparency between the retailers and the suppliers as both parties would be more willing to share truthful information.

In terms of shortfalls, sustainability reports are often inadequate in remedying the social issues that are the cause for the reporting. This is true for both mandatory reporting and voluntary reporting. The mandatory reports submitted are only adequate in addressing surface-level issues such as communicating whether there is adherence to local laws of where the factories are located, and as explained in the previous sections, government audit authorities are either not equipped with sufficient authority to profoundly effect change or the reports requested are filled with obscure and sometimes falsified information.

Compliance through basic reporting and adherence to local laws can lead to a lack of justice for workers who become victims of their unsafe working environments, especially when the country where the work took place does not have strong labour protection laws or a strong legal system. This lack of justice was the case for several victims and families of victims of the Rana Plaza disaster who attempted to bring a claim in Ontario against Loblaws, a Canadian clothing retailer who was outsourcing manufacturing to a company who operated in the Rana Plaza building. The victims sought to hold Loblaws and the manufacturing company liable for all damages they suffered due to the building collapse. However, the Ontario Court of Appeal agreed with the trial judge that, since the dispute was governed by the law of Bangladesh where there would not be a duty of care found in these circumstances and where the statute of limitations of bringing such a claim had already lapsed, the claim could not succeed.[69] Loblaws' central argument was that it had no obligation to protect the workers or ensure they were working in a safe environment.[70] While the court agreed that Loblaws had no obligation to do so, the fact that Loblaws was not willing to ensure compliance with its own CSR standards because it was not mandatory to do so[71] shows that sustainability reporting is sometimes not enough to ensure the safety of the vulnerable workers put at risk by the practices of fast fashion brands. Notably, in Loblaws's 2012 CSR Report,[72] there was no information on building safety. This information only began being reported in 2013,[73] after the collapse occurred.

As a result of shortcomings like the one described, compliance with sustainability standards have been attacked as an "annual 'tick the box' ritual"[74] that only requires fast fashion retailers to provide vague assertions of their business practices. Sustainability reports are used by fast fashion retailers as "a mechanism to legitimize and protect their business interests, rather than as a tool to detect and address social and environmental problems."[75] In other words, there is an inconsistency between fast fashion retailers' claims of promoting sustainability and their action of making vague assertions and using sustainability reporting more like an advertisement opportunity than as an internal audit.

As Patsy Perry notes, "given the highly complex nature of the fashion supply chain and the high level of outsourcing of manufacture, bureaucratic control mechanisms such as codes of conduct and supplier audits are not infallible."[76] Compliance monitoring via voluntary reporting, while beneficial in illuminating certain social issues, has led to an increase in certification labels and schemes that often counteract the purpose of compliance monitoring by making the facts behind the labels and schemes opaque.[77] Additionally, compliance monitoring, which may include burdensome audits, can lead to an increase of corruption within the auditing authorities, especially for countries with weak legal frameworks.[78] The NYU-Stern Report, *Business as Usual is Not an Option: Supply Chain and Sourcing after Rana Plaza* noted:

> Code of conduct audits have provoked a veritable industry of falsified wage and hour records as suppliers attempt to 'comply' with code standards … Social auditors have become adept at exposing fake records but this cat-and-mouse game has not gotten them off the treadmill … But overall, code of conduct audits are not changing the culture of non- compliance that reigns in many exporting countries.[79]

Simply having a code of conduct and a mandatory reporting system based upon whether the corporation complies with the code of conduct or a minimum standard established by the legislation is insufficient. For countries that have weak legal frameworks, "SSMC based on the pass/fail compliance approach has proved to be more of an incentive to 'drive problems underground' than to revamp management systems to sustain compliance and encourage improvement over time."[80] The workers in these countries were already at a substantially increased risk of labour exploitation because of weak legal frameworks. This would be exacerbated by the further pressure to conceal the exploitation on the part of the factory owners.

EFFECTIVE DISCLOSURE AND OTHER IMPROVEMENTS FOR SUSTAINABILITY REPORTING

There are external initiatives that can be undertaken by government and non-government organizations alike to assist corporations in lowering the cost for disclosure.[81] For example, an incentive to engage in sustainability reporting and disclosure of a supply chain could consist of educational projects to help raise customer awareness of the benefits of sustainability and thus leading to higher incremental market gain/loss.[82] The more benefit that a fast fashion retailer can derive from engaging in sustainable practices, the lower the cost of the disclosure will be to them and thus, the more inclined to practicing sustainability reporting they will be.

Internal initiatives such as re-orienting sustainability reporting, which has been mostly reporting about the current economic, environmental, and social impacts, to more of an action-oriented reporting would essentially transition sustainability reporting from that of passive fact reporting to proactive conduct reporting. The focus shifts from looking at *what* companies are currently doing in terms of sustainability issues to *how* are companies combating sustainability issues.

Current reporting mechanisms, as explained above, have been engaging in what I consider to be a twofold promotion of sustainability within their supply chains. First, fast fashion retailers, through sustainability reporting, are creating a database of information and allowing for further research to be conducted regarding their supply chain, thus creating an incentive for third-party organizations to audit their conduct. Second, sustainability reporting serves as an internal mechanism that allows corporations to "clean up their act" before they air their dirty laundry out in the public. Beyond the effects of this passive *communicative* reporting, a shift towards impact *action-oriented* reporting could assist in the company's goals of promoting sustainability. The KPMG Survey of Corporate Responsibility Reporting 2017 found that the United Nations Sustainable Development Goals (UNSDGs) are "fueling demands for impact data," noting that

> simply linking corporate responsibility activity thematically to the SDGs is not enough. *People want to know how companies are contributing to achieving the goals and what the actual impact of those positive contributions is.* Similarly, they want to know how company activities are exacerbating the challenges the SDGs seek to solve, and what that negative impact is in real terms. It is not just civil society and NGOs that want this information, we are seeing a number of large institutional investors exploring how they can align their investment approaches with the SDGs. Such investment strategies will inevitably require impact disclosure from business.[83]

The current information that is disclosed, while claiming to be about the social, economic, and environmental *impacts* of a company's everyday activities, is more of a description of the company's everyday activities. The supplier lists that are being provided by the seventeen companies as per the Transparency Pledge only require that the companies provide information regarding the full name of all authorized production units and processing facilities, the addresses, the parent company of the supplier, types of products made, and the worker numbers.[84]

Disclosures that are currently employed report on the measurements and indicators of actions of a corporation as opposed to actions taken by the fast fashion retailers towards sustainability.[85] Modern sustainability reporting has evolved into Integrated Reporting, which can be defined as "a concise communication about how an organization's strategy, governance, performance, and prospects, in the context of its external environment, lead to the creation of value over the short, medium, and long term." Its vision is to "align capital allocation and corporate behaviour to wider goals of financial stability and sustainable development."[86] The current reporting standards lack the authority to effect change as companies can choose what to disclose; they are positioned to enhance sustainability, transparency, and value creation in the supply chains of the fast fashion retailers through communication. Arguably, this model of reporting results in a gap between the walk of a fast fashion retailer and their talk, in that fast fashion retailers' talk is not matching up to their actions. This gap between stated goal and conduct is what needs to be overcome for sustainability reporting to evolve into effective disclosure.

By integrating the concept of disclosure, which is "the revelation of information that was previously secret or unknown,"[87] into the concept of reporting, which is a "detailed periodic amount of a company's activities, financial condition, and prospects that is made available to shareholders and investors,"[88] it is possible to move sustainability reporting into the realm where "[fast fashion retailers] become agents of change, stimulating the questioning and constructive criticism of corporate practices."[89] Instead of getting to choose what they disclose in their annual sustainability reports, fast fashion retailers would be forced to disclose any situation with regards to labourers that arises in their supply chain, in addition to how they plan to remedy the situation.

This change would be similar to the continuous disclosure requirements under Canadian securities regulations. According to section 1(f) of Form 51-102F1: *Management's Discussion & Analysis* of NI 51-102,[90] public companies are required to disclose material information that would influence or change a reasonable investor's decision of treatment of the securities of the company. However, the category of information that is disclosed should be expanded so as to encompass not just material information that would influence how a reasonable investor views the securities of the fast fashion retailers but should also include information regarding specific instances of exploitation in their supply chain. Using the OECD Due Diligence Guidance for Responsible Supply Chains in the Garment and Footwear Sector[91] as a benchmark for the types of information that should be disclosed would help to ensure all types of exploitation are addressed and reported.

By making this switch, fast fashion retailers are no longer afforded a grace period where they can tidy up their supply chain before reporting on the issue with their annual sustainability report. Instead, the fast fashion retailer will need to immediately disclose upon knowledge of the situation. The requirement would push fast fashion retailers to be proactive in the prevention of exploitation, as opposed to remedying exploitation. The goal is a move away from the treatment of reporting standards as mere technical compliance tools, and instead, allowing the reports to also take on the role of an effective and constructive tool for the continuous monitoring of fast fashion retailers' supply chains.

The Fast Fashion Sustainability Scorecard was proposed as an alternative to communicative sustainability reporting, such as the GRI standards. It seeks to facilitate understandings of how exactly sustainability is managed in complex supply chains and promote improvements of certain practices.[92] It seeks to do so via the disclosure of five different elements: UNSDGs,[93] Common Material Issues (CMIs),[94] Reported Actions towards Sustainability (RAS)[95] Topics, RAS Instruments, and actors involved. Each element disclosed seeks to address an issue with the current sustainability reporting standards. Forcing companies to report on their compliance with UNSDGs is an attempt to decrease the possibility of orphan issues[96] or easy-to-solve problem biases.[97] CMIs are disclosed to prevent fast fashion retailers leaving issues unaddressed and reporting on accessory issues, while RAS Topics and RAS Instruments are disclosed to make it harder for companies to fill their reports with disclosure on irrelevant information and makes it easier for a third-party auditor to establish a baseline for comparison between the companies in the fast fashion industry.[98] Finally, a shortlist of actors participating in the execution of RASs allows for the empowerment of partnerships to pursue a common goal.[99]

This re-orientation of sustainability reporting seeks to shift the focus to immediate solutions and actions to address sustainability issues that arise in the supply chains of fast fashion companies.[100] It will also facilitate partnerships within the industry and avoid situations where reporting fast fashion retailers are the ones that can "cherry pick" the information that they want to disclose and how it's disclosed.[101] Effective disclosure will be able to bridge the gap between action and talk and more importantly, be able to do so in real time. Instead of having to wait a year for the next sustainability report to be provided by the companies, through the re-orientation of passive annual reports to active-real-time-conduct reports, sustainability reporting can provide continuous monitoring that forces proactive conduct to engage with SSCM.

CONCLUSION

The fast fashion industry is "one of the most global industries in the world, with closely coordinated production and distribution lines spread out in regions with great variations in government regulation, employment and environmental protection, and wage levels."[102] It has one of the most complex supply chains, with numerous contractors and sub-contractors spanning several countries, and often, the characteristics of the fast fashion industry can pressure suppliers of the industry into situations where they ignore ethical treatment of workers. The complexity of the industry also results in low transparency within the industry, making it difficult for third-party auditing organizations to hold retailers accountable for their supply chains.

To fulfill their corporate social responsibilities, fast fashion retailers engage with SSCM to promote sustainability within their supply chain. In an effort to hold themselves accountable, fast fashion retailers participate in sustainability reporting to help promote transparency within the industry. Specifically, we see that fast fashion retailers are recognizing the importance of establishing their reputations as sustainable producers. In addition to the government-required disclosures, fast fashion retailers also engage in voluntary reporting using standards such as the GRI standards and participating in the Transparency Pledge. However, currently, sustainability reporting, while adequate in its purpose of communicating the social, environmental, and economic impacts of a company's activities, is insufficient to effect proactive change in behaviour. Thus, for sustainability reporting to be more effective in implementing SSCM, a transition from passive communicative sustainability reporting to a proactive effective disclosure system is needed.

Fast fashion is a double-edged sword. For tens of millions of workers across the world, the fashion industry is a significant employer that "spurs economic growth, generates tax revenue, provide valuable skills and training, and delivers crucial foreign exchange."[103] But it is also "a source of exploitation for millions."[104] Because the fast fashion industry is a potential source of exploitation for the millions of workers employed by it, it is crucial for the fast fashion industry to practice sustainable behaviour. The industry has demonstrated its willingness to communicate regarding its supply chain so third parties can hold them accountable. Now, it is time for fast fashion retailers to adjust their conduct to promote internal accountability by taking proactive steps to prevent exploitation.

NOTES

1 Sarah Labowitz, "'We Have One Eye Open and One Eye Closed': The Dirty Labor Secrets of Fast Fashion," *Quartz*, 24 April 2017, https://ca.finance.yahoo.com/news/one-eye-open-one-eye-175437011.html.

2 "Rana Plaza Collapse: 38 Charged with Murder over Garment Factory Disaster," *The Guardian*, 18 July 2016, https://www.theguardian.com/world/2016/jul/18/rana-plaza-collapse-murder-charges-garment-factory.

3 Nadra Nittle, "What the Rana Plaza Disaster Changed About Worker Safety," *Racked*, 13 April 2018, https://www.racked.com/2018/4/13/17230770/rana-plaza-collapse-anniversary-garment-workers-safety.

4 Mark Anner, "Binding Power: The Sourcing Squeeze, Workers' Rights, and Building Safety in Bangladesh Since Rana Plaza," PennState Centre for Global Workers' Rights (CGWR), 22 March 2018, 18, https://ler.la.psu.edu/gwr/documents/CGWR2017ResearchReportBindingPower.pdf.

5 Karan Khurana and Marco Ricchetti, "Two Decades of Sustainable Supply Chain Management in the Fashion Business, an Appraisal," *Journal of Fashion Marketing and Management* 20, no. 1 (March 2016): 95. After the Rana Plaza building collapse, some of the involved brands' first reactions demonstrate that they were unaware of who their indirect subcontractors were.

6 Patsy Perry and Neil Towers, "Conceptual Framework Development: CSR Implementation in Fashion Supply Chains," *International Journal of Physical Distribution & Logistics Management* 43, nos. 5/6 (June 2013): 478.

7 Hyo Jung Chang and Tun-Min Jai, "Is Fast Fashion Sustainable? The Effect of Positioning Strategies on Consumers' Attitudes and Purchase Intentions," *Social Responsibility Journal* 11, no. 4 (October 2015): 855.
8 Anner, "Binding Power."
9 Dean Nelson, "Bangladesh Building Collapse Kills at Least 82 in Dhaka," *The Telegraph*, 23 April 2013, https://www.telegraph.co.uk/news/worldnews/asia/bangladesh/10014778/Bangladesh-building-collapse-kills-at-least-82-in-Dhaka.html.
10 Dana Thomas, "Why Won't We Learn from the Survivors of the Rana Plaza Disaster?" *The New York Times*, 24 April 2018, https://www.nytimes.com/2018/04/24/style/survivors-of-rana-plaza-disaster.html.
11 Ibid.
12 Duygu Turker and Ceren Altuntas, "Sustainable Supply Chain Management in the Fast Fashion Industry: An Analysis of Corporate Reports," *European Management Journal* 32, no. 5 (October 2014): 837.
13 Perry and Towers, "Conceptual Framework Development," 480.
14 Alessandra Vecchi, *Advanced Fashion Technology and Operations Management* (Hershey: Business Science Reference, 2017).
15 Ana Isabel Escalona Orcao and David Ramos-Pérez, "Los Transportes y La Logística En Las Cadenas Globales de Producción Del Sector de La Moda Rápida: El Caso de La Empresa Española Inditex," *Investigaciones Geográficas* 0, no. 85 (2014): 116.
16 Turker and Altuntas, "Sustainable Supply Chain Management," 847.
17 Ibid., 838.
18 Ibid.
19 John S. Ahlquist and Layna Mosley, "Firm Participation in Voluntary Regulatory Initiatives: The Accord, Alliance, and US Garment Importers from Bangladesh," *The Review of International Organizations* 16, no. 2 (April 2021): 7.
20 Ibid., 7–9.
21 Ibid., 9.
22 Thomas, "Why Won't We Learn."
23 Stephen A. Pike, "Sustainability Reporting: The Lawyer's Response," *Gowling* WLG, 1 February 2015, https://gowlingwlg.com/en/insights-resources/articles/2015/sustainability-reporting-the-lawyer-s-response.
24 Ibid.
25 Global Reporting Initiative, "About GRI," accessed 18 August 2021, https://www.globalreporting.org/about-gri.
26 Turker and Altuntas, "Sustainable Supply Chain Management," 838.
27 Khurana and Ricchetti, "Sustainable Supply," 97.

28 Ibid., 96.

29 Ibid. Sustainability-lab.net found that the most widespread role that CSR played is "rule setting with no decision power" among eighteen European and American brands and leaders in their market segments with a total of more than €50 billion in sale in 2014. Marco Ricchetti et al., "2014 Fashion Brands Sustainable Procurement Survey," Sustainability-lab, 20 October 2014, https://www.researchgate.net/publication/269113916_2014_Fashion_Brands_Sustainable_Procurement_Survey.

30 Turker and Altuntas, "Sustainable Supply Chain Management," 846.

31 Anika Kozlowski, Cory Searcy, and Michal Bardecki, "Corporate Sustainability Reporting in the Apparel Industry: An Analysis of Indicators Disclosed," *International Journal of Productivity and Performance Management* 64, no. 3 (March 2015): 386–8.

32 David J. Doorey, "The Transparent Supply Chain: From Resistance to Implementation at Nike and Levi-Strauss," *Journal of Business Ethics* 103, no. 4 (Summer 2011): 588.

33 Jen-Yi Chen and Susan A. Slotnick, "Supply Chain Disclosure and Ethical Sourcing," *International Journal of Production Economics* 161 (March 2015): 19.

34 Doorey, "Transparent Supply Chain," 598.

35 Lucia Gatti et al., "Are We Moving Beyond Voluntary CSR? Exploring Theoretical and Managerial Implications of Mandatory CSR Resulting from the New Indian Companies Act," *Journal of Business Ethics* 160, no. 4 (December 2019): 964.

36 Elmer Lenzen. "Between Voluntary and Mandatory CSR," *United Nations Global Compact International Yearbook* (November 2014): 177.

37 Gatti et al., "Beyond Voluntary," 964.

38 *National Instrument 51-102 Continuous Disclosure Obligations*, BC Reg. 110/2004, https://www.canlii.org/en/bc/laws/regu/bc-reg-110-2004/latest/bc-reg-110-2004.html.

39 California Code, Civil Code, CIV § 1714.43, subd. (a)(1).

40 *Modern Slavery Act 2015, UK Public General Acts* 2015, c. 30, https://www.legislation.gov.uk/ukpga/2015/30/contents/enacted.

41 *Modern Slavery Act 2018, Australian Government* 2018, no. 153, https://www.legislation.gov.au/Details/C2018A00153.

42 Gershon Nimbalker et al., *The 2018 Ethical Fashion Report: The Truth Behind the Barcode* (New Zealand: Baptist World Aid Australia 2018), 29.

43 Paul Redmond, "At Last, Australia Has a Modern Slavery Act. Here's What You'll Need to Know," *The Conversation*, 2 December 2018, https://theconversation.com/at-last-australia-has-a-modern-slavery-act-heres-what-youll-need-to-know-107885.

44 Ibid.
45 Global Reporting Initiative, "About GRI."
46 José Luis Blasco and Adrian King, "The Road Ahead: KPMG's Survey of Corporate Responsibility Reporting 2017," KPMG, October 2017, 6, https://integratedreporting.org/wp-content/uploads/2017/10/kpmg-survey-of-corporate-responsibility-reporting-2017.pdf.
47 Turker and Altuntas, "Sustainable Supply Chain Management," 845.
48 Ibid.
49 Doorey, "Transparent Supply Chain," 592.
50 Ibid.
51 Ibid.
52 Ibid.
53 Perry and Towers, "Conceptual Framework," 479.
54 See e.g., Brian Stauffer, "Follow the Thread: The Need for Supply Chain Transparency in the Garment and Footwear Industry," *Human Rights Watch*, 20 April 2017, https://www.hrw.org/report/2017/04/20/follow-thread/need-supply-chain-transparency-garment-and-footwear-industry.
55 Aruna Kashyap, "Soon There Won't Be Much to Hide: Transparency in the Apparel Industry," Human Rights Watch, accessed 19 August 2021, https://www.hrw.org/sites/default/files/transparency.pdf.
56 ASOS plc, "Factory List," 31 January 2020, https://www.asosplc.com/~/media/Files/A/Asos-V2/documents/asos-plc-factory-list-jan-2020.pdf.
57 Imran Amed et al., "The State of Fashion 2019," McKinsey & Company, accessed 19 August 2021, https://www.mckinsey.com/~/media/mckinsey/industries/retail/our%20insights/the%20state%20of%20fashion%202019%20a%20year%20of%20awakening/the-state-of-fashion-2019-final.ashx.
58 Ibid.
59 Chen and Slotnick, "Supply Chain Disclosure," 27.
60 Lindsey Clark and David Master, *2012 Corporate ESG/Sustainability/Responsibility Reporting – Does It Matter?* (New York: Governance & Accountability Institute, Inc. 2012), 10, https://www.ga-institute.com/fileadmin/user_upload/Reports/SP500_-_Final_12-15-12.pdf.
61 Ibid., 36.
62 Ibid.
63 Ibid.
64 Wim Bartels et al., *Carrot & Sticks: Global Trends in Sustainability Reporting Regulation and Policy* (KPMG, 2016), 9.
65 Redmond, "Australia Has a Modern Slavery Act," 7.
66 Ibid., 8.
67 Ibid.
68 Perry and Towers, "Conceptual Framework," 492.

69 *Das v. George Weston Limited* [2018] OJ No. 6742, 2018 ONCA 1053, http://canlii.ca/t/hwqco.

70 David Doorey, "Vacuousness of CSR on Display in Loblaws' Victory in Rana Plaza Class Action Lawsuit," *International Union Rights* 24, no. 4 (Summer 2017): 18–20.

71 Ibid.

72 Loblaws, "2012 Corporate Social Responsibility Report," 2012, https://www.loblaw.ca/en/responsibility.

73 Loblaws, "2013 Corporate Social Responsibility Report," 2013, https://www.loblaw.ca/en/responsibility.

74 Sofia Garcia-Torres, Marta Rey-Garcia, and Laura Albareda-Vivo, "Effective Disclosure in the Fast-Fashion Industry: From Sustainability Reporting to Action," *Sustainability* 9, no. 12 (December 2017): 3.

75 Genevieve LeBaron, Jane Lister, and Peter Dauvergne, "Governing Global Supply Chain Sustainability through the Ethical Audit Regime," *Globalizations* 14, no. 6 (April 2017): 961.

76 Perry and Towers, "Conceptual Framework," 492.

77 Khurana and Ricchetti, "Sustainable Supply," 93.

78 Ibid.

79 Justine Nolan and Auret van Heerden, "Engaging Business in the Business of Human Rights," in *Principled Engagement: Negotiating Human Rights in Repressive States* (London: Routledge 2013), 163.

80 Khurana and Ricchetti, "Sustainable Supply," 93.

81 Chen and Slotnick, "Supply Chain Disclosure," 27.

82 Ibid., 27.

83 Blasco and King, "Survey of Corporate Responsibility Reporting 2017," 7.

84 Human Rights Watch, "The Apparel and Footwear Supply Chain Transparency Pledge," 2017, https://cleanclothes.org/transparency/transparency-pledge.

85 Garcia-Torres, Rey-Garcia, and Albareda-Vivo, "Effective Disclosure," 1.

86 Ibid., 4.

87 John Dumay, "A Critical Reflection on the Future of Intellectual Capital: From Reporting to Disclosure," *Journal of Intellectual Capital* 17, no. 1 (January 2016): 178.

88 Ibid.

89 Garcia-Torres, Rey-Garcia, and Albareda-Vivo, "Effective Disclosure," 3.

90 *Management Discussion & Analysis,* Form 51-102F1, BC Regs. 370/2006, s. 1(f).

91 OECD, *OECD Due Diligence Guidance for Responsible Supply Chains in the Garment and Footwear Sector* (Paris: OECD Publishing, 2018).

92 Ibid., 19.
93 See Garcia-Torres, Rey-Garcia, and Albareda-Vivo, "Effective Disclosure," 7–8.
94 See ibid., 6. CMIs are defined as a minimum number of material issues that summarize all the reported material issues.
95 See ibid. RAS are actions that are undertaken by companies to address the reported material issues as stated in their sustainability reports.
96 See ibid., 16.
97 Ibid., 19.
98 Ibid.
99 Ibid.
100 Ibid., 21.
101 Ibid., 22.
102 Thomas Laudal, "An Attempt to Determine the CSR Potential of the International Clothing Business," *Journal of Business Ethics* 96, no. 1 (September 2010): 63–4.
103 Libby Sanders et al., *The 2019 Ethical Fashion Report: The Truth Behind the Barcode* (New Zealand: Baptist World Aid Australia, 2019).
104 Ibid.

PART THREE

Corporate Accountability and Regulation

9

The Return of Robin Hood: A New Kind of Shareholder Activism

Bikaramjit S. Sandhu

The folklore character Robin Hood is known for his controversial philosophy of stealing from the rich to give to the poor.[1] Activist shareholders were once thought to embody this ideology in corporate culture; they were believed to reclaim and redistribute what was perceived to have been stolen from shareholders by corporations.[2] In doing so, they fulfilled the function of monitoring corporate spending and activity. Any waste or failure to realize maximization of shareholder wealth sprung activist shareholders into action to exert pressure on boards to restore equilibrium and return corporate value back to its supposed rightful "owners"[3] – the shareholders.[4] While activist shareholders have been steadily addressing corporate complacency, they have been relatively silent regarding companies' corporate social responsibility (CSR) policies,[5] until now. The emergence of environmental, social, and governance (ESG) investing and growing research supporting the business case for ESG creates new potential for activist shareholders to reinvent themselves as Robin Hood once again, this time with aligned goals of benefiting the corporation as a whole, its shareholders, and other stakeholders in the consideration of environmental and social impacts of corporate activity.

Recent trends in investing include the integration of ESG factors into investment strategies and decision-making.[6] In the past, the process of forming an investment thesis was based solely on financial analysis with other factors playing only a minor role. ESG issues such as climate change, wage disparities, and gender inequality were not given the full attention they deserved.[7] Now, many investors are beginning to understand the seriousness of the diverse and complex challenges that fall under the umbrella of ESG.[8] As a result, investors have begun to push public companies to consider their broader societal and environmental impacts.[9] Despite this trend, there is a noticeable lag in the adoption of ESG policies by publicly traded companies.[10] As it becomes clearer that ESG issues are inextricably tied to business activity, any valuation of these companies based on traditional methods of financial forecasting will necessarily be inaccurate and not indicative of true value. Further, board consideration of stakeholder interests in corporate decision-making was not only interpreted favourably in the leading case of *BCE v. 1976 Debentureholders* but is now codified in statute under s. 122(1.1) of the *Canada Business Corporations Act* (CBCA).[11] Stakeholders are cognizant of ESG issues and by failing to adopt ESG policies, corporations are vulnerable to stakeholder pressures and litigation.[12] Falling behind on ESG responsibilities can also result in failure to maximize shareholder wealth and thereby potentially trigger takeover activity or other like action from shareholders. Therefore, boards of directors will continue to face increased scrutiny and greater expectations from stakeholders to incorporate ESG policies.

Research has shown that the market rewards companies that integrate ESG in their policies and both short- and long-term planning. Therefore, companies that fail to incorporate ESG in their business strategies may be taking unnecessary risks and failing to maximize their value. Activist shareholders look to find gaps that could potentially lead to additional gains. The ESG valuation gap creates an environment where activist shareholders can pressure companies to adopt ESG policies. This chapter focuses on publicly listed companies and begins, in the first section, by defining the concept of ESG investing, along with characterizing the "activist shareholder" and their motivations and identifying the tools that activist shareholders possess in this context. While acknowledging the limitations and challenges facing activist shareholders in public companies, this section also argues that such shareholders are nevertheless uniquely capable of pressuring corporations into action to adopt policies that improve their ESG footprint. The second section examines the role hedge funds can play in fostering ESG in companies, and the third section discusses why a lack of political will necessitates this new kind of shareholder activism.

THE ROAD TO ESG AND SHAREHOLDER ACTIVISM

ESG is a general term that is used in the investing community to refer to non-financial performance indicators.[13] These indicators include corporate governance metrics and various other factors that are used to measure the sustainability and ethical impact of an investment.[14] The current trend includes examining ESG factors that cover a wide spectrum of issues such as how a corporation is combating climate change, waste management and water usage, human resources, supply chain management, among other environmental and social issues.[15] The governance in ESG includes analyzing the corporate governance structures of a company, such as ensuring transparency, accountability, and compliance with increasing policy developments on whether boards have policies in place regarding board diversity and sustainability.[16]

Investors understand that ESG impacts the bottom line.[17] The days of ESG as a secondary issue for shareholders have passed. Canadian proxy voting guidelines released by proxy advisors such as Glass, Lewis & Co. have begun to recommend voting against board slates that are responsible for any failure to design policies that effectively manage environmental and social risks.[18] Greater awareness of ESG issues is widespread and their impact on corporate governance and investing activities is becoming increasingly clear. Evidence of this movement can be found in the United Nations Principles for Responsible Investment (UNPRI), which serves as a set of voluntary, aspirational investment principles that the United Nations recommends be incorporated into investment practice.[19] The entities that become signatories to these principles agree that they have a duty to act in the best long-term interests of their beneficiaries.[20]

Currently, at over US$20 trillion in assets under management, ESG investing is estimated to be around a quarter of all professionally managed assets around the world, with its rapid growth "build[ing] upon the socially responsible investment (SRI) movement that has been around much longer."[21] While there is significant interplay between SRI and ESG, they remain distinct concepts. SRI is defined as ethical and moral criteria that ensure no investments are made in certain sectors, typically "SIN firms" (tobacco, alcohol, gambling, or firearms).[22] On the other hand, ESG is more focused on indicators that factor directly into financial valuation. The importance of ESG information lies in the fact that it plays a vital role in understanding the corporation's purpose, strategy, and management culture.[23]

Despite its obvious relevance, ESG has not always had investors' support. In the early days of the ESG movement, investors were reluctant to embrace the concept, arguing that they had a fiduciary duty to focus only on maximizing shareholder return and that ESG factors had no impact on maximization.[24] For retail and institutional investors, ESG offers the opportunity to not only make more informed choices with their capital and thereby reap greater returns, but it also allows them to vote on social issues with the same capital.[25] Specifically, investors will be able to allocate their capital towards projects where ESG factors are considered and elevated. Activist shareholders have begun to put forward shareholder proposals that require management to adopt ESG policies for and within the corporation.[26] Policymakers should, therefore, welcome these shareholder proposals, which are put forward for voting to ensure development for the common good.

Shareholder activism is premised upon investors who are dissatisfied with some aspect of a corporation, which leads the activist to pursue actions that could bring about change to the unsatisfactory aspect; in theory, activism should work to enhance overall shareholder value.[27] The activist usually targets the operations of the company or its management and is generally looking to transform the company, but not necessarily change effective control.[28] This phenomenon dates back to 1942, when the US Securities Exchange Commission began allowing shareholders to submit proposals for inclusion in corporate ballots.[29] This meant that shareholders could voice their opinion regarding choices for the company through shareholder proposals. From the 1940s to the 70s, shareholder activism was primarily dominated by individual investors; however, in the 80s, there was a rise in institutional investors pressuring management behind closed doors to implement change.[30] In the past decade, hedge funds and private equity funds have assumed prominent positions in the activism arena with their distinct investment theses.[31] These funds play a vital role in the financial markets, especially in their capacity to monitor corporate performance and champion leaders for change.

Activist shareholders can be divided into two subcategories. First, shareholders are considered to be "active" simply by trading a company's shares.[32] This group signals its feelings about the corporation's performance outlook by selling (or holding) its position on the stock market. In other words, the first group is actively engaged in the practice of voting with their "feet"[33] – selling their shares. Studies show that this simple act of selling shares can lead to real changes in corporate governance.[34] For example, if a corporation were to lose a large institutional investor such as the Ontario Teachers' Pension Plan, it would most likely lead to significant changes in their governance structure. On the other hand, the second group of activist shareholders is viewed as a draconian group essentially looking for corporate control. Corporate control is obtained through takeovers and leveraged buyouts and is generally pursued with the intention of making fundamental changes to the corporation.[35] Ultimately, the purpose of shareholder activism is fuelled by the quest for additional value.

At its core, shareholder activism is about rectifying agency conflicts that exist in large public companies, the purpose of which is largely perceived to be enhancing shareholder value and increasing monetary gains. Agency conflicts arise from the corporate structure. Shareholders are part and parcel of a corporation but pursuant to s. 102(1) of the CBCA, directors have the power and duty to manage and deal with all business affairs of the corporation on behalf of the corporation.[36] This power includes hiring and firing members of management; therefore, activism is triggered when the board fails to perform these tasks.[37] There are a number of remedies for inadequate boards, such as voting or selling shares, but not all shareholders are likely to be active or have sufficient incentive to punish the board. Institutional investors may be reluctant to initiate activism against corporations due to business relationships and some institutional investors may feel obligated to vote with management even as they believe that management behaviour is failing to meet the board's fiduciary obligations (i.e., the board is failing to consider the best interests of the corporation).[38]

Both types of activist shareholders can effect change within companies to an extent; however, this chapter will focus on activists that seek corporate control. This group of activists use a few tools to disrupt complacency in a company. Two common methods used by activist shareholders to effect meaningful change to the corporation are takeover bids and proxy contests. Using these mechanisms, activist shareholders can pressure companies into keeping with the times, which contemporarily includes incorporating ESG policies into their investing strategies.

Tools to Launch Campaigns

When activist shareholders are looking to generate greater returns, they will do whatever is necessary to see gains. One commonly used tool in this context is a proxy fight. Proxy fights are like a political election campaign. A dissident or insurgent group of shareholders attempts to win the hearts, minds, and – most of all – votes of the majority of the corporation's shareholders, such that the dissident's slate of directors will be elected to the board instead of the candidates nominated by the corporation's incumbent managers.[39] Proxy fights are initiated when activist shareholders (or groups of shareholders) who hold views in opposition to management make a public filing of their activist intent, supplemented by a filed news release.[40] A proxy fight reaches the status of a contest when the activist shareholder requisitions a meeting and the activist shareholder nominates their own slate, which is an alternative to the management slate. Generally, shareholders can requisition meetings if they hold at least 5 per cent equity in the company.[41]

The requisition of a meeting serves the purpose of officially announcing the intention to nominate alternative board members, or it can be used to conduct a "vote no" campaign on either the election of directors or mergers and acquisitions transactions. The latter occurs when the corporation intends to enter into an agreement to merge with another company; however, the activist shareholder may communicate their disapproval by instigating a "vote no" campaign to halt the transaction.[42] The goal of the activist shareholder is to inform the public of its opposition and that it has publicly targeted the company, implying that a fight has started. In Canada, it is not unheard of for larger shareholders, particularly institutional investors such as pension plans, to undertake a proxy contest to persuade other shareholders to vote against such planned transactions.[43]

In most cases, proxy fights are initiated in relation to board independence, executive pay, and other similar issues. However, activist shareholders are also using their positions in companies to drive social change. According to Kingsdale Advisory, there were a record number of majority-supported proposals in the US and Canada that were led by activist funds.[44] For example, JANA Partners (a top-tier activist fund in the US), along with the California State Teachers' Retirement System, pressured Apple Inc. to create new features to restrict children's access to iPhones and also to create a study to learn more about the impacts of iPhones on teenagers.[45] Both activist funds publicly stated that addressing this specific issue will lead to long-term value for all shareholders. Blue Harbour Group has publicly stated that social and environmental factors will play a significant role in its determination to deploy and invest US$3 billion in assets.[46] In Canada, the BC Government & Service Employees' Union General Fund filed a shareholder proposal where they raised concerns on Thomson Reuters's record on human rights and asked the company to provide a human rights report.[47] Thomson Reuters had contracts with the US Immigration and Customs Enforcement where their software was being used to assist in the Trump administration's inhumane family separation and indefinite family detention policies.

Activist shareholders introduce shareholder proposals prior to meetings, which companies generally perceive as being a threat. Shareholder proposals are also often viewed as an essential tool for monitoring corporate accountability. These proposals are introduced and voted on during an annual meeting or at a special meeting requisitioned by the shareholders. In recent years, a number of proposals dealing with environmental and social issues have been introduced.[48] Whereas most shareholder proposals are not withdrawn, there appears to be an opposite trend for ESG-specific proposals: in 2018, 48 per cent of ESG proposals were withdrawn by proponents.[49] Public companies usually will not negotiate on shareholder proposals when they believe that the proposals will not garner enough support from other shareholders anyway.[50] Conversely, public companies will negotiate with shareholders if there is a realistic possibility of the proposal going through. In the latter case, the company will engage in negotiations because they perceive the proposals as questioning management's competency and undermining their control. Therefore, in most cases, these proposals are adopted with some modifications. The current trend demonstrates that public companies feel obligated to listen to activist shareholders' proposals with regards to ESG policies, or else the company must defend itself in a public proxy fight.

The UNPRI suggest that shareholders should be active and incorporate ESG issues into their policies and practices. Activist shareholders can rely on this principle as the philosophy behind their investment thesis and gain a sense of legitimacy for their investment practices. Currently, there are numerous companies across the world that are bracing for direct and indirect impacts on their balance sheets due to climate change. Activist funds are willing to exert enormous amounts of pressure to meet their goal of realizing gains. Their strategy is to be very public about their concerns as publicity would create leverage over the boards of corporations.[51] The purpose of an activist fund is to target companies that have weak corporate governance structures, as well as those that are not fulfilling their fiduciary obligations to the corporation. Poor board diversity, lack of plans for tackling climate change, and lack of disclosure of ESG policies will likely lead to activist shareholders targeting those companies. As a result, one can anticipate activist shareholders expecting greater disclosure from public companies due to the pressure being exerted.[52]

A public battle with an activist shareholder is not a good look for a publicly traded company. Indications of severe disruptions to the operations of a company caused by the actions of a significant shareholder tend to lead to stock prices declining.[53] Efficient market hypothesis states that all the information that exists about a company is reflected in the company's stock price.[54] Therefore, any negative news is usually followed by a decline in the stock price, in conjunction with a decline in the company's market capitalization and possibly the alienation of other investors. More importantly, a public proxy fight will not only lead to some investors voting with their feet, but it can also lead to other investors not investing at all. Institutional investors in particular do not want to be associated with any proxy fight as it wastes valuable assets. A publicly traded company is viewed as a blue-chip company if the stock is owned by a large institutional investor. But if there is a proxy fight related to ESG matters, institutional investors will not only divest but might actually support the activist shareholder in their conquest to shake up the board.[55] In the post-Enron period, there is increasing evidence that shareholder proposals affect target firms' governance structures and, in some cases, enhance the firms' values.[56]

Since proxy contests can be expensive, companies often reach settlement agreements with activists that include standstill provisions and support of activist board nominations.[57] Activists use these strategies to obtain greater control of a target company's board, which can then be used to push for changes.[58] Additionally, large proxy advisory firms, such as Glass Lewis and Institutional Shareholder Services, serve the purpose of providing independent research and recommendations for investors to vote for a particular slate in a proxy contest. Institutional investors rely heavily on these proxy advisory firms since they do not have the capacity to perform their own research.[59] Both advisory firms have stated that they will not support any board slate that lacks diversity, which includes women and minority groups.[60]

Activist funds can gain support from proxy advisory firms and thus institutional investors by introducing ESG proposals. In 2018, TransCanada Corporation voted on a shareholder proposal asking management to create a report on climate change.[61] It passed with 99 per cent of shareholders' support along with management's recommendation.[62] Consequently, these companies will develop their own ESG policies, enhance disclosures, understand the ESG policies of shareholders, and ensure the board has environmental and social risk expertise.[63] If not, proxy fights based on shareholder proposals in the ESG space will likely proliferate. Even if such shareholder proposals do not receive majority support, it is reported that similar proposals will later be adopted.[64]

A takeover bid refers to the purchase of shares or offer to purchase under statutorily defined circumstances that legislators have decided could likely result in the purchaser attaining practical or effective control over a corporation.[65] Hostile takeovers can come about in a number of ways. Often, a bidder will initially approach a prospective target hoping to pursue a friendly deal, but when these advances are rebuffed by the intended target, the bidder may switch tactics and "go hostile" instead.[66] A hostile takeover may also be launched by a bidder immediately after the intended target has announced its own intention to complete a friendly deal with another party; the fact that a company has chosen to undertake a friendly acquisition is typically understood in the business community to have placed that company on the market, or "in play."[67]

In Canada, takeover bids are rarer due to new statutory requirements that have made takeover bids expensive to undertake.[68] However, if activist shareholders believe that there are fundamental errors of judgment on the part of management and the board in running the company, they may launch a takeover bid despite the cost. For a bid to be tendered, there must be a good potential for significant synergies that could lead to additional gains for the activist shareholder.

Why are activist funds that are normally focused exclusively on short-term returns and wealth generation so interested in ESG? The simple answer might be that like retail investors and institutional investors, activist funds have also become passionate about ESG issues that prioritize sustainable growth, positive impact on a company's long-term brand, and simply making the world a better place.[69] Also, it may be that UNPRI principles of active investment in ESG practices and policies have motivated activist funds to be more proactive in that realm. However, the more likely answer is that activist shareholders are publicly supportive of ESG initiatives to court major institutional investors who have had positive results with ESG investing in the past, so that such investors will invest in companies in which the activists maintain positions.

Takeover bids and proxy contests are just some of the tools that activist shareholders can use to demand change in pursuit of increased value and potential gains. As stated before, ESG factors are extra-financial factors that impact the bottom line. By not considering or incorporating ESG factors into corporate frameworks, corporations cannot present their true worth since they have not reached their full potential. Activist shareholders often use this as leverage to acquire a position in the company with the promise of delivering greater returns. Activist shareholders can take this opportunity to ensure that the company does maximize value by using different strategies to make changes to the corporation's operations.

TREND OF HEDGE FUND ESG ACTIVISM

In the past decade, hedge funds have become a dominant force in the arena of shareholder activism. The goal of an activist hedge fund is to generate outsized returns for its investors.[70] Unlike passive investors, activist funds and activist hedge funds use a variety of tools to proactively engage with companies in ways that passive investors do not.[71] Recent examples include hedge fund activist Paul Singer's Elliott Management Corp. and their proxy battle over Hyundai Motor Group, and Bill Ackman's Pershing Square Holdings Ltd in its activist campaigns over Wendy's International and Herbalife.[72] Hedge funds have a variety of goals in activism that are usually centred around changing management strategy or board decisions, affecting corporate governance changes, forcing sales or buyouts of divisions, and increasing dividend or share repurchases.[73] Their strategies are quite similar to activist funds, which include shareholder proposals, direct negotiations, use of media, proxy contests, litigation, and outright takeover.[74]

Research demonstrates that even hedge funds can play a role in bringing on ESG policies.[75] When examining the various components that make up ESG, the most common subset of issues touched on by activist campaigns is corporate governance.[76] Hedge funds target issuers that deal with executive compensation, weak governance structures, poor ownership structure, and business ethics.[77] With respect to environmental and social issues, there has been a shareholder proposal filed regarding food waste reporting,[78] and in November 2020, TCI Fund Management Limited submitted a shareholder proposal to Canadian Pacific Railway Limited requesting the company provide a climate action plan addressing greenhouse gas emission levels.[79]

Although hedge funds are not fully active in this arena, certain developments could lead to hedge funds entering this field on a regular basis. First, hedge funds could be more active in ESG investing if there were disclosure requirements for companies to report on ESG issues, as this would allow hedge funds to fully analyze what a company is doing in comparison to its peers and whether the fund believes the company is doing a poor job such that it should apply pressure to that company. All of this could serve to set the standard for how and to what degree ESG should be prioritized.[80] Disclosure would allow hedge fund activists to express their views on ESG issues and examine how companies are dealing with such issue; essentially, this would allow hedge funds to keep companies accountable on ESG issues. It would also encourage hedge funds to examine these factors since it confirms that ESG issues have a material impact on the valuation of a company.[81] Third, hedge funds can target companies with their long and short-term strategies.[82] Hedge funds are attuned to the fact that corporations that have not implemented ESG policies are susceptible to drops in their stock price since existing valuations would not represent the true value of the corporation.[83]

The current state of the hedge fund industry faces performance challenges that might require it to adopt new strategies. Lynette DeWitt points out that there is currently no clear hedge fund leader in impact investing and so it may be wise for leading hedge funds to become first movers to gain a competitive advantage. Hedge funds could build practice groups that focus entirely on impact investing, not only placing hedge funds higher on social rankings but also allowing them to differentiate themselves from competitors.[84] The core competency of this business proposition is built around the fact that there are growing numbers of consumers and investors who prefer SRI and ESG investment products compared to other investment options.[85] Competition is quite fierce in the hedge fund industry and impact investing strategies will create opportunities to bring in new clients and deepen relationships with existing clients.[86] Ultimately, impact investing could allow hedge funds to be reborn as the "Robin Hood" of capital markets.

Materiality to Returns

Over the past few years, the rise in prominence of ESG in the investment sectors has occurred at a rapid pace. The consensus is that corporations with ESG policies are rewarded with stellar long-term performance.[87] On the other hand, corporations with poor ESG policies are deemed to be risky and not as efficiently managed as their peers.[88] Credit agencies have also been playing a part in the rise[89] – for example, Standard & Poor's and Moody's have publicly acknowledged that climate change is a major risk that had not been previously factored into their rating system.[90] Furthermore, Moody's has warned coastal cities that they need to show evidence of climate change preparations or else they will see a downgrade on their bonds.[91] If cities such as New York City or Los Angeles see a downgrade in their credit rankings, they would experience negative impacts such as an increase in the cost of borrowing and impediments in their ability to fund future city projects.[92] Similarly, investors believe that a corporation's treatment of ESG factors will impact the investors' financial returns and long-term sustainability. There is a robust relationship between ESG and credit ratings.[93] Specifically, strong ESG factors allow companies to obtain lower financing costs even though ESG does not translate into an instant positive impact. Overall, a company's credit rating improves through improving relations with stakeholders, signalling operational and financial efficiency, and reducing the risks of bad behaviour.[94]

According to a 2018 State Street survey report, the driving force that is pushing investors to support ESG investing comes from the recognition that these issues are simply material to long-term financial outcomes.[95] The report states that "developments such as the [UNPRI] are helping investors seek ESG policies in terms of both opportunity and risk."[96] Recently, BlackRock Chairman and CEO Larry Fink issued an open letter to CEOs of companies that are held in its portfolio requesting that they develop long-term strategies in the context of non-financial metrics.[97] JANA Partners in January 2018 announced the creation of the "JANA Impact Capital Fund," which will invest in companies that are "good to the world" and focus on "social activism."[98] KKR, a renowned private equity firm, also just recently announced their creation of an ESG fund.[99]

Shareholders believe that good ESG performance is an indication of efficient management and that the company is performing well, but it also demonstrates that the company has a strong financial standing. A positive correlation has been found between corporations prioritizing environmental responsibility and long-term stock performance.[100] This correlation further indicates that outperformance of peers starts after three years and continues thereafter, which suggests that good environmental practices create long-term value.[101] Therefore, ESG factors are an important consideration when making investment decisions that are intended to generate sustainable returns. Activist shareholders often target reporting issuers that are yet to implement ESG policies as those companies have not attained their true value. These shareholders are looking for higher returns and ESG factors allow them to realize those higher returns. Furthermore, activist shareholders want to see reporting issuers hedge themselves against potential risks. Research indicates that risk stems from a lack of ESG policies and weak corporate governance structures, which hinder a company from seeing full returns.[102] The lack of both components will lead to activist shareholders targeting these companies.

Shareholders see such a chain of events as a major disruption and will demand strategies to be developed to mitigate the resulting risks. If mitigation processes are weak and not comprehensive, activist shareholders will put forward shareholder proposals that might lead to serious disruptions for the entire company. For example, with respect to Canada – a natural resource-based economy and leading mining nation – Canada's mining sector has attractive asset classes but is particularly susceptible to climate change impacts. Canada's mining industry in the North relies on winter supplies brought in on ice roads and summer access over permafrost roads. Climate change has led to shorter and milder winters. As a result, there is a significant loss of permafrost that makes it more difficult for workers to transport supplies, leading to supply shortages and inability to access mine sites.[103]

Furthermore, robust ESG disclosure practices by a public company have the potential to mitigate the risk of activist campaigns. A public company should look to incorporate a business and human rights (BHR) lens when developing and disclosing ESG practices. There have been disruptions in operations to a company that do not have proper human rights practices incorporated within their supply chains. In 2020, the US government banned all shipments from Sime Darby Planation Berhad after claims of forced labour and other abuses on the planation.[104] Disruption to operations would not only impact shareholders but other stakeholders. For instance, workers who rely on these operations for income would be impacted. Furthermore, public companies can predict stronger top-line growth but also stronger relationships when all stakeholders believe in the ESG policies of a company.[105] Specifically, by adopting a BHR lens practice, a company can expect to attract more loyal customers because customers would feel a sense of trust and thus achieve more success through the company's strong community relations. If the community lacks the trust, it could disrupt operations, leading to a loss of customers through poor sustainability practices and the perception of unstable and unsafe products being offered. By developing ESG practices that include all stakeholders, a corporation has the potential to mitigate many risks to its business by aligning all stakeholder interests. Therefore, a lack of social policies that include human right protections for stakeholders could seriously disrupt the supply chain and logistics of a company.

By implementing strong ESG policies, a company could also be offered more strategic freedom due to deregulation. Government can be perceived as an influential stakeholder but if the government supports the strong ESG policies and disclosures, the government can act as an ally. The government could assist with providing subsidies and grants instead of launching enforcement actions against the company.[106] Ultimately, a public company that has mandated proper ESG disclosure, through the incorporation of policies from a BHR lens, mitigates the corporation from potential activist campaigns. The activist mandate is based upon a new investment philosophy that is built around an increased awareness for climate change, wealth gaps, and gender inequality with the intention of mitigating future risk or expecting each investment dollar to go further.[107] The integration of these factors can be used as part of a risk mitigation screening process when evaluating which companies to invest in.[108] In conjunction with the belief that an investor should invest for the purposes of future returns, investors should also invest in companies that make products that are important to the investor.[109]

In Canada, a dramatic shift in investor demographics has increased the need for ESG integration. According to the Responsible Investment Association, millennials account for a larger proportion of reporting issuers' shareholder base on an annual basis and are 65 per cent more likely than older generations to examine the company's environmental and social records and policies when deciding to invest.[110] In addition, studies show that women are more attuned to ESG issues than men.[111] As a result, as women and millennials begin to control more wealth, Canadian companies can expect increased pressure to pursue environmental and social initiatives as well as equal representation in the boardroom.[112]

ROBIN HOOD REQUIRED DUE TO LACK OF POLITICAL WILL

Rules and regulations affect nearly every aspect of our daily lives and provide monitoring for various industries. In capital markets, there are disclosure requirements, prospectus requirements, and insider trading rules that serve the purpose of facilitating fair and efficient markets. Rules and regulations are the products of widely held beliefs that are then codified into statutes, but it can be a lengthy process to create these statutes. The government has been working on being more proactive when it comes to implementing positive rules and regulations; however, it has failed in most cases. Some would argue that the government is the best entity to force corporations to adopt ESG policies since it has the legislative power at its disposal to do so, and has the tools and resources needed to define ESG policies. Yet the government has generally proven to be successful only in dealing with crises on an ad hoc basis; it has been unable to create statutes that anticipate society's needs for regulation in a swift and efficient manner. These failures set a precedent for the proposition that a similar result would occur if the government were to be relied upon to lead the charge to ensure that corporations adopt ESG policies.

Government would not be efficient in forcing corporations to adopt ESG policies for numerous reasons. First, the government is quite slow in creating public policy unless it is an election year and its constituents demand such change. For instance, the federal government passed the Deferred Prosecution Agreement (DPA) through an ombudsperson bill along with the Budget in 2018.[113] Now, the federal government has been examining how to provide SNC-Lavalin with a DPA to not only save the company but also to demonstrate support of Quebec.[114] The lack of accountability and oversight by the federal government suggests that one's reliance on the state to solely protect public interests may be misguided. Second, governments are focused on their election mandates. Specifically, they are focused on completing multiple tasks from a bird's eye view. The government only has a mandate to govern for a short period of time; therefore, they are more focused on completing only those tasks that would get them re-elected.

Since there is no real consensus on the scope of these ESG policies, governments would have considerable difficulty forcing corporations to adopt ESG policies prior to attaining some form of consensus-building. All corporations are different; they have different structures and operations and produce different products, so the one-size-fits-all approach would likely not be feasible nor in the best interests of these corporations and the public. Instead, corporations themselves should integrate ESG policies that best fit their unique needs, as ultimately, the government lacks the capacity to create frameworks that allow for a smooth integration of ESG policies into a corporation's business model.

CONCLUSION

There are understandable disagreements from those opposing the idea that activist shareholders can effectively pressure corporations to adopt ESG policies. In many cases, activist shareholders have not actually introduced shareholder proposals that demand more board diversity or that tackle climate change policies, etc. Activist shareholders are perceived to be self-interested and focused on creating potential gains for themselves and their investors only. This chapter highlights the research that demonstrates corporations see more returns when ESG policies are implemented. ESG policies can lead to untapped gains, which motivates activist shareholders to launch campaigns.

Other arguments have been made with respect to the likelihood of campaigns being effective or successful. Although activist shareholders do have tactics and strategies that can be effective, skeptics note that companies fight back and certain corporate structures make it easy for corporations to defend themselves.[115] For instance, in a company with a staggered board, only a third of those directors are subject to re-election each year.[116] This defense limits the extent to which the makeup of the board can be changed and inhibits significant changes to corporate governance. Furthermore, along with the activist shareholder, proxy advisors and institutional investors also play a large role in activist campaigns. Institutional shareholders can influence the campaign if they decide that they are going to be working with the board instead of activist shareholders. As well, institutional investors cannot simply divest of a corporation's stock if they lack ESG initiatives since they have previous positions in index funds and mutual funds.[117] More importantly, divesting of publicly traded shares will distort the market price for those shares, which can lead to large losses for other investors. Finally, as Dominic Barton and Mark Wiseman have stated, if activist funds apply too much pressure to reporting issuers, they might just go private and avoid all these responsibilities.[118]

The above arguments are not insignificant, but it is important to note the marked trends that are developing that will likely minimize these arguments in the future. The weapons with which corporations have to defend themselves against activist shareholders are starting to become obsolete since activists can launch a proxy fight on those exact issues. Therefore, if a corporation uses such defensive tactics, it makes itself vulnerable to future proxy battles and would have to defend itself on multiple fronts. Furthermore, institutional investors rely on the research of proxy advisors for their voting decisions.[119] Proxy advisors have been noted to support board slates and shareholder proposals that include ESG initiatives. Activists can gain the support of institutional investors by ensuring that they consider ESG policies that proxy advisors agree with in their proposals. Finally, if reporting issuers elect to go private due to pressures, they will lose the ability to raise capital through the public markets and that alone heavily disincentivizes large corporations from going private.

Although society has started to turn more of its attention to social issues and reward environmentally friendly behaviour, not enough corporations have followed suit to significantly alter the trajectory of climate change or mitigate other social and environmental risks. Up until now, public companies have not had to face the kind of pressure that can be exerted by stakeholders that really push for ESG policies to be implemented. However, activist shareholders have the tools to force these companies to incorporate ESG policies, including the ability to negatively impact the valuation and stock price of these companies by initiating proxy fights and hostile takeover bids. As a result, companies are forced by activist shareholders to incorporate ESG policies and reach their true worth to enhance shareholder value.

Institutional investors and the government have some ability to encourage these companies to adapt; however, shareholder activism should be seen as a legitimate tool to hold companies accountable to their ESG policies and one of the most powerful in forcing these companies to transform. Given that more gains are realized through the implementation of ESG policies, activist shareholders should be particularly motivated to pursue these policies. It should be noted that prestigious funds such as JANA Partners and KKR have created new funds for just this purpose. These funds are attempting to capitalize on ESG policies as they recognize that passive investors have an appetite for investing in companies that are committed to bettering society. In this way, activist shareholders are the modern-day version of Robin Hood that society desperately needs.

NOTES

1 Kent L. Steckmesser, "Robin Hood and the American Outlaw: A Note on History and Folklore," *The Journal of American Folklore* 79, no. 312 (June 1966): 348.

2 Rusty O'Kelley, Anthony Goodman, and Melissa Martin, "2019 Global & Regional Trends in Corporate Governance," *Harvard Law School Forum on Corporate Governance*, 30 December 2018, https://corpgov.law.harvard.edu/2018/12/30/2019-global-regional-trends-in-corporate-governance.

3 The naming of shareholders as "owners" is, however, problematic. More accurately, shareholders own a bundle of interrelated rights in the corporation. See Lynn Stout et al., "The Modern Corporation Statement on Company Law," SSRN, 6 October 2016, https://papers.ssrn.com/sol3/papers.cfm?abstract_id=2848833.

4 See Yuliya Ponomareva, "Shareholder Activism is on the Rise: Caution Required," *Forbes*, 10 December 2018, https://www.forbes.com/sites/esade/2018/12/10/shareholder-activism-is-on-the-rise-caution-required/?sh=515 1e0e34844.

5 Clara Herzberg, "Why Are 'Activist Investors' Silent on Corporate Social Responsibility?" *Truthout*, 3 August 2017, https://truthout.org/articles/why-are-activist-investors-silent-on-corporate-social-responsibility.

6 Hélène Roy and Laura Gitman, "Trends in ESG Integration in Investment: Summary of the Latest Research and Recommendations to Attract Long-Term Investors," BSR, August 2012, https://www.bsr.org/reports/BSR_Trends_in_ESG_Integration.pdf.

7 Lauren Caplan, John S. Griswold, and William E. Jarvis, *From SRI to ESG: The Changing World of Responsible Investing* (Connecticut: Commonfund Institute 2013), 2, https://files.eric.ed.gov/fulltext/ED559300.pdf.

8 Roy and Gitman, "Trends," 5–6.

9 Sara Bernow, Bryce Klempner, and Clarisse Magnin, "From 'Why' to 'Why Not': Sustainable Investing as the New Normal," *McKinsey & Company*, 25 October 2017, https://www.mckinsey.com/industries/private-equity-and-principal-investors/our-insights/from-why-to-why-not-sustainable-investing-as-the-new-normal.

10 O'Kelley, Goodman, and Martin, "2019 Global & Regional Trends."

11 *BCE Inc. v. A Group of 1976 Debentureholders* [2008] 3 SCR 560, 2008 SCC 69.

12 See Canada Climate Law Initiative, https://ccli.ubc.ca.

13 ADEC Innovations, "What is ESG Investing?" accessed 25 August 2021, https://www.adecesg.com/resources/faq/what-is-esg-investing.

14 Gunnar Friede, Timo Busch, and Alexander Bassen, "ESG and Financial Performance: Aggregated Evidence From More Than 2000 Empirical Studies," *Journal of Sustainable Finance & Investment* 5, no. 4 (October 2015): 210.

15 Ibid.

16 Bernow, Klempner, and Magnin, "From 'Why.'"

17 "Issues that Keep Boards Awake at Night," *Law Times*, 25 February 2019, https://www.lawtimesnews.com/practice-areas/corporate-commercial/issues-that-keep-boards-awake-at-night/263431.

18 Ibid.

19 United Nations Principles of Responsible Investment, "What are the Principles for Responsible Investment?," 1 December 2017, https://www.unpri.org/pri/what-are-the-principles-for-responsible-investment.

20 Ibid.

21 Georg Kell, "The Remarkable Rise of ESG," *Forbes,* 11 July 2018, https://www.forbes.com/sites/georgkell/2018/07/11/the-remarkable-rise-of-esg/?sh=35c8da5e1695.

22 Ibid. For more on CSR and the alcohol industry see Catherine L.H. Lee, "Reputation or Reparations: The Paradox of CSR and the Alcohol Industry," chapter 7 of this book.

23 Ibid.

24 Ibid.

25 Matthew J. Kiernan, "Universal Owners and ESG: Leaving Money on the Table?" *Corporate Governance: An International Review* 15, no. 3 (May 2007): 478–85.

26 Joseph P. Kalt et al., *Political, Social, and Environmental Shareholder Resolutions: Do They Create or Destroy Shareholder Value?* (National Association of Manufacturers 2018), https://corpgov.law.harvard.edu/wp-content/uploads/2018/06/ESG-Paper-FINAL_reduced-size-002.pdf.

27 Ibid.

28 Stuart Gillan and Laura T. Starks, "The Evolution of Shareholder Activism in the United States," *Journal of Applied Corporate Finance* 19, no. 1 (Winter 2007): 55–73.

29 Ibid.

30 Ibid.

31 Mary Ann Cloyd, "Shareholder Activism: Who, What, When, and How?" *Harvard Law School Forum on Corporate Governance*, 7 April 2015, https://corpgov.law.harvard.edu/2015/04/07/shareholder-activism-who-what-when-and-how.

32 Ibid., 56.

33 Ibid.

34 Anat R. Admati, Paul Pfleiderer, and Josef Zechner, "Large Shareholder Activism, Risk Sharing, and Financial Market Equilibrium," *Journal of Political Economy* 102, no. 6 (December 1994): 1124.

35 Gillan and Starks, "The Evolution of Shareholder Activism," 56.

36 *Canada Business Corporation Act, Revised Statutes of Canada* 1985, c. C-44, s. 102(1) and s. 122, https://laws-lois.justice.gc.ca/eng/acts/C-44/INDEX.HTML.

37 Gillan and Starks, "The Evolution of Shareholder Activism," 58.

38 *Canada Business Corporation Act*, s. 102(1).

39 Christopher C. Nicholls, *Mergers, Acquisitions and Other Changes of Corporate Control, 2/e* (Toronto: Irwin Law, 2012), 332.

40 Cloyd, "Shareholder Activism," 3.

41 *Canada Business Corporation Act*, s. 167.

42 Trevor Zeyl, "Holding up the Deal: The Threat of 'Bumpitrage' to M&A," *Deal Law Wire – Norton Rose Fulbright*, 18 October 2018, https://www.deallawwire.com/2018/10/18/holding-up-the-deal-the-threat-of-bumpitrage-to-ma.

43 Ibid.

44 Wes Hall et al., "2018 Canadian Proxy Season Review," *Harvard Law School Forum on Corporate Governance*, 28 October 2018, https://corpgov.law.harvard.edu/2018/10/28/2018-canadian-proxy-season-review.

45 Robert G. Eccles, "Why an Activist Hedge Fund Cares Whether Apple's Devices are Bad for Kids," *Harvard Business Review*, 16 January 2018, https://hbr.org/2018/01/why-an-activist-hedge-fund-cares-whether-apples-devices-are-bad-for-kids.

46 Blue Harbour Group, "News & Press," 9 December 2013, https://www.bhgrp.com/about-us/news-press.

47 *BCGEU News*, "BC Union's Shareholder Proposal Questions Thomson Reuters on Human Rights Record, Connections to ICE," 17 April 2020, https://www.bcgeu.ca/bc_union_s_shareholder_proposal_questions_thomson_reuters_on_human_rights_record_connections_to_ice.

48 Kosmas Papadopoulos, "The Long View: The Role of Shareholder Proposals in Shaping U.S. Corporate Governance (2000–2018)," *Harvard Law School Forum on Corporate Governance*, 6 February 2019, https://corpgov.law.harvard.edu/2019/02/06/the-long-view-the-role-of-shareholder-proposals-in-shaping-u-s-corporate-governance-2000-2018.

49 Ibid.

50 Cloyd, "Shareholder Activism," 7.

51 Ibid., 10.

52 Caroline Flammer, "Shareholder Activism and Firms' Disclosure of their Exposure to Climate Change," *United Nations Principles for Responsible Investing*, 25 November 2019, https://www.unpri.org

/pri-blog/shareholder-activism-and-firms-disclosure-of-their-exposure-to-climate-change-risks/5142.article.

53 Nicholls, *Mergers*, 333.

54 See Andrew W. Lo, "Efficient Markets Hypothesis," in *The New Palgrave: A Dictionary of Economics 2/e*, by Lawrence E. Blume and Steven Durlauf (New York: Palgrave McMillan, 2007), citing Paul Samuelson and Eugene Fama as originators of the concept.

55 Nicholls, *Mergers*, 333.

56 Gillan and Starks, "Evolution," 56.

57 Karl Valentini, "Hedge Fund Activism and ESG: Examining the Role of Activist Hedge Funds as Protagonists in Capital Markets," *Social Impact Research Experience (SIRE)* 61, (September 2018).

58 Ibid.

59 Institutional Shareholder Services Inc., "2019 Americas Proxy Voting Guidelines Updates," November 2018, 3, https://www.issgovernance.com.

60 Kern McPherson, "2019 Policy Guideline Updates: United States, Canada, Shareholder Initiatives, Israel," *Glass, Lewis & Co.*, 24 October 2018, https://www.glasslewis.com/2019-policy-guideline-updates-united-states-canada-shareholder-initiatives-israel.

61 Hall et al., "2018 Canadian Proxy."

62 Ibid.

63 Ibid.

64 Papadopoulos, "The Long View."

65 Cloyd, "Shareholder Activism," 3.

66 Nicholls, *Mergers,* 110.

67 Ibid.

68 British Columbia Securities Commission, "National Instrument 62–104: Take-Over Bids and Issuer Bids," 9 May 2016, https://www.bcsc.bc.ca/-/media/PWS/Resources/Securities_Law/Policies/Policy6/62104-NI-May-9-2016.pdf.

69 Hall et al., "2018 Canadian Proxy."

70 Martin Lipton et al., "Dealing with Activist Hedge Funds and Other Activist Investors," *Harvard Law School Forum on Corporate Governance,* 20 January 2020, https://corpgov.law.harvard.edu/2020/01/20/dealing-with-activist-hedge-funds-and-other-activist-investors-3.

71 Gillan and Starks, "Evolution," 68.

72 Jim Rossman et al., "Profiles of Selected Shareholder Activists," *Harvard Law School Forum on Corporate Governance,* 8 April 2019, https://corpgov.law.harvard.edu/2019/04/08/profiles-of-selected-shareholder-activists.

73 Gillan and Starks, "Evolution," 70.
74 Ibid.
75 Valentini, "Hedge Fund Activism," 17.
76 Ibid.
77 Ibid.
78 Gillan and Starks, "Evolution," 71.
79 *PR Newswire,* "TCI Fund Management Limited Announces Submission of Climate Change Shareholder Proposal to Canadian Pacific Railway Limited," 19 November 2020, https://www.prnewswire.com/news-releases/tci-fund-management-limited-announces-submission-of-climate-change-shareholder-proposal-to-canadian-pacific-railway-limited-301177108.html.
80 Valentini, "Hedge Fund Activism," 31.
81 Jyothika Grewal, George Serafeim, and Aaron Yoon, "Shareholder Activism on Sustainability Issues," SSRN, 6 July 2016, 11, https://papers.ssrn.com/sol3/papers.cfm?abstract_id=2805512
82 Valentini, "Hedge Fund Activism," 31.
83 Ibid.
84 J. Lynette DeWitt, "Impact Investing: A Sustainable Strategy for Hedge Funds," Deloitte Centre for Financial Services, 2016, https://www2.deloitte.com/us/en/pages/financial-services/articles/impact-investments-hedge-funds-esg-business.html.
85 Ibid.
86 Valentini, "Hedge Fund Activism," 35.
87 O'Kelley, Goodman, and Martin, "2019 Global & Regional Trends."
88 Hall et al., "2018 Canadian Proxy."
89 Ibid.
90 Michael Wilkins, Nicole D. Martin, and Kurt E. Forsgren, "S&P Global Ratings' Proposal for Environmental, Social, and Governance (ESG) Evaluations," *S&P Global*, 24 September 2018, https://www.spglobal.com/en/research-insights/articles/sp-global-ratings-proposal-for-environmental-social-and-governance-esg-evaluations.
91 *Moody's Investors Service,* "Announcement: Moody's: Climate Change is Forecast to Heighten US Exposure to Economic Loss Placing Short- and Long-Term Credit Pressure on US States and Local Governments," 28 November 2017, https://www.moodys.com/research/Moodys-Climate-change-is-forecast-to-heighten-US-exposure-to--PR_376056.
92 Wilkins, Martin, and Forsgren, "S&P Global Ratings."
93 Ibid.
94 Ibid.

95 State Street Global Advisors, "ESG Investing," 24 July 2019, https://www.ssga.com/international/en/institutional/ic/capabilities/esg.

96 Ibid.

97 Larry Fink, "Larry Fink's 2019 Letter to CEOs: Purpose & Profit," *BlackRock*, 2019, https://www.blackrock.com/corporate/investor-relations/2019-larry-fink-ceo-letter.

98 Svea Herbst-Bayliss, "Exclusive: Jana Liquidates Two Hedge Funds, to Focus Only on Activism," *Reuters*, 15 January 2019, https://www.reuters.com/article/us-hedgefunds-jana-exclusive-idUSKCN1P927L.

99 David French and Joshua Franklin, "Exclusive: KKR Launches Unit Focused on Impact Investing - Sources," *Reuters*, 26 April 2018, https://www.reuters.com/article/us-kkr-privateequity-investment-exclusiv-idUSKBN1HX3CA.

100 Friede, Busch, and Bassen, "ESG and Financial Performance."

101 Ibid.

102 Grewal, Serafeim, and Yoon, "Shareholder Activism."

103 Hall et al., "2018 Canadian Proxy."

104 Margie Mason and Robin McDowell, "Rape, Abuses in Palm Oil Fields Linked to Top Beauty Brands," *The Associated Press*, 17 November 2020, https://apnews.com/article/palm-oil-abuse-investigation-cosmetics-2a209d60c42bf0e8fcc6f8ea6daa11c7.

105 Witold Henisz, Tim Koller, and Robin Nuttall, "Five Ways that ESG Creates Value," *McKinsey Quarterly*, 14 November 2019, https://www.mckinsey.com/business-functions/strategy-and-corporate-finance/our-insights/five-ways-that-esg-creates-value.

106 Ibid.

107 Hall et al., "2018 Canadian Proxy."

108 Ibid.

109 Grewal, Serafeim, and Yoon, "Shareholder Activism."

110 Responsible Investment Association, "2016 Millennials, Women, and the Future of Responsible Investing Report," April 2016, 1, https://www.riacanada.ca/research/millennials-women-and-the-future-of-responsible-investing.

111 Ibid.

112 Christie Stephenson, "How Women and Millennials Will Redefine Ethical Investing," *The Globe and Mail*, 27 February 2018, https://www.theglobeandmail.com/report-on-business/rob-commentary/how-women-and-millennials-will-redefine-ethical-investing/article38131537; for more on representation in corporate boardrooms see Oludolapo Makinde,

"Gender Diversity on Corporate Boards: Much Ado About Mandatory Quotas?," chapter 3 of this book.

113 *Dentons*, "Canada's 2018 Budget Heralds Introduction of Deferred Prosecution Agreements for Corporate Wrongdoing," 16 March 2018, https://www.dentons.com/en/insights/alerts/2018/march/16/canadas-2018-budget-heralds-introduction-of-deferred-prosecution-agreements-for-corporate-wrongdoing.

114 Diana Swain, "An Economic Reality Check on SNC-Lavalin: Are 9,000 Jobs Really at Stake?" *CBC News*, 8 March 2019, https://www.cbc.ca/news/business/snc-lavalin-scandal-economics-jobs-risk-1.5047248.

115 Valentini, "Hedge Fund Activism," 12.

116 Ibid., 29.

117 Ibid.

118 Dominic Barton and Mark Wiseman, "Focusing Capital on the Long Term," *Harvard Business Review*, January 2014, https://hbr.org/2014/01/focusing-capital-on-the-long-term.

119 Valentini, "Hedge Fund Activism."

10

Avoiding Tax Avoidance as the Socially Responsible Thing to Do

Julie Liang

Corporate social responsibility (CSR) invokes powerful notions about sustainability, diversity, change, and more socially responsible business practices. Conversely, tax avoidance and paying a fair share of tax is not usually regarded as a CSR component.[1] However, as multinational corporations (MNCs) become larger and increasingly complex and powerful, their behaviour and social responsibilities with respect to taxation have garnered interest and scrutiny from governments, international organizations such as the Organisation for Economic Co-operation and Development (OECD), the media, and the general public. This chapter explores the relationship between CSR and tax avoidance, examines how aggressive tax avoidance schemes pose a social problem that should be addressed through CSR, and proposes some suggestions as to how corporations and governments can work together to mitigate this problem.

This chapter focuses on the form of tax avoidance that involves a "payment of less tax than might be required by a reasonable interpretation of a country's laws" or a "payment of tax on profits declared in a country other than where they were really earned."[2] Tax avoidance must be distinguished from the concept of tax evasion. Under Canadian law, tax evasion is a criminal offence that involves deliberately ignoring provisions of the relevant legislation to produce tax benefits. In contrast, tax avoidance is legal under Canadian law. It involves constructing tax benefits in a way that complies with the letter of the law but does not necessarily conform with the spirit or intent of the law.[3] One example of tax avoidance is Base Erosion and Profit Shifting (BEPS), as indicated by the OECD.[4] With the growth of MNCs and the economy becoming globally integrated, opportunities have opened for MNCs to greatly reduce their tax burden. BEPS involves arrangements that achieve low to no taxation by shifting profits away from the jurisdiction in which they are generated.

Examples of specific ways that MNCs engage in BEPS include transfer pricing, surplus stripping, and treaty shopping.[5] At a high level, transfer pricing involves inflating the price paid for goods and services bought by a corporation in a high-tax jurisdiction from a related company in a low-tax jurisdiction to lower the overall tax liability of the corporate group.[6] Income can also be shifted out of high-tax jurisdictions through surplus stripping, which involves payments of interest, rents, royalties, and management fees to related corporations that are located in tax havens and hold legal title to the debt, tangible property, or intellectual property.[7] Treaty shopping involves MNCs artificially setting up a business entity in a jurisdiction in which treaty benefits such as lower withholding tax rates are available, but they do not actually conduct business in that jurisdiction other than to take advantage of those treaty benefits.[8] These techniques help MNCs maximize shareholder value by minimizing income tax liability; however, the depletion of the global tax base caused by aggressive tax avoidance practices such as these poses a significant problem to the global community.[9]

This chapter comprises four parts. The first section outlines the social problem with tax avoidance and examines the relationship between CSR and tax avoidance by looking at empirical studies conducted by various scholars and academics from around the globe. The chapter then focuses on theoretical and business arguments regarding tax avoidance in conjunction with CSR approaches. The third section outlines the main aspects of responsible tax planning – governance, compliance, relationships with authorities, and transparency. It also looks toward the future, analyzing the role that both corporations and governments could play in using CSR to combat tax avoidance. Finally, the fourth section evaluates the practical considerations and limitations of using CSR to address aggressive tax avoidance behaviours.

THE SOCIAL PROBLEM WITH TAX AVOIDANCE

The main problem with BEPS is that it causes a deprivation of government resources across the globe through both decreased revenue collection and increased costs of ensuring compliance.[10] It has been calculated that global revenue losses due to profit-shifting amount to US$500 billion.[11] Governments are in charge of providing and maintaining public goods and services such as health care, education, infrastructure, public transportation, national defense, and the legal system (including the regulation of markets and industry).[12] As the payment of corporate taxes helps to fund the provision of these public goods, one inference we can make is that the quality of these public goods and services will be in jeopardy on a global scale if tax revenues cannot keep up.[13]

From a human rights perspective, governments rely on tax revenue to progressively realize economic, social, and cultural rights such as water and sanitation, as well as civil and political rights, such as access to justice, freedom of expression, and personal security.[14] Aggressive tax avoidance by corporations (and high net worth individuals) reduces the resources available to governments and forces them to raise revenues from other sources, shifting the burden to people who have significantly less ability to pay.[15] Regressive tax structures where people making less money are paying more tax would limit the effectiveness of redistribution programs, since these programs would be funded by the people that they are supposed to benefit.[16] In addition to economic inequality, gender equality is also undermined when women are forced to take on additional unpaid care (due to deteriorating public services) and disproportionately bear the burden of a regressive tax system.[17]

Another detrimental effect is a decrease in trust and respect for the law leading to a decrease in compliance, since the tax system will be generally perceived to be lacking in fairness when some wealthy taxpayers succeed in avoiding tax.[18] If aggressive tax avoidance consistently leads to tax advantages, then the corporations who usually pay their fair share of tax may follow suit and implement aggressive tax avoidance measures to make sure that they have a fair competitive playing field. If the opposite norm where corporations plan their taxes responsibly is implemented, then the competition will be fairer and there will also be more general compliance.[19]

Taxes are also an important policy tool for sustainable development, as incentives can be used to encourage investment in areas such as research and development in environmentally friendly technologies.[20] Governments also need the resources to implement and enforce environmental regulations, which is another key aspect of sustainable development.[21] Relying on external borrowing to fund public objectives will contribute to unsustainable debt, increasing the cost of borrowing for governments, and making it even more difficult to fund public expenditures and sustainability initiatives.[22] Given these social detriments, caused by aggressive tax avoidance, one might assume that MNCs that claim to be socially responsible will veer as far away from tax avoidance as possible.[23] However, empirical studies conducted within the most recent decade have shown that that is not necessarily the case. This will be examined in the following section.

In the literature on the relationship between CSR and tax avoidance, there are two competing theories on the relationship between an MNC's CSR and tax avoidance activities: corporate culture theory and risk management theory.[24] Corporate culture theory suggests that all the decisions of an MNC should reflect a "shared belief of right behaviour" and CSR engagement in areas other than tax would indicate a decrease in tax avoidance activities.[25] Under this theory, CSR and tax avoidance are substitutes, thus enhancing overall welfare because society benefits from both CSR activities and the decline in aggressive tax avoidance.[26] Risk management theory, on the other hand, argues that there is a positive correlation between CSR and tax avoidance because firms will increase other CSR activities to hedge against reputational risks that might arise from aggressive tax avoidance practices.[27] If CSR and tax avoidance are complements as suggested by risk management theory, then an MNC's intention to benefit society through CSR activities may have adverse welfare consequences in the form of underpaid tax.[28]

Empirical studies have shown mixed results, using varying proxies for CSR performance and tax avoidance. The most popular proxy for CSR performance is the Kinder, Lydenberg, Domini & Co. (KLD) rating system, which evaluates firms based on community, corporate governance, diversity, employee relations, environment, human rights, and product quality and safety.[29] Proxies used for tax avoidance include tax disputes,[30] offshore entities in a tax haven jurisdiction,[31] effective tax rate,[32] and book-tax difference.[33] An entity's effective tax rate is the percentage of actual tax paid in comparison to pre-tax profits, and book-tax difference involves looking at the difference between what a corporation reports for accounting or investment purposes versus what it reports to taxation authorities.[34]

In a 2013 study of US public firms, Chun Keung Hoi et al. concluded that firms that engage in more irresponsible CSR activities are also more aggressive in avoiding taxes, providing support for the corporate culture theory.[35] A 2016 study conducted by Roman Lanis and Grant Richardson also involving publicly listed US firms concluded that CSR and tax avoidance are inversely related, in that the higher the level of CSR performance, the lower the likelihood of tax avoidance.[36] Their additional analysis revealed that community relations and diversity are particularly important elements of CSR performance that reduce tax avoidance.[37] A study of Korean firms also concluded that CSR activities are negatively related to tax avoidance, specifically CSR activities for social services, satisfaction of employees, and contributions to economic development.[38] A 2018 study of Nigerian firms found that firms who engage in CSR related to environmental remediation generally pay more corporate taxes, but firms engaging in CSR related to poverty alleviation and educational development (which is more dominant in Nigeria) are more likely to have more aggressive tax avoidance behaviour.[39]

Conversely, other empirical studies have presented a different result. These studies support the risk management theory, which suggests that CSR and tax avoidance are complementary. Burcin Col and Saurin Patel conducted a study of US firms that opened offshore tax haven affiliates and found that these firms' KLD ratings substantially increased after these offshore entities were established.[40] They also concluded that the main areas of CSR with increased positive activities are the more visible areas of environment, diversity, and human rights, implying that the subject firms use these CSR activities to rebuild their corporate image or to hedge against the negative connotations associated with tax avoidance practices.[41] Another study conducted by M.A. Gulzar et al. of listed Chinese companies also produced a similar result, finding that corporate tax payments and CSR activities are negatively associated (tax avoidance would then be positively associated with CSR).[42] They concluded that socially responsible firms do not necessarily view paying taxes as socially responsible behaviour.[43] A more recent study published in 2019 based on a sample of 614 companies from the European Union also found that CSR performance is positively related to the level of tax avoidance, using both effective tax rate and book-tax difference as proxies.[44]

Since empirical studies provide support for both the corporate culture and risk management theories, even when they look at similar CSR ratings and use similar proxies for tax avoidance, it is not safe to assume that MNCs engaging in CSR activities will automatically refrain from aggressive tax avoidance as part of their CSR policy. In fact, tax issues are seldom mentioned as a key aspect of CSR in corporate codes of conduct,[45] especially firms with their headquarters in low-tax jurisdictions such as Bermuda and the Cayman Islands.[46] It has been argued that corporations are justified in paying fewer taxes by compensating society through investing in other CSR initiatives,[47] but as seen in the next section, there are further theoretical arguments to be made to support the proposition that MNCs should incorporate responsible tax planning as at least one aspect of their overall CSR policy.

TAX AVOIDANCE INCORPORATED INTO CSR: THEORETICAL AND PRACTICAL ARGUMENTS

One theoretical argument in favour of MNCs incorporating responsible tax planning is the corporate citizen theory. According to David Stephenson and Veselina Vracheva, it is generally agreed that "CSR firms should strive to make a profit, obey the law, be ethical, and be a good corporate citizen."[48] Good citizenship involves certain duties, responsibilities, and participation in a community.[49] Under this theory, these responsibilities are intrinsic to a corporation's very existence as a social entity.[50] It can, therefore, be argued that the duty to pay a fair share of tax as a contributing citizen of society is also intrinsic to a corporation's existence as a social entity. The corporation, as a separate legal person,[51] should be subject to the same tax responsibility as the natural person who pays tax based on income and ability to pay. The expectation of a good corporate citizen would then be to refrain from aggressive tax avoidance practices and plan their affairs in a socially responsible way.[52]

Another theoretical argument for MNCs to engage in responsible tax planning is premised on the internal morality of law, which is based on the claim that the legal system has a normative core that consists of legal principles that are influenced by morality.[53] Examples of these principles include legal certainty, equality, proportionality, and distributive justice, which includes the proposition that taxes should be levied based on ability to pay.[54] According to Hans Gribnau, CSR can be defined as corporations accepting ethical obligations beyond mere compliance with the law, and paying tax is a moral obligation fixed by an institutional decision in the form of laws.[55] The resulting argument is that CSR companies should go beyond strict compliance with the letter of the law and refrain from tax avoidance activities that appear to be against the spirit of the law and its underlying principles. For example, one basic principle in international taxation is that MNCs should pay their taxes to the place where the economic value is created.[56] Since it is highly unlikely that governments intended for their tax base to be transferred away to low-tax or tax-free jurisdictions, activities resulting in BEPS would be against the spirit of the law and the underlying moral obligation to pay tax.

A third theoretical argument for MNCs to incorporate responsible tax planning into their CSR agendas is organizational legitimacy. Organizational legitimacy involves a certain degree of consistency between stated corporate values, actual corporate activities, and the norms of acceptable behaviour in wider society.[57] The adoption of CSR tools is a good way of building legitimacy; however, companies that claim to act socially responsible when they do not meet their economic responsibilities to society may be undermining the basis of CSR from a legitimacy perspective.[58]

One example of when an organization's legitimacy came into jeopardy is the case of Starbucks in the UK.[59] From 1998–2012, Starbucks had paid corporate tax in the UK only once in fifteen years of business.[60] Total sales during that time amounted to more than £3 billion, but the total amount of taxes paid was only £8.6 million (compared to its closest competitor Costa Coffee who paid £15 million in tax for a similar volume of sales).[61] To investors and analysts, Starbucks communicated that its UK operations were profitable, but to the UK tax authorities, it reported losses.[62] Starbucks achieved this result through shifting taxable income using legal tax avoidance tools such as transfer pricing, royalty payments, and interest expense deductions.[63] While making use of these tax avoidance tools, Starbucks also claimed to be socially responsible through areas such as ethical sourcing, environmental impact, and community improvement.[64] When this ethically contradictory behaviour was revealed, Starbucks's organizational legitimacy took a hit and public backlash ensued in the form of protests and boycotts.[65] To mitigate the damage to its reputation, Starbucks announced that it would voluntarily pay £31 million in taxes.[66] This course of action can be seen in two ways: Starbucks is either taking a step towards socially responsible tax practices, or it is providing further support for risk management theory. The result is beneficial for both Starbucks, who pays the price for restoring legitimacy in the eyes of the public, and the UK government, who recoups some revenue from its previously eroded tax base.

There are also business case arguments to be made for including tax as a CSR issue. According to Arjo van Eijsden, there are five reasons for integrating tax strategies with corporate responsibility:

1 Increased compliance costs associated with the growing complexity of tax legislation enacted in response to aggressive tax avoidance;
2 The reputational risk from adverse publicity;
3 An increased risk of litigation and costs associated with being challenged by tax authorities;
4 Uncertainty with regards to actual tax liability caused by aggressive tax avoidance plans; and
5 Decreased investor confidence because of tax uncertainty, since they evaluate after-tax profit when making investment decisions.[67]

Taxes are a cost of doing business that corporations want to reduce to maximize shareholder value, but there are also business costs and risks involved with the avoidance of taxes that could also negatively affect shareholder value.[68]

A corporation's commitment to responsible tax behaviour will help its own long-term interest.[69] Paying tax can be seen as an investment by companies in the institutional environment in which they operate, supporting the development of profitable and sustainable societies.[70] Conducting business will be much easier in a peaceful and stable environment, with functioning transportation networks and infrastructure, educated and healthy workforces, and strong consumer bases with purchasing power.[71] In a study of the effects of both aggressive and responsible corporate tax strategies on corporate success with consumers, Inga Hardeck and Rebecca Hertl found that aggressive tax strategies diminish corporate success with consumers while responsible tax strategies enhance corporate success.[72] They also found that consumers had a lower willingness to pay for products sold by companies with aggressive tax avoidance strategies and these companies had a lower brand purchase intention when compared to the neutral control group.[73] These results suggest that implementing responsible tax strategies can help maintain the integrity of the corporate brand and build a relationship of trust between a corporation and its customers.

RESPONSIBLE TAX PLANNING: WHAT DOES IT LOOK LIKE?

Given the theoretical arguments proposed in this chapter, the next step is to examine what responsible tax planning would look like through the corporation's lens. In February 2018, the B Team established seven principles for corporations to follow with regard to responsible corporate tax strategies.[74] Also in 2018, the United Nations Principles of Responsible Investment (UNPRI) published a report for investors to use as a tool for engaging with companies on corporate tax disclosure practices.[75] In March 2019, CSR Europe and PwC Netherlands came together to put together "A Blueprint for Responsible and Transparent Tax Behaviour," which also breaks down responsible tax behaviour into six theme areas.[76] All three reports contain principles and guidance to help companies implement responsible tax planning, the four main themes being governance, compliance, cooperation with authorities, and transparency.

Governance

The first principle deals with internal accountability and governance, starting from the top with the board of directors, to allow for consistency for the MNC across different jurisdictions. Some specific suggestions made by the B Team with respect to this principle include:

1. Having a tax strategy and principles approved by the board;
2. Holding the board accountable for tax risk management;
3. Putting in place mechanisms to ensure awareness and adherence to the board-approved tax strategy and principles;
4. Implementing procedures to carry out risk assessments before entering into any tax planning transactions;
5. Annual reporting on tax risks;
6. Having the strategy and principles permeate throughout the corporate group; and
7. Employing qualified tax professionals with the required level of expertise.[77]

CSR Europe and PwC have identified that an increased collaboration between an organization's tax managers and the CSR department is emerging as a way to ensure consistency with the overall company sustainability strategy.[78] To be effective and credible, a tax strategy must also be aligned with the company's business vision, philosophy, mission, and values.[79] Investors can also encourage their representatives on the board of directors to articulate the process of identification and management of tax risks.[80]

A corporate tax strategy can be viewed as an implementation of corporate culture theory to achieve organizational legitimacy since the board of directors will make accountable decisions at the top regarding the tax strategy for the entire corporation or corporate group to follow, and having these decisions be consistent with other CSR decisions will help increase credibility and bolster legitimacy.[81]

Compliance

The second main theme involves compliance with tax legislation, but not mere compliance with the letter of the law. "Active tax responsibility" would require that value creation is taken into account in the context of taxation and that the purpose or the spirit of the tax law (not only the letter of law) of each operating state is followed.[82] Thus, active tax responsibility means paying the right amount of tax at the right time, in the jurisdictions where value is created, and applying reasonable interpretations of the legislation to the actual economic substance of commercial activities.[83] However, it is important to consider different forms of tax avoidance, specifically within the Canadian jurisdiction. Tax avoidance involves meeting the textual requirements of the legislation, but not necessarily the intent of the legislation. Tax planning, on the other hand, meets both the letter and intent of the legislation but is still considered to be a form of tax avoidance.[84] Under Canadian law, the common law principle that taxpayers are permitted to minimize their tax liability to a legally allowed extent has resulted in tax planning being viewed favourably by the judiciary, because it is seen as legitimate.[85] However, because instances of tax planning are highly contextual, it is not necessarily clear whether these activities would fully embrace the idea of "responsibility" promoted by international organizations, as tax planning may still be carried out in a way that disadvantages populations, as highlighted in the first section of this chapter.

The principle of compliance also suggests an undertaking not to create transactions whose sole purpose is to create a tax benefit in excess of a reasonable interpretation of the relevant legislation, regulation, or treaty.[86] Examples include avoiding the use of tax havens, artificial structures, or contracts. The implementation of this principle will be the most effective in addressing BEPS because if the taxing of profits is aligned with the economic substance of commercial activities, the jurisdiction where the economic activity takes place will not have its tax revenue shifted somewhere else where it may not be taxed at all. A real-world example of this is Iberdrola, a Spanish multinational utility company, who included the following language in its corporate tax policy: "not to use artificial structures unrelated to the Group's business for the sole purpose of reducing its tax burden, nor enter into transactions with related entities solely to erode the tax basis or to transfer profits to low-tax territories."[87] This principle also conforms with the theory of the internal morality of law, since it involves applying reasonable interpretations of the law to commercial activities with economic substance, thus complying with the spirit and intent of most income tax legislation.[88]

Relationship with Authorities

The third aspect of responsible tax planning is for corporations to develop cooperative relationships with tax authorities based on respect, transparency, and trust. Some specific actions include:

1. Establishing professional, courteous, and timely procedures for dealing with tax authorities and government officials;
2. Being responsive to enquiries;
3. Building relationships of cooperative compliance;
4. Providing full disclosure of all the relevant facts and circumstances; and
5. Entering into dialogue with tax authorities if there is significant uncertainty as to the interpretation or application of the relevant rules.[89]

In recent years, the OECD developed a "co-operative compliance framework" that recommends tax authorities and large taxpayers engage in a relationship based on transparency, cooperation, trust, and mutual understanding.[90] The authorities benefit from this relationship by efficiently allocating resources based on the risk profile of the taxpayer, and taxpayers who are more transparent can also benefit from decreased compliance costs.[91] Regularly cooperating and communicating with tax authorities will help MNCs with reducing the risk of litigation and having an uncertain tax liability, which provides some stability to shareholder value as well.[92]

A cooperative relationship with authorities can also help a company invest in its institutional environment,[93] especially with the development of technology. An example of this is Safaricom, the largest corporate taxpayer in Kenya.[94] Safaricom not only proactively engages with the

Kenyan Revenue Authority (KRA) when its tax position is unclear or may be subject to challenge, but it also worked with the KRA to develop a mobile billing and payment platform though which taxpayers can remit their tax payments to the KRA, bringing about improved efficiency, simplified processes, and enhanced convenience for taxpayers.[95] Engaging in dialogue with governments supports the development of effective tax systems, legislation, and administration.[96]

Transparency

The final principle is transparency, which is arguably the most important from a CSR perspective. The operation of this principle involves providing information about the corporation's tax approaches, strategies, and liabilities to stakeholders, including investors, employees, and the public.[97] For example, investors and shareholders have an interest in tax transparency because they need to know how much of the company's performance is based on the underlying business and how much is based on subsidies, credits, and artificially shifting profits.[98]

Examples of disclosure items include the tax strategy chosen, updates on tax issues, a corporate structure diagram that lists all the entities in the corporate group, explanations as to the existence of certain entities in low-tax jurisdictions, annual information on the MNC's overall effective tax rate as well as taxes paid to each jurisdiction, and information on tax incentives used.[99] One way to make disclosures more effective is including clarifications and context in the form of a narrative describing the approach, internal processes, and operations that support the implementation and execution of a tax strategy in greater detail.[100]

CSR Europe and PwC introduced Vodafone Group plc as an example of a company that provides annual disclosure on its tax affairs through a transparency report, which includes country-by-country tax payments with supporting narrative using non-technical language.[101] The reporting process is a collective effort between the tax, sustainability, and communications teams, with input from audit and risk committees, the chief financial officer, and the chief executive officer.[102] Having all hands on deck in the tax reporting process will allow companies to make sure that their tax-related communications are clear, credible, and consistent with their overall business vision, values, and strategy.[103] Transparency is important from a CSR perspective because it helps a corporation build a trust relationship with its stakeholders, which can lead to more business from consumers,[104] as well as a more informed public debate on the appropriate approach to responsible tax planning.[105]

Next Steps: Role of Corporations and Governments

In addition to the four aspects of responsible tax planning mentioned above, Troels Boerrild et al. give some suggestions to go above and beyond expectations.[106] One suggestion is for MNCs to develop internal systems to assess the human rights impact of any significant tax-advantageous transaction.[107] They also suggest that MNCs with operations in poorer countries and intellectual property held in low-tax jurisdictions progressively improve international equity by shifting tax liabilities out of low-tax jurisdictions and into economies with greater fiscal needs, in which the MNC is already creating value.[108] To maximize the effectiveness of CSR from a tax perspective, MNCs should incorporate these suggestions into their tax strategies. Investors of MNCs also have a role to play. By asking the MNCs questions on their tax strategy and practices, investors can help push the agenda of responsible tax behaviour and advance the conversation of increased disclosure.[109]

An important stakeholder MNCs should engage with for their responsible tax plans to work as intended is the government. According to the OECD, BEPS can be attributable to the interaction of different tax rules from different jurisdictions that lead to double non-taxation or less than single taxation.[110] Cooperation between governments would be critical to ensure that the tax base is intact for everyone to share. However, countries are usually reluctant to cede tax sovereignty to any international agency,[111] and there is no hard law in place preventing governments from engaging in tax competition to attract investment.[112]

One solution offered by the OECD is the *Multilateral Convention to Implement Tax Treaty Related Measures to Prevent Base Erosion and Profit Shifting* (MLI).[113] The MLI helps signatory countries reform their bilateral tax treaties to implement measures to address treaty-related tax avoidance issues like treaty shopping.[114] As of 23 January 2020, there are ninety-three signatories, forty-one of which have already domestically ratified, accepted, or approved of the MLI, and six other jurisdictions who have expressed intent to become a signatory.[115]

Another important aspect of the government's role is to improve the global tax system in the long run by simplifying the rules.

Governments have tended to make tax rules increasingly complicated with each response to avoidance behaviour, but according to Gribnau, continuous changes and complexity in tax law have a negative effect on the level of compliance.[116] The dynamism creates a vicious cycle of increased avoidance and more complex rules, leading to more creative forms of avoidance and more complexity to the rules to catch that one instance.[117] Therefore, to foster socially responsible compliance with tax legislation, governments have a responsibility to make it easier for MNCs to comply with both the letter of the law and with the spirit of the law. One practical difficulty to taking the next steps towards socially responsible tax behaviour is determining the proper interpretation of some legislative provisions with multiple reasonable interpretations. MNCs and governments may have to resort to litigation to solve this problem, along with discrepancies in the application of the law to specific situations, including the assessment of where value is created.

One example of current government reliance on litigation to solve problems relating to interpretation and specific tax planning actions is the Canadian context and the utilization of the General Anti-Avoidance Rule (GAAR). This rule was introduced to address tax planning that was determined to be aggressive, although still in compliance with the letter of the law.[118] As per the 2005 decision in *Canada Trustco Mortgage Co. v. Canada*, the rule can be applied if three criteria are met: the taxpayer has gained a tax benefit as a result of a transaction or series of transactions; there has been an avoidance transaction; and there has been a misuse or abuse of any provision of the *Income Tax Act*, a tax treaty, or other federal tax laws.[119] Although a specific test was set out by the court, it has been deemed vague and easily applied to both sides in a given dispute.[120] Thus, the Canadian context highlights the importance of simplifying and clarifying rules, as within the thirty-year period that the GAAR has been in application, the number of cases that have used the rule successfully is limited.[121]

CONCLUSION

Aggressive tax avoidance is a social problem that can have serious human rights and sustainable development implications, and the solution is for socially responsible corporate taxpayers to incorporate responsible tax planning into their daily operations and high-level decision-making. Currently, the relationship between CSR firms and tax avoidance practices is unclear, since empirical studies have shown that there are firms who treat CSR and tax avoidance as substitutes, following corporate culture theory, and there are also firms who treat CSR as a means of hedging against the reputational risk associated with aggressive tax avoidance. Various theoretical arguments support the proposition to incorporate responsible tax strategies into overall CSR strategies, including the corporate citizen theory, the moral obligation to pay one's fair share, organizational legitimacy, and enhancing corporate reputation, as well as the business case that paying tax will invest in the company's long-term institutional and business environments. This chapter does not address the situation where a corporation avoids tax by making charitable donations, although it has been suggested that aggressive tax planning practices potentially cost the state much more than it gains from philanthropic corporate gestures.[122] Some may argue that they prefer to have corporations investing their money in other worthwhile initiatives, and governments are not trustworthy enough to achieve the objectives that are important to them. It could also be argued that the more philanthropic corporations are not doing any net harm to society by simultaneously engaging in tax avoidance, but would it be desirable for these corporations to oversee resource allocation when they are already immensely powerful on the global stage? This chapter also assumes that governments can effectively allocate resources, at least in the provision and maintenance of public goods, but corrupt government officials who misappropriate taxpayer money present another issue that is beyond the scope of this chapter.

Responsible tax planning involves holding directors accountable for tax strategies, complying with tax laws on an economic substance basis, being cooperative with tax authorities, and being transparent with stakeholders about tax-related matters. In taking steps towards achieving socially responsible tax planning, corporations, investors, and governments all have a role to play. Corporations should incorporate responsible tax strategies into their CSR objectives, their annual reporting, and their daily operations, with everyone within the organization on the same page from a tax strategy and implementation perspective. Consistency between CSR values and tax practices will help businesses increase corporate credibility and gain trust from various stakeholders, including consumers, investors, and authorities. Investors can help by asking the right questions about tax strategy and transparency and by holding corporations accountable for inappropriate tax practices. Governments can help facilitate the implementation of responsible tax practices by engaging more actively with corporations, communicating expectations more efficiently, and modifying laws to simplify interpretation. Together, corporate law and sustainability can work together to bring about a result that will benefit everyone.

NOTES

1 Burcin Col and Saurin Patel, "Going to Haven? Corporate Social Responsibility and Tax Avoidance," *Journal of Business Ethics* 154, no. 4 (February 2019): 1033–50.
2 David Stephenson and Veselina Vracheva, "Corporate Social Responsibility and Tax Avoidance: A Literature Review and Directions for Future Research," SSRN, 13 November 2015, https://papers.ssrn.com/sol3/papers.cfm?abstract_id=2756640. Illegal tax evasion is clearly problematic and wrong, but this is a legal and less a "CSR" issue, thus this chapter does not address illegal tax evasion.
3 Ibid.
4 See OECD, *Action Plan on Base Erosion and Profit Shifting* (Paris: OECD Publishing 2013), 8.
5 See Jinyan Li, Arthur Cockfield, and J. Scott Wilkie, *International Taxation in Canada: Principles and Practices*, 3rd ed. (Markham: LexisNexis Canada 2014).
6 Ibid., 371.
7 Ibid., 370.
8 Ibid., 372
9 OECD, *Action Plan,* 8.
10 Ibid.
11 Laszlo Goerke, "Corporate Social Responsibility and Tax Avoidance," *Journal of Public Economic Theory* 21, no. 2 (February 2019): 310.
12 Roman Lanis and Grant Richardson, "Is Corporate Social Responsibility Performance Associated with Tax Avoidance?" *Journal of Business Ethics* 127, no. 2 (March 2015): 442.
13 See ibid.
14 Juan Pablo Bohoslavsky, "Tax-Related Illicit Financial Flows and Human Rights," *Journal of Financial Crime* 25, no. 3 (Summer 2018): 754.
15 Ibid., 755.
16 Ibid.
17 Ibid.

18 Robert McMechan, *Economic Substance and Tax Avoidance: An International Perspective* (Toronto: Carswell 2013), 43.
19 Ibid.
20 The B Team, "A New Bar for Responsible Tax," 9 February 2018, 3, https://bteam.org/assets/reports/A-New-Bar-for-Responsible-Tax.pdf.
21 Lanis and Richardson, "Corporate Social Responsibility," 442.
22 Bohoslavsky, "Tax-Related," 757.
23 This is an instance of corporate culture theory, to be discussed further the following section. See Col and Patel, "Going to Haven," 1034.
24 Ibid.
25 Ibid.
26 Goerke, "Corporate Social Responsibility," 311–12.
27 Col and Patel, "Going to Haven," 1034.
28 Goerke, "Corporate Social Responsibility," 312.
29 See Col and Patel, "Going to Haven," and Lanis and Richardson, "Corporate Social Responsibility."
30 Lanis and Richardson, "Corporate Social Responsibility," 440.
31 Col and Patel, "Going to Haven."
32 M.A. Gulzar et al., "Does Corporate Social Responsibility Influence Corporate Tax Avoidance of Chinese Listed Companies?" *Sustainability* 10, no. 12 (Winter 2018): 4549.
33 Chun Keung Hoi, Qiang Wu, and Hao Zhang, "Is Corporate Social Responsibility (CSR) Associated with Tax Avoidance? Evidence from Irresponsible CSR Activities," *The Accounting Review* 88, no. 6 (November 2013): 2025–59.
34 See Gulzar et al., "Corporate Tax Avoidance," and Stephenson and Vracheva, "Tax Avoidance," 6.
35 Hoi, Wu, and Zhang, "CSR Associated," 2051.
36 Lanis and Richardson, "Corporate Social Responsibility," 454.
37 Ibid.
38 SungJong Park, "Corporate Social Responsibility and Tax Avoidance: Evidence from Korean Firms," *Journal of Applied Business Research; Laramie* 33, no. 6 (October 2017): 1067.
39 Asian Umobong and Uche T. Agburuga, "Corporate Tax and Corporate Social Responsibility of Firms in Nigeria," *Research Journal of Finance and Accounting* 9, no. 10 (Summer 2018): 8.
40 Col and Patel, "Going to Haven," 1034.
41 Ibid., 1035.
42 Gulzar et al., "Corporate Tax Avoidance," 10.
43 Ibid.

44 Yosra Makni Fourati, Houda Affes, and Ikram Trigui, "Do Socially Responsible Firms Pay Their Right Part of Taxes? Evidence from the European Union," *Journal of Applied Business and Economics* 21, no. 1 (March 2019): 40.
45 Stephenson and Vracheva, "Tax Avoidance," 9.
46 Lutz Preuss, "Tax Avoidance and Corporate Social Responsibility: You Can't Do Both, Or Can You?" *Corporate Governance: International Journal of Business in Society* 10, no. 4 (Summer 2010): 365–74.
47 See Fariz Huseynov and Bonnie K. Klamm, "Tax Avoidance, Tax Management and Corporate Social Responsibility," *Journal of Corporate Finance*, 18, no. 4 (September 2012): 804–27.
48 Stephenson and Vracheva, "Tax Avoidance," 5.
49 Domènec Melé, "Corporate Social Responsibility Theories," in Andrew Crane et al., eds., *The Oxford Handbook of Corporate Social Responsibility* (Oxford University Press 2008), 26.
50 Ibid.
51 Reuven S. Avi-Yonah, "Corporate Social Responsibility and Strategic Tax Behavior," in Wolfgang Schön, ed., *Tax and Corporate Governance* (Berlin: Springer 2008): 190.
52 Ibid., 184.
53 Hans Gribnau, "Corporate Social Responsibility and Tax Planning: Not by Rules Alone," *Social & Legal Studies* 24, no. 2 (Summer 2015): 241.
54 Ibid.
55 Ibid., 228, 241.
56 Reijo Knuutinen, "Corporate Social Responsibility, Taxation and Aggressive Tax Planning," *Nordic Tax Journal*, no. 1 (May 2014): 54.
57 See Preuss, "Tax Avoidance," 366.
58 Ibid.
59 Katherine Campbell and Duane Helleloid, "Starbucks: Social Responsibility and Tax Avoidance," *Journal of Accounting Education* 37, (December 2016): 38–60.
60 Ibid.
61 Sabina Mexis and Pablo Caballero, "Socially Responsible Taxation: Smelling the Coffee," Ontario Bar Association, July 2013, http://www.oba.org/en/pdf/sec_news_tax_jul13_mex_cof.pdf.
62 Campbell and Helleloid, "Starbucks," 41.
63 Ibid., 42.
64 Ibid., 43.
65 Ibid.
66 Mexis and Caballero, "Smelling the Coffee," 2.

67 Arjo van Eijsden, "The Relationship between Corporate Responsibility and Tax: Unknown and Unloved," EC *Tax Review* 22, no. 1 (February 2013): 58.
68 Ibid.
69 Troels Boerrild et al., *Getting to Good – Towards Responsible Corporate Tax Behaviour* (UK: ActionAid, Christian Aid, and Oxfam International, 2015).
70 Ibid.
71 Ibid.
72 Inga Hardeck and Rebecca Hertl, "Consumer Reactions to Corporate Tax Strategies: Effects on Corporate Reputation and Purchasing Behavior," *Journal of Business Ethics* 123, no. 2 (Summer 2014): 309.
73 Ibid., 322
74 The B Team, "New Bar"; see also The B Team, "Our Mission," accessed 26 August 2021, http://www.bteam.org/who-we-are/mission.
75 UN Principles for Responsible Investment, "Evaluating and Engaging on Corporate Tax Transparency: An Investor Guide," 17 May 2018, https://www.unpri.org/Uploads/t/r/l/PRI_Evaluating-and-engaging-on-corporate-tax-transparency_Investor-guide.pdf.
76 CSR Europe and PwC Netherlands, "A Blueprint for Responsible and Transparent Tax Behaviour," March 2019.
77 The B Team, "New Bar," 5.
78 CSR Europe and PwC Netherlands, "A Blueprint," 13.
79 Ibid.
80 United Nations Principles for Responsible Investment, "Encouraging Responsible Tax Behaviour: What Investors Need to Know," 26 April 2019, https://www.unpri.org/tax-avoidance/encouraging-responsible-tax-behaviour-what-investors-need-to-know/4346.article.
81 Preuss, "Tax Avoidance," 366.
82 Knuutinen, "Corporate Social Responsibility," 54.
83 The B Team, "New Bar," 5.
84 Canada Revenue Agency, "Tax Avoidance," last modified 23 December 2013, https://www.canada.ca/en/revenue-agency/corporate/about-canada-revenue-agency-cra/tax-alert/tax-avoidance.html.
85 Mary Anna Bueschkens and Benjamin Mann, "Canada and the GAAR: A Catch-all for Abusive/Avoidance Tax Planning," *Trusts & Trustees* 25, no. 1 (February 2019): 76.
86 The B Team, "New Bar," 5.
87 CSR Europe and PwC Netherlands, "A Blueprint," 12.
88 Gribnau, "Tax Planning," 235.
89 The B Team, "New Bar," 7.

90 CSR Europe and PwC Netherlands, "A Blueprint," 19.
91 OECD, *Co-operative Compliance: A Framework – From Enhanced Relationship to Co-operative Compliance* (Paris: OECD Publishing 2013), 41.
92 van Eijsden, "Unknown and Unloved," 59.
93 Boerrild et al., *Getting to Good*, 11.
94 The B Team, "The B Team Responsible Tax Principles in Action: Safaricom's Efforts to Promote Tax Compliance in Kenya," 21 October 2019, https://bteam.org/our-thinking/news/the-b-team-responsible-tax-principles-in-action-safaricoms-efforts-to-promote-tax-compliance-in-kenya.
95 Ibid.
96 The B Team, "New Bar," 8.
97 Ibid.
98 United Nations Principles for Responsible Investment, "Encouraging."
99 The B Team, "New Bar," 8.
100 CSR Europe and PwC Netherlands, "A Blueprint," 24.
101 Ibid., 26.
102 Ibid.
103 Ibid., 24.
104 Hardeck and Hertl, "Consumer Reactions."
105 The B Team, "New Bar," 14.
106 Boerrild et al., *Getting to Good*.
107 Ibid., 28.
108 Ibid., 15–16.
109 Athanasia Karananou and Anastasia Guha, "Engagement Guidance on Corporate Tax Responsibility," UN Principles for Responsible Investment, 2015, 32, https://www.unpri.org/download?ac=5601. For more on the role investors can play, see Bikaramjit S. Sandhu, "The Return of Robin Hood: A New Kind of Shareholder Activism," chapter 9 of this book.
110 OECD, *Action Plan*, 10.
111 Jinyan Li, Arthur Cockfield, and J. Scott Wilkie, *International Taxation in Canada: Principles and Practices*, 4th ed. (Markham: LexisNexis Canada 2018), 474.
112 See ibid., 474–5.
113 OECD, "Multilateral Convention to Implement Tax Treaty Related Measures to Prevent Base Erosion and Profit Shifting," 2019, https://www.oecd.org/tax/treaties/multilateral-convention-to-implement-tax-treaty-related-measures-to-prevent-BEPS.pdf.
114 Li, Cockfield, and Wilkie, *International Taxation*, 4th ed., 445.
115 OECD, "Multilateral Convention."
116 Gribnau, "Tax Planning," 234.

117 See ibid.

118 Bueschkens and Mann, "GAAR," 76.

119 Ibid., 76.

120 Benjamin T. Kujinga, "Factors that Limit the Efficacy of General Anti-Avoidance Rules in Income Tax Legislation: Lessons from South Africa, Australia, and Canada," *The Comparative and International Law Journal of Southern Africa* 47, no. 3 (November 2014): 446–7.

121 Bueschkens and Mann, "GAAR," 91.

122 A 2011 study of Israeli public companies concluded that the state's tax loss resulting from tax avoidance practices far exceeds the public benefit from corporate donations: Moran Harari, Ofer Sitbon, and Ronit Donyets-Kedar, "Aggressive Tax Planning and Corporate Social Responsibility in Israel," *Accountancy Business and the Public Interest* (2013): 34, 43.

11

Closing the Accountability Gap? Early Lessons from the Canadian Ombudsperson for Responsible Enterprise

Erica Sandhu

On 17 January 2018, the Canadian federal government formally announced the creation of the Canadian Ombudsperson for Responsible Enterprise (CORE). This position was created in response to decades-long criticism regarding the misconduct of Canadian corporations operating abroad, specifically those in the extractives sector. As per the government's 2018 announcement, the mandate of the CORE is "to investigate human rights abuses by Canadian companies operating abroad in the oil and gas, mining and garment sectors."[1] This independent watchdog was described as the first of its kind, with the power to independently investigate companies without their prior authorization.

The initial response to the CORE was immensely positive. Civil society groups had been strongly pushing for the creation of an ombudsperson to close the accountability gap, as corporations often face minimal consequences for their actions abroad. The positive response, however, soon turned into criticism as months went by without the government filling the position or taking further action. Finally, on 8 April 2019, almost fifteen months after the initial announcement, the federal government reported that it had appointed Sheri Meyerhoffer for the CORE position.[2] As of August 2021, the CORE has the mandate to review alleged human rights abuses arising from a Canadian company's operations abroad, make and monitor recommendations, recommend trade measures for companies that do not cooperate in good faith, and report publicly throughout the process.[3]

To the dismay of critics and civil society groups, the CORE has a significantly limited scope than what was originally announced. Specifically, in an Order in Council dated 8 April 2019, the CORE was merely set out as a "special adviser to the Minister for International Trade."[4] In July 2019, all fourteen civil society and labour union representatives sitting on the Multi-stakeholder Advisory Body on Responsible Business Conduct (which was created alongside the CORE) unanimously decided to resign in protest as the Canadian government had not fulfilled its commitment to create an independent ombudsperson.[5] In September 2019, a more recent Order in Council confirmed the mandate of the CORE as follows:

1 Promote the implementation of the UN Guiding Principles and the OECD Guidelines;
2 Advise Canadian companies on their practices and policies with regard to responsible business conduct;
3 Review a complaint that is submitted by or on behalf of an individual, organization, or community concerning an alleged human rights abuse where the abuse allegedly occurred after the day on which the first Ombudsperson is appointed;
4 Review, on the Ombudsperson's own initiative, an alleged human rights abuse where the abuse allegedly occurred after the day on which the first Ombudsperson is appointed;
5 Offer informal mediation services; and
6 Provide advice to the Minister on any matter relating to their mandate, including issues related to the responsible business conduct of Canadian companies operating abroad.[6]

This chapter aims to provide an analysis of the CORE and early lessons learned from the challenges in its implementation. In the first section, I offer brief context on the history and human rights concerns of Canadian companies operating abroad, and provide an overview of the CORE's predecessor, the Corporate Social Responsibility (CSR) Counsellor, and its limitations. Next, I discuss the judicial and non-judicial mechanisms that exist alongside the CORE. By identifying the shortcomings of each, I argue that an accountability gap still exists and that the implementation of the CORE or its equivalent is necessary to help fill this gap. In the second section, I argue that for the CORE to truly be effective and address the existing accountability gap, it must be independent, mandatory, have broad investigative powers, and have the power to issue a range of remedies. If the CORE is not equipped with these powers moving forward, it will be a hollow body, indistinguishable from its predecessor and the existing judicial and non-judicial mechanisms that currently exist to address corporate misconduct.

ISSUE OF CANADIAN CORPORATIONS ABROAD AND HUMAN RIGHTS

To advance the case that the ombudsperson body created by the Canadian federal government needs to be equipped with wide-ranging powers, some context is important. Ethical questions regarding the behaviour of Canadian extractive companies in developing nations have been garnering attention since the late 1990s.[7] Human rights and other abuses committed by Canadian companies abroad have become an unfortunate reality, or, as some have said, the "cost of doing business."[8] Further, while most attention has been focused on the extractives sector, as it accounts for most acts of corporate wrongdoing, it is also important to recognize that human rights as well as environmental and other abuses are present across a range of other industries.[9]

Canadian-headquartered mining and mineral exploration companies account for 31 per cent of global exploration expenditures, and over 50 per cent of the world's publicly listed mining exploration and mining companies are headquartered in Canada.[10] These 1,500 Canadian companies have operations in over one hundred countries.[11] Allegations against Canadian companies abroad have been extensive and include environmental issues such as contamination and effects on human health, violations of failing to obtain "free, prior, and informed consent" with Indigenous communities, gross human rights violations committed by companies' security personnel, and serious labour violations, including the use of slave labour.[12] A 2009 report by the Canadian Centre for the Study of Resource Conflict found that since 1999, there were 171 incidents involving international mining and exploration companies carrying out unethical practices, environmental degradation, community conflict, and human rights abuses.[13] Canada was responsible for 33 per cent of total violations, with four times the number of incidents as Australia and India (which accounted for 8 per cent), followed by the United Kingdom (UK) and the United States (4 per cent each). Most of these incidents took place in Latin America (32 per cent) followed by Sub-Saharan Africa (24 per cent).[14] A report from the Justice and Accountability Project echoes these findings, reporting that between years 2000–15, Canadian companies operating in Latin America were responsible for forty-four deaths and over four hundred non-workplace related injuries.[15]

Based on these statistics, it is apparent that Canadian companies operating abroad – specifically those in the extractives sector – have been committing significant wrongdoing in a manner disproportionate to other countries. Because of this, there is a need for an ombudsperson body that has teeth or, in other words, is equipped with wide-ranging powers. Before describing an ideal ombudsperson, I will provide further context. First, I will address the shortcomings of the CSR Counsellor, Canada's previous response to corporate wrongdoing. Second, I analyze the existing judicial and non-judicial processes that exist in Canada to address corporate accountability.

The CSR Counsellor: CORE's Predecessor

Canada's previous response to addressing human rights abuses committed by Canadian companies abroad was the Office of the Extractive Sector CSR Counsellor. This predecessor to the CORE was introduced in 2009 as part of the federal government's strategy on CSR for the Canadian extractive sector operating abroad. The strategy, "Building the Canadian Advantage: A CSR Strategy for the International Extractive Sector," was developed in response to stakeholder pressure and was informed by consultations with civil society, industry, and other actors.[16]

As set out in the 2009 strategy, the CSR Counsellor was appointed by the Governor in Council and reported directly to the Minister of International Trade.[17] Its mandate related exclusively to Canadian extractive companies operating abroad. Duties of the CSR Counsellor were limited to the review of CSR practices of these companies and advising stakeholders on the implementation of CSR performance guidelines. The review process included five stages: initial assessment, informal mediation, fact finding, access to formal mediation, and reporting.[18] Importantly, the CSR Counsellor would only undertake reviews with the consent of the parties involved.[19] Requests for review could be initiated by individuals, groups, or communities who believed that they were or could be adversely affected by activities of a Canadian extractive company operating abroad, as well as from extractive companies that believed they were the target of unfounded allegations regarding their conduct abroad.[20] The CSR Counsellor's mandate did not include the power to independently review the activities of a Canadian company on its own initiative. Further, the CSR Counsellor was not empowered to make binding legislative, policy, or other recommendations; create new performance standards; or formally mediate between parties.

In 2014, Canada launched an updated policy to provide a "more robust role" for the CSR Counsellor.[21] This updated CSR strategy, "Doing Business the Canadian Way: A Strategy to Advance Corporate Social Responsibility in Canada's Extractive Sector Abroad" reportedly "refocused the role of the CSR counsellor and strengthened the Office's mandate."[22] Specifically, the CSR Counsellor was now empowered to work closely with Canada's National Contact Point (NCP) for the Organisation for Economic Co-operation and Development's (OECD) Guidelines for Multinational Enterprises on responsible business conduct.[23] If formal mediation was required, the CSR Counsellor could refer parties to the NCP where they could then engage in the OECD dispute resolution process (discussed further below).

An overview of the criticism and limitations of the CSR Counsellor role provides a clearer understanding of why the CSR Counsellor was discontinued and replaced with the CORE. The CSR Counsellor faced criticism from the outset due to its extremely limited mandate. Penelope Simons has referred to the CSR Counsellor as a "toothless dispute mechanism" and civil society groups labelled it as a "bogus, PR job."[24] The review process, as mentioned above, was completely voluntary and lacked independent powers. It, therefore, did not provide an effective dispute resolution mechanism. Further, during its nine-year tenure, the CSR Counsellor only received a handful of complaints and failed to resolve a single dispute between mining companies and victims of corporate wrongdoing.[25]

According to the registry of requests for review, which provides a record of the requests received and registered by the office of the CSR Counsellor, there were six complaints during the CSR Counsellor's tenure, with the first one in 2011 and last in 2013.[26] All six requests for review were initiated by individuals abroad alleging wrongdoing by Canadian extractive companies. The first complaint and request for review involved a mining union and workers accusing Excellon Resources Inc., a Vancouver-based company at the time, of human rights abuses.[27] The CSR Counsellor received the request in January 2011 and closed it shortly after (in April 2011) as the company refused to participate in the process.[28] A review of the five subsequent requests shows that they were generally closed one to five months within receipt of the initial request and without any resolution. A complaint against First Quantum, another Vancouver-based company, further reflects the CSR Counsellor's ineffectiveness. This complaint was filed in August 2011 by a community in Mauritania and specifically concerned labour and consultation issues, as well as concern that there was no existing company grievance mechanism at the company's project site.[29] First Quantum reported to the CSR Counsellor that a grievance mechanism was available 3.9 kilometres away from the mine site at the company's liaison office. The CSR Counsellor closed the case and referred the community to First Quantum's grievance office. In a follow-up investigation by MiningWatch Canada, it was found that no grievance mechanism existed, and the community's complaint was never addressed.[30] This example reflects the serious limitations of the CSR Counsellor, namely the voluntary participation, lack of independent powers, and inability to provide effective dispute resolution and remedies.

Further, the updated 2014 policy, which aimed to expand the CSR Counsellor's mandate, had little impact as the CSR Counsellor still lacked substantive powers. As mentioned above, the 2014 policy "refocused" the role of the CSR Counsellor. Specifically, the 2014 changes allowed the CSR Counsellor to refer parties to Canada's NCP for the OECD Guidelines on responsible business conduct.[31] The OECD NCPs are voluntary, non-judicial grievance mechanisms, and as I will discuss below, just as toothless as the CSR Counsellor. As the NCP does not provide any additional investigative authority, the 2014 policy changes did not enhance the role of the CSR Counsellor. On 18 May 2018, the CSR Counsellor ended its mandate,[32] as the government had earlier announced that it would be replaced with the new CORE position.

Existing Judicial and Non-Judicial Mechanisms and their Limitations

Independent from the CSR Counsellor and CORE, there are other judicial and non-judicial mechanisms to which victims of Canadian corporate wrongdoing can bring their complaints; specifically, company-created grievance mechanisms, the OECD National Contact Point, and Canadian courts. Though non-judicial mechanisms such as state-enhanced company grievance mechanisms or reformed NCPs may have potential, in their current form they have failed to provide meaningful remedies for victims. Judicial mechanisms have recently shown that they may provide opportunities for achieving justice, but significant questions persist about the extent to which they can address corporate wrongdoing. In other words, the accountability gap still exists and for CORE to be meaningful, it must provide more than these existing mechanisms. What follows is an overview of company-created grievance mechanisms, the OECD National Contact Points, and how victims may bring their claims to Canadian courts, along with the shortcomings of each.

COMPANY-CREATED GRIEVANCE MECHANISMS

In the absence of any government body, individuals and communities affected by human rights abuses committed by Canadian companies abroad are forced to turn to grievance mechanisms offered by the companies themselves. These grievance mechanisms are generally referred to as company-created operational-level grievance mechanisms (OGMs).[33]

OGMs are non-state, non-judicial grievance mechanisms through which companies receive complaints and provide dispute resolution or remedies at the operational or project level to those who have suffered human rights abuses or other harms because of the company's operations.[34] OGMs have been endorsed by the United Nations Guiding Principles on Business and Human Rights (Guiding Principles).[35] In particular, Guiding Principle 29 (GP 29) states that "to make it possible for grievances to be addressed early and remediated directly, business enterprises should establish or participate in effective operational-level grievance mechanisms for individuals and communities who may be adversely impacted."[36] As set out in the commentary to GP 29, these mechanisms "need not require that a complaint or grievance amount to an alleged human rights abuse before it can be raised, but specifically aim to identify any legitimate concerns of those who may be adversely impacted."[37] In other words, OGMs are encouraged to address any degree of complaint, whether it is a gross human rights violation or a minor issue.

To provide a specific example, Barrick Gold Corporation, the largest gold mining company in the world, established one of the first OGMs at the Porgera mine in Papua New Guinea to offer reparations to women who had been sexually assaulted by company security guards and employees.[38] This OGM, however, was grossly inadequate and attracted significant criticism as the ability of the claimants to receive remedy was conditional upon them waiving their legal rights to sue Barrick in any jurisdiction in the world.[39] In 2018, a MiningWatch report reviewed another OGM for Barrick's North Mara Gold Mine in Tanzania and noted that the process lacked transparency, was procedurally unfair, did not have legitimacy, and was used by the mine to evade legal action on behalf of victims.[40]

The consensus on OGMs is that, especially in their earliest forms, they have been inadequate when it comes to addressing human rights abuses and providing remedies and justice for victims. However, emerging literature seeks to improve upon the initial failures of OGMs by suggesting improvements, such as an increased state role in ensuring access and effectiveness of non-state-based grievance mechanisms and placing the onus on the non-state entities themselves to ensure these processes are cooperative, transparent, rights compatible, and equitable.[41] The Annex of the United Nations General Assembly Human Rights Council report on non-state-based mechanisms for corporate accountability provides a detailed accounting of how these aims might be achieved.[42]

OECD NATIONAL CONTACT POINTS

Unlike OGMs, the OECD NCPs are state-based grievance mechanisms that exist to help hold corporations around the world to account for their actions.[43] Like OGMs, they are non-judicial in nature. States that adhere to the OECD Guidelines for Multinational Enterprises commit to establishing an NCP. The NCPs are then tasked with implementing and promoting the OECD Guidelines, as well as handling complaints regarding non-compliance, thus playing "both a preventative proactive role and a reactive remedial one."[44] The OECD Guidelines cover all areas of business responsibility and, therefore, are not solely focused on human rights. According to the OECD, the NCP's handling of cases is a three-step process.[45] First, there is an initial assessment where the NCP evaluates whether the complaint warrants further examination. Second, if the complaint is accepted, the NCP offers dialogue, mediation, and conciliation services to both parties. Third, the NCP will publish a statement regarding the issues in the case and the outcomes.

Scholars have acknowledged that NCP statements can enable a corporation to change its practices and stop human rights abuses through "naming and shaming" as the statements are made public.[46] Apart from this, however, the NCPs are arguably toothless and rarely result in remedies for victims.[47] For example, NCPs cannot award financial compensation, cannot impose sanctions, and cannot compel parties to engage in mediation or conciliation.[48] Like the CSR Counsellor discussed above, NCPs provide little for the actual victims of corporate misconduct. As Mona Paré and Tate Chong point out, "the inability to compel participation from business and provide remedies leads to a lack of confidence in the mechanism."[49]

MiningWatch Canada, a civil society group, was involved in seven cases brought to the Canadian NCP between 2005–13 involving Canadian companies.[50] They identified several issues with the NCP process of handling complaints. With regards to the NCPs initial assessment, MiningWatch reported that the NCP often dismissed cases on "dubious and non-transparent grounds."[51] Further, during the second stage (mediation and conciliation), MiningWatch identified a serious power imbalance between the complainants and companies as the latter would send their legal team over to deal with the process and the former were unrepresented and often faced considerable language barriers. Finally, the organization highlighted that the statements issued by the NCP have been harmful to victims, resulting in a loss of trust "in the ability of the Canadian NCP to carry out its function as a grievance mechanism in a professional, equitable, and unbiased manner."[52]

There is potential that a reform of Canada's NCP to align with the best practices of the most effective NCPs might lead to better outcomes. In 2011, a report by the European Center for Constitutional and Human Rights found that the UK's NCP was an example of how NCP can be most effective and transparent in dealing with complaints. They found that their use of an external mediator agreed upon by both parties allowed for an impartial process. The NCP also refrained from commenting on the case content and did not dictate the mediation process. It was also found that the UK's NCP had detailed binding rules for the complaint procedure that helped to ensure a level of practicability of outcomes. The UK's NCP also maintained a high level of transparency towards the public as well as the participants themselves and ensured relevant information was shared with the parties in a prompt manner.[53] If Canada's NCP is able to reach or even exceed the standard of the UK's NCP, there may be a chance of it being an effective means of resolution that the Canadian government can support more fully, though the issue of corporations being unwilling to voluntarily participate in the process remains.

THE COURTS

When OGMs and NCPs fail to provide any remedy for victims of Canadian corporate misconduct abroad, parties may turn to Canadian courts and file civil claims as a last resort. These transnational lawsuits, however, face significant hurdles in Canadian courts for multiple reasons.

First, plaintiffs must establish that a Canadian court has the jurisdiction to hear the case, proving that there is a substantial connection between the plaintiff's case and the province or territory over which the court presides.[54] Even if a court has the jurisdiction to hear the case, it is within the court's discretion to decline to exercise its jurisdiction because of the legal principle of *forum non conveniens*.[55] According to *forum non conveniens*, a court can dismiss a claim if it decides that another court is better positioned to hear the case. In the majority of claims brought by victims of human rights abuses by Canadian companies operating abroad, corporate defendants have argued that the host state (i.e., state in which the abuses occurred) is a more appropriate venue to hear the case. The foreign plaintiffs thus bear the difficult burden of proving that the court in their home state is unable to provide them with a fair trial. For example, *Das v. George Weston Limited* involved foreign plaintiffs from Bangladesh who brought a class action against Loblaws,[56] a Canadian company whose workers were killed in a building collapse. In that case, the Ontario Court of Appeal declined jurisdiction and held that Bangladeshi law applied to the plaintiffs' claims.[57] Foreign plaintiffs are faced with an additional challenge owing to the legal structure of multinational corporations that they are claiming against. Due to the "corporate veil" doctrine that treats parent companies and their subsidiaries as separate legal entities, the former can be shielded from liability.[58] Alternatively, plaintiffs can argue that the parent company is personally liable for the actions that occurred abroad; however, this is also an issue that has not yet been settled.

Another challenge that foreign plaintiffs have faced when attempting to hold Canadian corporations legally accountable for wrongs committed abroad is that Canadian courts historically had not recognized private causes of action for breaches of international legal norms (i.e., customary international law) such as torture and slavery.[59] Even if customary international law does create private law remedies, there is the further question of whether customary international law applies to corporations.[60] Each of these questions were recently before the Supreme Court of Canada (SCC), in *Nevsun Resources Ltd v. Araya* (*Nevsun*).[61]

The case involves allegations against Nevsun Resources Ltd, a Vancouver-based company, for gross human rights abuses at its Eritrean mine. A group of Eritrean plaintiffs are claiming damages against Nevsun alleging that through its Eritrean subsidiary, Nevsun committed gross human rights violations including forced labour, torture, slavery, and crimes against humanity.[62] The plaintiff's claims are based in customary international law. The British Columbia Court of Appeal rejected Nevsun's arguments and upheld the BC Supreme Court decision, which dismissed Nevsun's forum application and their application that the customary international law claims were "bound to fail."[63] The SCC agreed with this decision, finding that customary international law was part of Canadian law that must apply to all Canadian corporations and, therefore, Nevsun can be sued in Canadian court for their breach of international law.[64] The decision has been regarded as a significant victory for human rights, setting the precedent that Canadian companies who commit human rights violations abroad can be held accountable within the Canadian court system. While only time can determine whether these types of complaints will lead to substantive justice for victims, the court system has an increased potential to be a meaningful arena in which to address corporate human rights abuses.

In sum, existing non-judicial mechanisms including OGMs and NCPs are largely inadequate when it comes to addressing the human rights abuses of Canadian companies abroad. While the *Nevsun* decision provides hope that plaintiffs will be able to achieve justice under the Canadian judicial system, it remains to be seen whether this will lead to positive outcomes for victims. The limitations and shortcomings of these existing mechanisms have created an accountability gap and environment of corporate impunity. Thus, there is an important role for the CORE to fill, but only if it is equipped with the necessary powers.

CORE: WHAT IT NEEDS TO BE EFFECTIVE

Ombudspersons are a common feature in most democracies and institutions, as "a broader association of an ombudsperson with accountability and the protection of human rights has developed over the years."[65] Ombudspersons are now identified as a "hallmark of good governance" in a variety of public, private, national, or international institutions.[66] Specifically, it is the independence and accountability that gives an ombudsperson legitimacy. Further, although ombudspersons are not fully judicial bodies and their remedial powers are usually recommendatory rather than binding, they provide a "cheap, flexible and accessible" means of redress.[67] Civil society groups and non-governmental organizations had been pushing for an ombudsperson to oversee Canadian companies operating abroad for almost a decade, so when the government made the announcement in 2018 regarding the creation of the CORE, the initial response was warm. However, as previously discussed, industry groups have been skeptical whether the CORE is necessary considering that other institutions already exist.[68] As I have outlined, these existing judicial and non-judicial mechanisms have significant limitations, and an accountability gap remains.

The federal government has displayed reluctance in going as far as needed to address this gap, with industry pressure being a central factor in this reluctance. A significant concern raised by members of the mining industry is the potential for stricter accountability standards to create a competitive disadvantage for Canadian companies; developing nations would be less willing to take on Canadian developers due to increased legal and financial risk associated with stricter operating rules.[69] This point is pervasive, being raised in 2011 in response to the ultimately failed Bill C-300, which sought to increase accountability for the mining, oil and gas sectors,[70] and again being raised in 2019 in opposition to the Supreme Court's decision in *Nevsun*.[71] Another factor raised in attempting to dissuade the government from closing the accountability gap is the potential infringement on state sovereignty where Canadian companies are operating.[72] This factor was a central concern in *Nevsun*,[73] and was also raised against Bill C-300.[74]

However, the *Nevsun* decision suggests that the Supreme Court is willing to prioritize human rights over economic and diplomatic concerns, perhaps opening the door for the federal government to do the same.[75] If the CORE is to address the shortcomings of the existing institutions and the previous CSR Counsellor, the CORE must be mandatory, independent, and have broad investigatory and remedial powers. In the absence of these powers, the CORE will remain an ineffective and inadequate body that simply upholds the status quo, much like the previous CSR Counsellor.

Mandatory Not Voluntary

For the CORE to be effective, it must be mandatory for companies to cooperate in investigations and participate in the grievance and mediation processes. As mentioned above, a key issue with the CSR

Counsellor and the OECD NCP is the fact that both were voluntary, meaning it was left up to the corporations to decide whether they wanted to cooperate and engage in grievance processes (i.e., dialogue and mediation). The federal government had initially confirmed: "the Ombudsperson is one of Canada's two *voluntary* dispute mechanisms, complementing Canada's National Contact Point."[76] As of August 2021, the CORE remains a voluntary process, although the ombudsperson has the power to recommend the denial of withdrawal of trade advocacy if companies do not comply. Keeping the CORE as a voluntary dispute mechanism is a serious flaw that impedes it from having any actual effect. As evidenced by the CSR Counsellor and NCPs, corporations clearly lack the will to participate in voluntary grievance processes.

Independent

In a discussion of human rights ombudspersons, Florian Hoffman and Frédéric Mégret note that "at minimum, ombudspersons are meant to be independent from both the body that created them and the agencies they oversee," and they must be empowered to carry out independent investigations.[77] What this means is that the CORE should be independent and operate at arms-length from the government. In 2019, the government announced that the minister of international trade diversification will be responsible for the CORE's budget.[78] Additionally, the CORE is also responsible for reporting directly to this minister's office. According to the Canadian Network for Corporate Accountability (CNCA), this compromises the CORE's independence. As the CNCA noted, to be truly independent, the CORE must have its own budget, operate out of its own office, and report directly to parliament.[79] To provide an example, under the previous CSR Counsellor who lacked independence, there were allegations that Canadian diplomats and trade commissioners interfered in a protest in Mexico against Excellon Resources. For example, emails accessed in a freedom of information request indicated that a Canadian ambassador and trade commissioner agreed to a meeting with the protestors "to listen, possibly to gather intel helpful to the company."[80] As the CORE reports directly to the minister of international trade diversification, there is no guarantee that the office will be free from interference, thus raising serious concerns about its independence (or lack thereof).

Investigatory Powers

When the federal government first announced the creation of the CORE to replace the CSR Counsellor, part of the announcement included a pledge that the CORE would have the power to conduct independent, complex investigations at their own discretion.[81] This power would be a great improvement from the previous CSR Counsellor who, as mentioned, was only empowered to conduct limited investigations when it received complaints and depended on the cooperation of both parties to provide information. Broad investigatory powers include the powers to compel witnesses and testimony and access all relevant documents. These powers are not different from those possessed by other Canadian ombudsperson offices, who have the power to compel the production of documents and testimony without a court order. To ensure the CORE's legitimacy and accountability, the CNCA has suggested that the CORE should be required to obtain judicial approval for acquiring documents and testimony to "enhance the procedural protections afforded to companies subject to a complaint."[82] This approach would strike a balance between accountability and a detrimental overreliance on the company's cooperation. Further, civil society groups have been pushing for the CORE to be appointed under the federal *Inquiries Act*.[83] Because the CORE office is not being created with its own implementation legislation, it does not have the legal authority to obtain documents on its own, nor compel witnesses and testimony. An appointment under the *Inquiries Act* would give it these powers. Specifically, under s. 4 commissioners appointed under the *Inquiries Act* have the power to summon witnesses and require them to give evidence (orally or in writing, and under oath), as well as the power to compel the production of documents "and things as the commissioners deem requisite to the full investigation of the matters into which they are appointed to examine."[84] By possessing such powers, the CORE would truly be able to distinguish itself from the previous ineffective CSR Counsellor position. In June 2019, an Order in Council set out that the CORE is to be appointed under the *Public Service Employment Act*,[85] thereby confirming fears of it being a toothless body.

Remedial Powers

By their very nature, ombudspersons' remedial powers are usually recommendatory rather than binding, and their ability to effect compliance typically rests on the publicity of their reports rather than on "formal prosecutorial competences."[86] Therefore, an ombudsperson does not have power to provide remedy in the form of monetary compensation to victims of corporate wrongdoing, nor can it make final determinations of guilt and liability. Despite this limitation, ombudspersons can provide remedies and enforcement in other forms. In addition to issuing public reports, the CORE possesses the following remedial powers: recommending the Canadian company pay financial compensation, apologize publicly, do what is needed to fix the harm, or make changes so that the same harm does not happen again; or recommend that the Canadian government stop trade support or refuse to give trade or financial support to the company in the future, send the complaint to another organization or to police, or change Canadian laws and policies.[87] Human rights scholars have long held that "naming and shaming" is a popular strategy to enforce international human rights norms and laws among states.[88] While this argument has also been extended to corporations, some scholars are skeptical whether naming and shaming actually results in changes to corporate behaviour with regards to human rights.[89] In other words, while it is important that the CORE has the power to publicly report on investigations and issue public recommendations, it is uncertain whether this will have an immediate effect on corporations, especially those in the extractive sector who may see human rights abuses as a cost of doing business.

CONCLUSION

This chapter has shown how the previous CSR Counsellor and existing judicial and non-judicial mechanisms have been generally ineffective in addressing corporate wrongdoing and closing the accountability gap, with the possible exception of recent judicial developments. The need for the CORE is clear, but it will only be an effective institution if it is equipped with a broad range of powers. Specifically, it must be independent, mandatory for corporations to participate, and possess strong investigatory and remedial powers.

The government's announcement in April 2019 and subsequent updates regarding the CORE indicate that it will not be given the same powers and mandate as the government had initially reported in January 2018 and will be unable to fill the accountability gap as needed. The government appeared to bow to corporate pressure by establishing a powerless advisory post.[90] As a result, it is unlikely that the CORE will be able to occupy an important role and adequately address the issue of corporate wrongdoing by Canadian companies abroad. While the CORE is necessary in light of the shortcomings of existing mechanisms, it will not be effective unless equipped with the powers discussed herein.

NOTES

1 Canada, Parliament, House of Commons, Mandate of the Canadian Ombudsperson for Responsible Enterprise, *Report of the Standing Committee on Foreign Affairs and International Development*, 2nd sess., 43rd Parliament, 2021, https://publications.gc.ca/collections/collection_2021/parl/xc11-1/XC11-1-1-432-8-eng.pdf.

2 Global Affairs Canada, "Minister Carr Announces Appointment of First Canadian Ombudsperson for Responsible Enterprise," 8 April 2019, https://www.canada.ca/en/global-affairs/news/2019/04/minister-carr-announces-appointment-of-first-canadian-ombudsperson-for-responsible-enterprise.html.

3 Sheri Meyerhoffer, *Operating Procedures for the Human Rights Responsibility Mechanism of the Canadian Ombudsperson for Responsible Enterprise (CORE)* (Quebec: CORE, 2021), https://core-ombuds.canada.ca/core_ombuds-ocre_ombuds/assets/pdfs/operating-procedures.pdf.

4 Government of Canada, "Orders in Council – PC Number: 2019–0299," 8 April 2019, https://orders-in-council.canada.ca/attachment.php?attach=37587&lang=en.

5 Jolson Lim, "Civil Society, Labour Groups Resign in Protest from Federal Panel on Corporate Responsibility Abroad," *iPolitics*, 11 July 2019, https://ipolitics.ca/2019/07/11/civil-society-labour-groups-resign-in-protest-from-federal-panel-on-corporate-responsibility-abroad.

6 Government of Canada, "Orders in Council – PC Number: 2019–1323," 6 September 2019, https://orders-in-council.canada.ca/attachment.php?attach=38652&lang=en.

7 Paul Alexander Haslam, Nasser Ary Tanimoune, and Zarlasht M. Razeq, "Do Canadian Mining Firms Behave Worse Than Other Companies? Quantitative Evidence from Latin America," *Canadian Journal of Political Science* 51, no. 3 (April 2018): 521.

8 Duncan Hood, "People Are Dying Because of Canadian Mines. It's Time for the Killing to Stop," *The Globe and Mail*, 19 February 2019, https://

www.theglobeandmail.com/business/rob-magazine/article-people-are-dying-because-of-our-mines-its-time-for-the-killing-to.

9 For more on the garment industry, particularly fast fashion, see Selena Chen, "Behind the Veil: Fast Fashion in Global Supply Chains," chapter 8 of this book.

10 Arlene Drake, "Canadian Global Exploration Activity," Natural Resources Canada, last modified 28 January 2019, https://www.nrcan.gc.ca/mining-materials/exploration/8296.

11 Ibid.

12 United Nations Human Rights Office of the High Commissioner, "Statement at the End of Visit to Canada by the United Nations Working Group on Business and Human Rights," 1 June 2017, https://www.ohchr.org/EN/NewsEvents/Pages/DisplayNews.aspx?NewsID=21680&LangID=E.

13 The Canadian Centre for the Study of Resource Conflict, "Corporate Social Responsibility: Movements and Footprints of Canadian Mining and Exploration Firms in the Developing World," October 2009, http://caid.ca/CSRRep2009.pdf.

14 Ibid.

15 Samuel E. Farkas, *Araya v. Nevsun and the Case for Adopting International Human Rights Prohibitions into Domestic Tort Law* (University of Toronto Faculty of Law Review 2018).

16 Global Affairs Canada, "Building the Canadian Advantage: A Corporate Social Responsibility (CSR) Strategy for the Canadian International Extractive Sector," last modified 22 April 2016, https://www.international.gc.ca/trade-agreements-accords-commerciaux/topics-domaines/other-autre/csr-strat-rse-2009.aspx?lang=eng.

17 Ibid.

18 Ibid.

19 Ibid.

20 José Carlos Marques, "Private Regulatory Fragmentation as Public Policy: Governing Canada's Mining Industry," *Journal of Business Ethics* 135, no. 4 (June 2016): 617–30.

21 Penelope Simons, "Canada's Enhanced CSR Strategy: Human Rights Due Diligence and Access to Justice for Victims of Extraterritorial Corporate Human Rights Abuses," *Canadian Business Law Journal* 167 (July 2015).

22 Global Affairs Canada, "Doing Business the Canadian Way: A Strategy to Advance Corporate Social Responsibility in Canada's Extractive Sector Abroad," last modified 13 May 2021, https://www.international.gc.ca/trade-agreements-accords-commerciaux/topics-domaines/other-autre/csr-strat-rse.aspx?lang=eng.

23 Ibid.
24 Simons, "Enhanced."
25 Global Affairs Canada, "Registry of Request for Review," 30 May 2017, https://www.international.gc.ca/global-affairs-affaires-mondiales/home-accueil.aspx?lang=eng.
26 Ibid.
27 Ibid.
28 Ghada Alsharif, "'No Real Role': Canada's Watchdog for Mining Abroad Struggles to Sharpen Its Teeth," *CBC News*, 20 November 2016, https://www.cbc.ca/news/canada/mining-watchdog-1.3855789.
29 Sakura Saunders, "Oh No Canada: The Canadian Mining Sector's Lack of Response to Human Rights Abuses Abroad Comes to a Head," *Alternatives Journal (AJ) – Canada's Environmental Voice* 40, no. 1 (February 2014): 26–7.
30 Ibid.
31 Simons, "Enhanced."
32 Global Affairs Canada, "Office of the Extractive Sector Corporate Social Responsibility (CSR) Counsellor," last modified 26 June 2018, https://www.international.gc.ca/csr_counsellor-conseiller_rse/index.aspx?lang=eng.
33 Sarah Knuckey and Eleanor Jenkin, "Company-Created Remedy Mechanisms for Serious Human Rights Abuses: A Promising New Frontier for the Right to Remedy?" *The International Journal of Human Rights* 19, no. 6 (Summer 2015): 801–27.
34 Ibid.
35 The third pillar of the United Nations "Protect, Respect, and Remedy" framework recognizes the need for greater access by victims to effective remedy.
36 United Nations Human Rights Office of the High Commissioner, *Guiding Principles on Business and Human Rights: Implementing the United Nations 'Protect, Respect and Remedy' Framework* (Geneva: United Nations, 2011), https://www.ohchr.org/documents/publications/guidingprinciplesbusinesshr_en.pdf.
37 Ibid.
38 Margaret Jungk, Ouida Chichester, and Chris Fletcher, *In Search of Justice: Pathways to Remedy at the Porgera Gold Mine* (San Francisco: BSR 2018), https://www.bsr.org/reports/BSR_In_Search_of_Justice_Porgera_Gold_Mine.pdf.
39 Catherine Coumans, "Brief on Concerns Related to Project-Level Non-Judicial Grievance Mechanisms," MiningWatch Canada, 25 September 2014, https://miningwatch.ca/sites/default/files/briefonnjgmsforcfe2014.pdf.

40 Catherine Coumans, "Review of Barrick Gold/Acacia Mining's Draft 'Community Grievance Process – Standard Operating Procedure' for the North Mara Gold Mine in Tanzania," MiningWatch Canada, 24 April 2018, https://miningwatch.ca/sites/default/files/review_of_new_north_mara_grievance_mechanism_april_2018_final_0.pdf.

41 UN High Commissioner for Human Rights, *Improving Accountability and Access to Remedy for Victims of Business-Related Human Rights Abuse through Non-State-based Grievance Mechanisms* (Geneva: UN 2020).

42 Ibid.

43 OECD Watch, "Our Campaign Demands for Policymakers," November 2017, https://www.oecdwatch.org/wp-content/uploads/sites/8/2017/11/OECD-Watch_-Campaign_demands.pdf.

44 Karin Buhmann, "Analysing OECD National Contact Point Statements for Guidance on Human Rights Due Diligence: Method, Findings and Outlook," *Nordic Journal of Human Rights* 36, no. 4 (December 2018): 390–410.

45 OECD, "Cases Handled by the National Contact Points for the OECD Guidelines for Multinational Enterprises," accessed 25 August 2021, https://www.oecd.org/investment/mne/ncps.htm.

46 Karsten Engsig Sørensen and Birgitte Egelund Olsen, "Strengthening the Enforcement of CSR through Mediation and Conflict Resolution by National Contact Points: Finding a New Balance between Hard Law and Soft Law," *Nordic & European Company Law Working Paper* (May 2013): 10–38.

47 OECD Watch, "Campaign Demands."

48 Ibid.

49 Mona Paré and Tate Chong, "Human Rights Violations and Canadian Mining Companies: Exploring Access to Justice in Relation to Children's Rights," *The International Journal of Human Rights* 21, no. 7 (Spring 2017): 908–32.

50 Catherine Coumans, "Peer Review of the Canadian National Contact Point on the OECD Guidelines for Multinational Enterprises," MiningWatch Canada, 23 January 2018, https://miningwatch.ca/sites/default/files/miningwatchcanadasubmissiontoncppeerreviewjanuary2018.pdf.

51 Ibid.

52 Ibid.

53 European Center for Constitutional and Human Rights, *A Comparison of National Contact Points – Best Practices in OECD Complaints Procedures* (Berlin: ECCHR, 2011), https://www.ecchr.eu/fileadmin/Publikationen/OECD_A_comparison_of_NCPs_Policy_Paper_2011-11.pdf.

54 *Araya v. Nevsun Resources Ltd* [2016] BCWLD 7429, 2016 BCSC 1856.

55 Paré and Chong, "Human Rights."

56 *Das v. George Weston Limited* [2018] OJ No. 6742, 2018 ONCA 1053.
57 Ibid.
58 *Salomon v. Salomon & Co Ltd* [1897] AC 22, 1896 WL 4725.
59 Farkas, "Araya v Nevsun."
60 *Araya v. Nevsun Resources Ltd* [2018] 2 WWR 221, 2017 BCCA 401.
61 *Nevsun Resources Ltd v. Araya* [2020] 4 WWR 1, 2020 SCC 5.
62 *Araya v. Nevsun Resources Ltd* [2018] 2 WWR 221, 2017 BCCA 401.
63 Ibid.
64 *Nevsun Resources Ltd v. Araya* [2020] 4 WWR 1, 2020 SCC 5.
65 Florian Hoffmann and Frédéric Mégret, "Fostering Human Rights Accountability: An Ombudsperson for the United Nations?" *Global Governance* 11, no. 1 (Winter 2005): 43.
66 Ibid.
67 Katja Heede, "Enhancing the Accountability of Community Institutions and Bodies: The Role of the European Ombudsman," *European Public Law* 3, no. 4 (December 1997): 587–605.
68 Sunny Freeman, "The Case For – And Against – An Ombudsperson to Resolve Mining Disputes," *Financial Post*, 7 March 2017, https://financialpost.com/business/the-case-for-and-against-an-ombudsperson-to-resolve-mining-disputes.
69 Sara L. Seck, "Canadian Mining Internationally and the UN Guiding Principles for Business and Human Rights," *Canadian Yearbook of International Law* 49, (2012): 72.
70 Ibid.
71 Amanda Coletta, "A Canadian Company Is Accused of Human Rights Abuses Overseas. Can It Be Sued in Canada?" *The Washington Post*, 24 January 2019, https://www.washingtonpost.com/world/the_americas/a-canadian-company-is-accused-of-human-rights-abuses-overseas-can-it-be-sued-in-canada/2019/01/24/8e763642-1feb-11e9-a759-2b8541bbbe20_story.html.
72 Seck, "Canadian Mining," 73.
73 *Nevsun Resources Ltd v. Araya* [2020] 4 WWR 1, 2020 SCC 5.
74 Seck, "Canadian Mining," 73.
75 For more on the *Nevsun* decision, please see Cristina Borbely, "The Search for Corporate Accountability in Transnational Business and Human Rights," chapter 12 of this book.
76 Global Affairs Canada, "Canada's Ombudsperson for Responsible Enterprise."
77 Hoffmann and Mégret, "Fostering."

78 Global Affairs Canada, "Responsible Business Conduct Abroad – Questions and Answers," last modified 8 July 2020, https://www.international.gc.ca/trade-agreements-accords-commerciaux/topics-domaines/other-autre/faq.aspx?lang=eng.

79 Jennifer Wells, "Canada Has a New Watchdog for Corporate Ethics. But Where Are Its Teeth?" *The Toronto Star*, 9 April 2019, https://www.thestar.com/business/opinion/2019/04/09/canada-has-a-new-watchdog-for-corporate-ethics-but-where-are-its-teeth.html.

80 Karen Pauls, "Canadian Embassy Went Too Far to Protect Mining Company Interests in Mexico, Critics Say," *CBC News*, 25 February 2015, https://www.cbc.ca/news/canada/manitoba/canadian-embassy-went-too-far-to-protect-mining-company-interests-in-mexico-critics-say-1.2970108.

81 Global Affairs Canada, "The Government of Canada Brings Leadership to Responsible Business Conduct Abroad," 17 January 2018, https://www.canada.ca/en/global-affairs/news/2018/01/the_government_ofcanadabringsleadershiptoresponsiblebusinesscond.html.

82 Canadian Network on Corporate Accountability, "Canadian Leadership in Business and Human Rights," 2018, https://cnca-rcrce.ca.

83 *Inquiries Act*, RSC 1985, c. I-11, https://laws-lois.justice.gc.ca/eng/acts/i-11/page-1.html.

84 Ibid.

85 *Public Service Employment Act, Statutes of Canada* 2006, c. 22, https://laws-lois.justice.gc.ca/eng/acts/p-33.01; Government of Canada, "Orders – 2019–1323."

86 Hoffmann and Mégret, "Fostering."

87 Government of Canada, "What Does the CORE do if it Finds there was Human Rights Abuse?" last modified 5 August 2021, https://core-ombuds.canada.ca/core_ombuds-ocre_ombuds/fact_sheet_3-fiche_descriptive_3.aspx?lang=eng.

88 Emilie M. Hafner-Burton, "Sticks and Stones: Naming and Shaming the Human Rights Enforcement Problem," *International Organization* 62, no. 4 (Fall 2008): 689–716.

89 David A. Skeel Jr, "Shaming in Corporate Law," *University of Pennsylvania Law Review* 149, no. 6 (2001): 1811–68.

90 Stacey Gomez, "Opinion: Still Waiting for an Effective Mining Ombudsperson," *The Chronicle Herald*, 11 April 2019, https://www.saltwire.com/halifax/opinion/opinion-still-waiting-for-an-effective-mining-ombudsperson-300804.

12

The Search for Corporate Accountability in Transnational Business and Human Rights

Cristina Borbely

Transnational corporations (TNCs) have become increasingly powerful in our globalized world. However, regulatory obstacles and inadequacies in both international and domestic legal frameworks prevent TNCs from being held accountable for corporate wrongdoing. This governance gap is particularly hazardous considering the ease and capability of TNCs to violate the human rights of people around the world.[1] While there have been attempts to close this governance gap,[2] this chapter examines the challenges faced in the development of international and domestic frameworks aiming to hold TNCs accountable for corporate wrongdoing. While corporate responsibility to respect human rights is making strides to becoming an international norm, corporate *accountability* for human rights violations is not achieving the same progress.

It is important to distinguish between these two concepts of corporate responsibility and corporate accountability. The United Nations Guiding Principles on Business and Human Rights (Guiding Principles) define corporate responsibility as the principle that corporations "should avoid infringing on the human rights of others and should address adverse human rights impacts with which they are involved."[3] Corporate accountability, as referred to in this chapter, describes a legal obligation that, when breached, either imposes a sanction against the corporation or allows the injured party to bring a legal action against the corporation in a court of law; a corporation is considered to be held accountable where it has been found liable for violations of international human rights.[4] The Guiding Principles, along with the United Nations Global Compact (Global Compact), are eminent examples of international instruments conceived to promote the principle of corporate human rights responsibility.[5] This chapter will examine the efficacy of these instruments, as well as domestic attempts to implement them. While these instruments do support the development of corporate responsibility for human rights, this chapter explores how they fall short of promoting actual corporate accountability where human rights violations do occur.

The underlying assumptions of this chapter are derived from business and human rights (BHR) discourse. Unlike the related and often intertwined concept of corporate social responsibility (CSR), which in the past has emphasized voluntary corporate responsibility, BHR emphasizes corporate legal accountability.[6] With respect to corporate violations of human rights, BHR discourse is, therefore, more compelling. BHR emerges from legal discourse, while CSR emerges from management discourse.[7] While the basic assumptions driving CSR are the separation of the public and private domains, strong states, and the emphasis on voluntary responsibility, the basic assumptions from which BHR operates are the blurring of the public and private domains, governance voids caused by weak states, and actual legal accountability.[8] BHR, described as an emerging research field, is thus driven by the desire to prevent human rights abuses and to hold corporations accountable for violations that occur.[9]

A BHR perspective promotes the view that corporate accountability for violations of human rights requires findings of legal liability, as respect for human rights is not voluntary. Human rights are unconditional, universal, and equal, holding irrespective of domestic laws.[10] Even where the corporate responsibility to respect human rights is not a domestic legal requirement, it nevertheless exists "independently of any government's abilities or willingness to act on its obligation."[11] Despite this, a legal vacuum arises in relation to transnational corporate human rights violations and perpetuates the perception of its voluntariness; it is thus "vital that the distinction between CSR policies and human rights protections is made forcibly to corporations,"[12] and it is essential that corporate human rights violations attract legal repercussions. Only through findings of legal liability can corporate accountability begin its journey to maturing into an international norm. The notion that corporate violations of human rights should attract legal liability distinguishes BHR from the voluntary essence of CSR. Unfortunately, as will be examined in this chapter, the current international and domestic legal frameworks render findings of legal liability elusive.

This chapter first examines the participation of TNCs in international decision-making through the policy-oriented process, as well as the international instruments that have emerged as a result. Domestic attempts to implement these international instruments are also discussed. The first section demonstrates that international instruments are nurturing the development of CSR as an international norm and prompting TNCs to avoid human rights violations before they occur; still, these instruments are not advancing the principle of corporate accountability. The second section assesses Canadian examples of the breakthrough of human rights litigation against TNCs, as well as the appropriateness of such a method in comparison with legislative-driven regulation. This section further demonstrates how transnational human rights litigation could be wielded by individual stakeholders to fill the global governance gap and support the development of corporate accountability as an international norm.

INTERNATIONAL AND MULTILATERAL INSTRUMENTS AND THE POLICY-ORIENTED PROCESS

The Policy-Oriented Process

International law recognizes both subjects and objects, and this framework can be seen as determinative of how human rights abuses are perceived and dealt with.[13] As subjects of international law, states and international organizations have international legal rights and duties.[14] The international human rights framework is premised on the assumption that states are the violators of human rights.[15] Objects of international law, such as corporations, do not have legal personality at international law but are instead characterized as nationals of states.[16] John Ruggie, the architect behind the Guiding Principles, notes how the power, authority, and relative autonomy of TNCs are shaped by the failure of international public law to fully recognize TNCs.[17] Accordingly, despite violating fundamental norms of international law, TNCs cannot be found legally accountable.[18] Though various theories attempt to describe the nature of the international legal framework and the role of the corporation within it, the policy-oriented process best explains how non-state entities such as TNCs can acquire both a prominent role and, eventually, legal accountability on the international stage.

The policy-oriented process, also dubbed the New Haven School (NHS), advances polycentric governance with a humanitarian focus and prominent role for TNCs. The NHS first intertwines law and policy.[19] Law is seen as a "social process of authoritative decision-making," rather than a "set of sovereign commands."[20] Non-state entities, TNCs included, increasingly play a role in influencing state decisions, particularly in relation to international law norms.[21] Second, the NHS places individuals, as opposed to states, at the forefront of decision-making, with individuals being recognized as international law stakeholders.[22] TNCs, as entities with which individuals are affiliated, are thus given a prominent role in the decision-making process.[23] Third, the NHS has a humanitarian focus as it "undertakes to improve the performance of decision processes themselves and enhance their capacity to achieve outcomes more consonant with human dignity."[24] As the NHS has evolved, a greater emphasis has been placed on the rule of law, accountability, human rights, and the process by which states and private actors internalize legal norms into domestic law.[25] Throughout this chapter, soft law instruments, public-private partnerships such as the Global Compact, international initiatives such as the Guiding Principles, and transnational adjudication will all be explored as examples of the policy-oriented process in action.

As products of polycentric governance, soft law instruments are also important for redefining the position of TNCs. While states remain relevant in international decision-making, new policy channels are emerging, with non-governmental organizations (NGOs) and TNCs playing an increasingly important role in the process of international norm development and implementation.[26] Such policy channels have led to the creation of soft law instruments, which can be adopted and implemented more quickly than international laws or treaties.[27] Soft law instruments demonstrate a compromise between two opposing views: first, that TNCs should be regulated by states in a way that is consistent with state sovereignty and territorial autonomy; second, that TNCs should instead be regulated at an international or supranational level, rather than domestic level.[28] These instruments, despite their soft law nature, are expected to acquire normative force and effectiveness through recognition and implementation, in a process similar to the codification of international human rights.[29] It was through soft law rather than through hard positivist decrees that the international consensus was changed.[30]

The Global Compact and the Guiding Principles are prime examples of the policy-oriented process theory in action. Such instruments represent a departure from the state-oriented instruments of the past, and the rise of public-private partnerships designed to address both state and market failures to regulate TNCs.[31]

United Nations Global Compact

The Global Compact, as a form of public-private partnership, exemplifies the policy-oriented process, representing an "outsourcing" of global governance to the private sector through the implementation of voluntary initiatives.[32] Public-private partnerships are means of financing, implementing, and operating public sector services through contract with the private sector.[33] In this context, a partnership between public state actors and private corporations attempts to ensure corporate accountability, which typically may be seen as a consequence under the sole control of states. From its foundation in 2000, the Global Compact has been a tool to advance the corporate sustainability initiatives of the United Nations (UN). Since 2015, the focus of the Global Compact has been on fulfilling the seventeen UN Sustainable Development Goals, aimed to be achieved by 2030. Examples of the goals include gender equality, quality education, climate action, and an end to poverty and hunger.[34] The Global Compact is seen as an effective means to achieve these goals through the help of private entities, as such goals "cannot be achieved solely with the support of states."[35] Indeed, TNCs are "capable of making and implementing decisions at a pace that neither governments nor international agencies can match."[36] The Ten Principles of the Global Compact (Ten Principles) promote corporate sustainability, focusing on human rights, labour, the environment, and anti-corruption.[37] Principle 1 instructs businesses to "support and respect the protection of internationally proclaimed human rights," while under Principle 2, businesses are to "make sure that they are not complicit in human rights abuses."[38]

The Global Compact has a broad reach and large-scale goals. Over 9,500 companies based in over 160 countries, both developed and developing, are participants in the Global Compact.[39] The vision of the Global Compact is "to mobilize a global movement of sustainable companies and stakeholders to create the world we want."[40] One way the Global Compact seeks to accomplish this is by providing members with the knowledge they need to meet their sustainability objectives via tools such as the Global Compact Local Networks.[41] These networks operate in countries where the Global Compact is active by promoting the Ten Principles within specific national and cultural contexts, while providing outreach and support to companies.[42] The Canadian Local Network launched in 2013 and includes seventy-eight participants. It seeks to facilitate dialogue among the members, promote best practices, and engage in peer review of the reporting each company undertakes.[43]

However, despite its ambitious goals and high rate of corporate acceptance, the Global Compact is not a mechanism that leverages corporate accountability. It is not designed to monitor or measure the performance of participants.[44] Rather, the Global Compact Office may, as a last resort, delist the corporation from the Global Compact where allegations of abuse are either admitted by a representative of the corporation or where a competent court or body finds the corporation guilty.[45] The Global Compact does not address the role of the state in facilitating processes to achieve a finding of guilt – and without state action, corporate accountability cannot be achieved.[46] Alternatively, the Guiding Principles do address the responsibility of states to provide access to remedies for corporate violations of human rights through findings of legal liability.

United Nations Guiding Principles on Business and Human Rights

The Guiding Principles, adopted in 2011, are another addition to the international framework addressing the regulation of TNCs in the field of human rights. Though created after the Global Compact, the Guiding Principles are the result of an effort to create global human rights standards that gained momentum in the 1990s. Early attempts to create legally binding norms of human rights failed, largely due to debate between activists and corporations about the extent of such initiatives. Attempting to resolve this issue, the UN appointed John Ruggie in 2005 as a Special Representative on the Issue of Human Rights. Through this mandate, Ruggie created the "Protect, Respect and Remedy" report in 2008 as a focal point around which expectations could be established.[47] In 2011, recommendations were presented as the Guiding Principles.[48] The long and intensive process behind the creation of the Guiding Principles can likely be explained by the fact that these principles apply to all states and business enterprises, unlike the Global Compact, which is voluntary.[49]

The three pillars of the Guiding Principles recognize the state obligation to respect, protect, and fulfill human rights, the responsibility of corporations to respect human rights, and the need for effective remedies where human rights violations occur.[50] A polycentric approach is taken to prop up these pillars, as the Protect, Respect and Remedy framework it is based upon is seen as "an attempt to build simultaneous public and private governance systems as well as coordinate, without integrating, their operations."[51] In this sense, rather than opting to ground corporate responsibility solely in state legal structures, societal and cultural expectations are intertwined to ensure that the characteristics of both states and enterprises as actors in the system are respected.[52] As Larry Backer explains in his work on the subject, "[t]hat essential governance binary then serves as the basis for building a structure of remedial rights and obligations – those of the state grounded in law and an expectation of legal harmonization (internally applied within domestic legal orders), and those of economic actors grounded in private webs of obligation to corporate stakeholders."[53] The inclusion of non-state actors, such as enterprises and civil society organizations, along with state governments as agents of corporate responsibility for human rights, seems to cast a wider net to catch abuses. However, once they are caught, rectifying such injustices remains a problem for the Guiding Principles.

The Guiding Principles are not legally binding, meaning that none of the actors involved have any obligations to ensure that a remedy is provided for human rights violations or that offenders are held accountable.[54] As a result, the UN has sought to strengthen the remedy aspect of the three pillars by identifying what makes an effective remedy and how they are best provided.[55] They have emphasized that the effectiveness and accessibility of remedies must be construed from the perspective of the rightsholders seeking remedies. Remedies should be varied depending on the situation, including compensation, rehabilitation, and guarantees of non-repetition. Moreover, effective remedies must not create a fear of any form of victimization, such as intimidation, arrest, or legal consequences.[56] To achieve these aims the UN has stressed the importance of a cooperative approach to remedies, requiring the participation of states, businesses, and civil society organizations. As a result, the UN encourages a multifaceted approach to remedies, including state-based judicial and non-judicial mechanisms, as well as operational-level grievance mechanisms established by businesses.

Judicial, non-judicial, and business-led grievance mechanisms have nevertheless each faced issues, preventing them from being truly effective.[57] Corporate grievance mechanisms have been plagued with a lack of transparency and inadequate remedies.[58] State-based mechanisms have failed to demonstrate a commitment to the cross-border cooperation necessary to achieve justice. Access to justice issues have limited the accessibility of judicial remedies. A lack of internal policy coherence has also limited the effectiveness of domestic mechanisms.[59] To understand the steps states are taking to improve these outcomes, the following section will examine the binding measures taken by the European Union (EU) to implement the non-binding Guiding Principles. By its actions, the EU is facilitating the creation of enforceable international norms.[60] However, considerable work remains with respect to the full implementation of corporate legal liability.

THE EU AND THE IMPLEMENTATION OF THE GUIDING PRINCIPLES

The EU has adopted both voluntary and mandatory measures to implement the Guiding Principles.[61] First, the EU has redefined CSR in a way that aligns with the Guiding Principles: references to CSR as "voluntary" have been removed, thus setting out "a clear expectation that business enterprises should respect human rights."[62] Second, the implementation of the Guiding Principles was one of the components of the EU Strategic Framework and Action Plan on Human Rights and Democracy in 2012.[63] A new Action Plan on Human Rights and Democracy was adopted in 2015, aiming to make advances in the field of business and human rights by inviting member states to develop and adopt National Action Plans (NAPs) implementing the Guiding Principles by 2017.[64] To date, nineteen of the twenty-seven EU member states have produced a NAP and two more have plans in development.[65] In a similar vein, in 2013, the European Commission issued Sector Guides on implementing the Guiding Principles, which expressly recognized that the corporate responsibility to respect human rights persists, regardless of whether a state has met its own duty to protect human rights.[66] Third, in alignment with the Guiding Principles, the EU issued a directive in 2014 requiring disclosure of non-financial and diversity information by certain large undertakings and groups, including reports on human rights policies, impacts, and due diligence processes.[67] The Directive establishes a comply-or-explain model, by which entities must disclose whether they have in place a human rights policy or else explain why they do not have one.[68]

Despite the EU's keen efforts to implement the Guiding Principles, problems persist in finding TNCs liable for human rights violations. The NAPs of EU Member States address the extraterritorial jurisdiction of states over corporate violations of human rights, but do not necessarily provide effective judicial remedies to victims of international human rights violations committed extraterritorially. To demonstrate this, consider the following sample of NAPs across the UK, the Netherlands, France, Italy, and Germany. The UK is included despite its departure from the EU in early 2020 due to its regional and economic importance.

The UK NAP does not significantly increase the effectiveness of remedies against TNCs violating international human rights. The NAP lists the remedies for corporate human rights abuses that are already in place in the UK. The NAP defines "remedy," stating that it "may include apologies, restitution, rehabilitation, financial or non-financial compensation and punitive sanctions, as well as the prevention of harm through, for example, injunctions or guarantees of non-repetition."[69] It lists judicial mechanisms that are available in the UK and overseas. These include employment tribunals, avenues to pursue civil law claims, as well as criminal provisions contained in the *Bribery Act 2010*,[70] the *Modern Slavery Act 2015*,[71] etc.[72] The NAP also lists actions taken to promote access to remedies, including encouraging companies to extend their UK grievance mechanisms to their overseas operations.[73]

The Dutch NAP references the polemic regarding both extraterritorial legislation and extraterritorial adjudication, without resolving the issue.[74] It also addresses the liability of a parent company for the actions of a foreign subsidiary, stating that in keeping with the principle of *lex loci delicti* of private international law,[75] the actions of the subsidiary will be judged according to the law of the state in which the conduct occurred.[76] While the Dutch NAP states that the Minister of Security and Justice will examine increasing transparency measures of parent companies and their subsidiaries in relation to the impact of their operations on human rights, it does not attempt to resolve the obstacles raised by separate legal personality in the pursuit of a finding of corporate liability.[77]

The French NAP provides a comprehensive description of the legal framework governing the actions of corporations abroad. Any company domiciled in France can be sued in a French court, "regardless of the victim's nationality and State of residence, and regardless of where the harm occurred"; moreover, proceedings may be filed in French courts for a "denial of justice" in foreign courts.[78] French law also allows parent companies to be found criminally liable for acts committed by their subsidiaries abroad where the parent company committed or was complicit in the offence. Nevertheless, while it is a criminal offence under French law for companies to engage in activities that breach people's rights, it must also be a criminal offence in the other jurisdiction in which the act was committed, and a judgment must have been obtained in that country before a finding of guilt can be made in France.[79] The French NAP acknowledges that this presents an obstacle for a finding of liability under these provisions, and France endeavours to examine national and international options to address denials of justice that can occur as a result.[80]

Oddly, the Italian NAP addresses access to Italian courts by foreign enterprises, rather than for victims of human rights abuses.[81] On the other hand, the German NAP states that any person who considers their rights to have been infringed abroad by actions of a German enterprise may bring an action in Germany.[82] As part of their NAP, Germany will produce a multilingual information brochure on access to justice and remedies available under German civil procedure law.[83]

Therefore, the British, Dutch, and Italian NAPs demonstrate that states are not necessarily inclined to challenge the status quo when it comes to facilitating the access to remedies as required by Pillar 3 of the Guiding Principles.[84] Under Pillar 3, "states must take appropriate steps to ensure, through judicial, administrative, legislative or other appropriate means, that when such abuses occur within their territory and/or jurisdiction those affected have access to effective remedy."[85] While the French approach acknowledges the denials of justice inherent in its current framework, it emphasizes that any future initiatives should not create an uneven playing field for French businesses abroad.[86] The desire to maintain a level playing field for businesses while searching for a remedy for extraterritorial corporate wrongdoing is also present in the German and Dutch NAPs.[87]

The implementation of the Guiding Principles aims to develop the norm of corporate responsibility to respect human rights.[88] While a norm of corporate responsibility to respect human rights is certainly becoming entrenched due to the recognition and implementation of the Guiding Principles,[89] the same cannot be said for a norm of transnational corporate liability. The Guiding Principles prioritize the abolition of root causes for human rights abuses over accountability measures for corporate human rights violations.[90] While it is an essential goal to stamp out human rights abuses at their root, it unfortunately appears evident that such a project will take many years and wide-reaching buy-in from corporations and states to be achieved. Therefore, in the meantime, there must be a legitimate commitment to preventing companies from carrying out human rights abuses and providing justice to those who suffer from them. The reluctance of states to implement effective avenues of remediation has not deterred victims of corporate human rights abuses from bringing claims against corporations in courts, despite the perceived improbability of success. Transnational adjudication presents another mechanism, driven by individuals rather than by states, by which transnational corporate liability can achieve normative force. The next section of this chapter discusses such transnational human rights litigation.

TRANSNATIONAL ADJUDICATION AND TRANSNATIONAL LEGISLATION

Victims of corporate human rights violations have sought remedies in the home states of corporations and their subsidiaries in actions referred to as "foreign direct liability cases," or "transnational human rights litigation."[91] In such cases, TNCs are sued in their home states for their involvement in human rights violations committed by their subsidiaries, or for their negligence in effectively preventing such violations.[92] Transnational adjudication is another manifestation of the policy-oriented process discussed earlier in this chapter; victims of corporate human rights abuses, as international law stakeholders, endeavour to compel states through the judiciary to contribute to the development of corporate legal liability as an international norm. Individuals seek to exert influence and engage in polycentric governance by urging courts to step into the governance gap left by the inaction of states that allow corporations to violate human rights with impunity. This section will examine three cases of transnational human rights litigation brought in Canada, Canada's reluctance to enact strong transnational legislation, and Australian and American jurisprudence on transnational human rights.

Though Canadian companies operating abroad are among the top offenders of human rights,[93] Canada is one of the many states yet to effectively regulate TNCs.[94] Despite endorsing international initiatives such as the Guiding Principles, Canada has not created a NAP to implement them. In the meantime, victims of human rights violations have brought forward actions in tort against Canadian companies and their foreign subsidiaries.[95] There have been several significant Canadian cases that have had the potential to redefine corporate liability for TNCs. Two of the cases, *Garcia v. Tahoe Resources Inc.* (*Garcia*)[96] and *Choc v. Hudbay Minerals Inc.* (*Choc*),[97] concern the liability of Canadian corporations for the actions of the security personnel of their subsidiaries at Canadian-owned mines in Guatemala. *Araya v. Nevsun Resources Ltd* (*Araya*)[98] and the resulting 2020 Supreme Court of Canada (SCC) decision, *Nevsun Resources Ltd v. Araya* (*Nevsun*),[99] grapple with the potential complicity of a publicly held British Columbia mining corporation in the human rights abuses of the Eritrean military and its indirect subsidiary in relation to the building of a mine. The plaintiffs' arguments in each case, while complex, are advanced from the same premise: the respect for international human rights is legally binding on corporations.[100]

In *Garcia*, the plaintiffs claimed that Tahoe Resources Inc.'s CSR policies bound it to observe international humanitarian and local law.[101] In *Choc*, as intervenor, Amnesty International submitted that the transnational element of the claim should not release a TNC from liability for the harm caused by its subsidiaries, as corporations owe a duty of care for the actions of their subsidiaries, particularly where subsidiaries operate in high-risk areas.[102] In *Araya*, the plaintiffs claimed that Nevsun had been negligent in failing to adhere to standards of CSR.[103] While these are remarkable and novel arguments in Canadian courts, the courts have yet to resolve and definitively comment on the merits of the arguments. Rather, the courts have been occupied by the procedural challenges raised by the defendants.

In *Garcia*, the defendants asserted the conflicts of law doctrine of *forum non conveniens*, requesting that the court decline to exercise its discretion on the grounds that Guatemala was clearly the more appropriate forum for the claim.[104] This challenge ultimately proved unsuccessful: the British Columbia Court of Appeal overturned the lower court's finding that Guatemala was the more appropriate forum.[105] The court concluded that "there is some measurable risk that the appellants will encounter difficulty in receiving a fair trial against a powerful international company whose mining interests in Guatemala align with the political interests of the Guatemalan state."[106] The case was accordingly allowed to proceed. However, the case was settled in July 2019 and the terms of the settlement are confidential.[107] Publicly, Pan American Silver Corporation (Pan American), which acquired the corporate defendant, Tahoe Resources Inc. (Tahoe), acknowledged that the human rights of the plaintiffs had been violated.[108] Pan American apologized on behalf of Tahoe, stating that Pan American is "assessing how [its] human rights and security practices are consistent with the *Voluntary Principles on Security and Human Rights*, as well as the *Child Rights and Security Checklist*."[109]

Pan American has also reviewed its security practices at its operations in Guatemala and has appointed a human rights officer who reports to Pan American's general counsel.[110] While the plaintiffs in *Garcia* achieved a beneficial resolution with Tahoe, which vindicated their human rights,[111] the end result of the litigation did not advance the development of the norm of corporate accountability through legal liability. Paradoxically, when cases of transnational human rights litigation are settled out of court, such results further the norm of CSR while stunting the development of corporate accountability where corporations fall short of their obligations to respect human rights.

In *Choc*, the defendants challenged the action on procedural grounds: first, the defendants argued that it was "plain and obvious" that the claims disclosed no reasonable cause of action; second, that the claim was statute-barred; and third, that the Ontario Superior Court of Justice did not have jurisdiction over a Guatemalan corporation.[112] The court ultimately did not dismiss the action, finding that it was not "plain and obvious" that Hudbay Minerals Inc. (Hudbay) did not owe the plaintiffs a duty of care.[113]

This case is significant for many reasons. It advances the potential of a novel duty of care between a parent company and the individuals with whom its subsidiary interacts in a foreign country. Furthermore, the public statements made by Hudbay concerning the standards it had adopted and its training of security personnel were seen as a potentially significant factor in grounding the proximity requirement for a novel duty of care.[114] This finding may imply that voluntary adoptions of policies by corporations will have legal implications on the level of accountability within an adjudicative process, similar to the pleadings in *Garcia*. Finally, *Choc* exemplifies the challenge of accessing justice in transnational human rights cases. The most recent development in the case followed examinations for discovery and a successful motion by the plaintiffs to amend their claim, decided in 2020,[115] making it almost a decade since the Ontario Superior Court of Justice dismissed the preliminary motions of Hudbay. Therefore, despite the success of the plaintiffs to date, an actual decision on the merits of the case has yet to be rendered.

Alternatively, the SCC's 2020 decision in *Nevsun* represents a breakthrough for transnational human rights litigation, buttressing claims based on breaches of customary international law. Customary international law is a form of international law that is universally binding on all states. An action becomes customary international law based on consistent patterns of state practice and the belief by most states that engaging in that practice is required by law.[116] In *Nevsun*, the plaintiffs alleged that they were subjected to forced labour and violent, cruel, inhuman, and degrading treatment. The prohibition against slavery, forced labour, and cruel, inhuman, and degrading treatment are peremptory norms and norms of customary international law.[117]

While Nevsun submitted that customary international law did not apply to corporations, Abella J. noted that international law has evolved to the point that

> there is no longer a tenable basis for restricting the application of customary international law to relations between states. The past 70 years have seen a proliferation of human rights law that transformed international law and made the individual an integral part of this legal domain, reflected in the creation of a complex network of conventions and normative instruments intended to protect human rights and ensure compliance with those rights.[118]

These remarks by the SCC demonstrate a marked manifestation of the policy-oriented process and the influence exerted by soft law instruments on shifting the international consensus to accept and facilitate corporate accountability. On a polycentric international stage, individuals are key stakeholders; modern international human rights law requires the enforceability of human rights against not just states, but by private actors as well.[119] The SCC affirmed that customary international law is part of Canada's common law[120] and held that, in the absence of conflicting legislation, customary international law may bind private actors.[121] Accordingly, it is not "plain and obvious" that corporations are excluded from direct liability or indirect liability for complicity in violations of customary international law in Canadian courts.[122]

Nevsun did not decide whether existing domestic torts capture violations of international human rights, only that it would not be against Canadian law for courts to develop civil remedies for corporate violations of customary international law norms.[123] The SCC noted, however, that "[r]efusing to acknowledge the differences between existing domestic torts and forced labour; slavery; cruel, inhuman or degrading treatment; and crimes against humanity, may undermine the court's ability to adequately address the heinous nature of the harm caused by this conduct."[124]

While Abella J. briefly contemplated the civil remedy that would be available for breaches of norms of customary international law that form part of the Canadian law, she concluded that the matter would ultimately be left for the trial judge to decide. While this case opened the door for Nevsun to be brought to court for their alleged abuses, it was settled out of court in October 2020.[125]

Nevsun is a landmark decision in terms of the acceptance of customary international law in Canada and in protecting against human rights abuses. The idea that corporations are subject to customary international law and can be held liable for breaches in Canadian courts is significant and was fiercely contested in dissent.[126]

These cases summarized above demonstrate that Canadian courts have created an opening for corporate liability for human rights violations committed abroad.[127] However, it is unclear whether plaintiffs in transnational human rights cases will be ultimately successful and what types of remedies will be fashioned as this area of the law develops. Even if corporate respect for human rights is deemed to be customary international law, it is unlikely that transnational *liability* has yet reached the level of customary international law; it is through the availability of robust remedies through the courts that transnational liability would truly crystallize and become customary international law:

> The fact that the judiciary of a particular State determines in a binding resolution that a given norm must be enforced, regardless of its character under international law as "soft" law or "hard" law, would give it at least a semibinding character under domestic jurisdiction, thus helping conform a normative precedent that could become the basis for the development of a customary norm.[128]

Thus *Nevsun* is a significant, but still preliminary, judicial step promoting access to remedies in keeping with the Guiding Principles. Transnational adjudication facilitates corporate accountability for human rights abuses that could not be achieved otherwise.[129] Plaintiffs in civil proceedings related to human rights abuses are often seeking acknowledgment of their rights and to promote public awareness, rather than purely financial compensation.[130] Recognizing that human rights violations have occurred has an important symbolic purpose both for plaintiffs and for society as a whole.[131] States that refuse to open up their judicial system to victims of corporate human rights abuses impede the implementation of all three pillars of the Guiding Principles, but particularly of Pillar 3, the access to remedy pillar.[132]

Even where states have been willing to take on transnational human rights claims, as Canada has recently demonstrated in *Nevsun*, remedies can still be largely inaccessible. The difficulty in accessing justice is evident in the lengthy delays experienced by the plaintiffs in *Choc*, and such issues are not limited to Canada. When Australian courts agreed to hear complaints from residents of Papua New Guinea who endured human rights violations at the Ok Tedi Mine, what seemed like a path to justice faced consistent obstructions.[133] Not only were the plaintiff's claims severely limited on jurisdictional grounds, but Broken Hill Proprietary Company Limited (Broken Hill), which led the mine, worked within the Papua New Guinean government to create legislation severely limiting the ability to receive compensation, essentially making any action of Broken Hill unactionable.[134] This legislation was to apply equally to lawsuits filed outside of Papua New Guinea and meant that any judgment against Broken Hill by a foreign court would not be enforceable.[135] While some monetary compensation has been provided to victims, it has not been clear exactly what harm is being compensated and environmental damage has continued.[136] As a result, we can see that even where courts are willing to be open to international corporate human rights claims, there are significant hurdles that plaintiffs continue to face.

Despite its potential contributions to the development of international norms, transnational adjudication has been criticized as inappropriate for dealing with corporate accountability for human rights abuses, with transnational legislation seen as less controversial.[137] In the case of Canada, it is considered to be the role of the legislature rather than the courts to make such substantial changes to the law, as would be required for rights of action in tort for corporate human rights abuses committed abroad.[138] The creation of such torts would require a balancing of complex policy considerations such as economics, foreign affairs, and human rights, which legislators are in a better position to do.[139] The dissenting opinion in *Nevsun* expressed strong concerns with the courts encroaching on the role of the legislature by permitting the creation of causes of action based in customary international law.[140] On the other hand, the majority opinion penned by Abella J. proclaims that there is "no reason for Canadian courts to be shy about implementing and advancing international law."[141]

Despite the apparent suitability of the legislature, attempts at transnational legislation have thus far failed in Canada. In 2016, a member of Parliament proposed a private member's bill, Bill C-331, to amend the *Federal Courts Act* to create a statutory civil cause of action for violations of international law.[142] This Bill was defeated in June 2019.[143] In other past parliamentary sessions, Bill C-300 and Bill C-584 were introduced as attempts to ensure that Canadian companies in the extractive industry respect international human rights.[144] However, legislators raised concerns that such bills might create an uneven playing field for investment opportunities for Canadian companies abroad, and these bills were both defeated.[145] Canadian legislators appear hesitant to enact strong transnational legislation and seem to be inhibited by the same apprehensions faced by Germany, France, and the Netherlands in their contemplation of remedies for extraterritorial corporate wrongdoing within their NAPs.

States apparently remain unconvinced about the advantages of transnational legislation (indeed, the Dutch NAP explicitly states as much),[146] while courts may remain too timid to make findings of transnational corporate liability without express legislative approval. For example, even though the United States has enacted a statute allowing foreigners to bring actions in front of American courts for torts committed in violation of the law of nations or a treaty, the Supreme Court of the United States (SCUS) stated in 2013 that the *Alien Tort Claims Act* does not apply to corporate wrongdoing that occurred outside of the US.[147] The SCUS reasoned that the presumption against extraterritoriality "ensures that the Judiciary does not erroneously adopt an interpretation of US law that carries foreign policy consequences not clearly intended by the political branches."[148] In 2018, in the case of *Jesner v. Arab Bank, PLC*, the SCUS held that the *Alien Tort Claims Act* does not apply to foreign corporations, again stating that it was the role of the political branches (i.e., the president and Congress) to address the violation of international norms by foreign corporations and not that of the judiciary.[149] Moreover, the SCUS noted that international law does not hold corporations liable for human rights violations.[150]

Though transnational adjudication and transnational legislation would serve to crystallize corporate accountability for human rights violations as a norm of international law, legislatures and courts have proved reluctant to take concrete steps to formally recognize corporate liability for human rights violations. Though the recent case of *Nevsun* has propelled Canada forward by contemplating novel torts or breaches of customary international law as potential causes of action, the dissenting opinions were strong, the true ramifications of transnational adjudication remain unclear, and there are still significant issues concerning access to justice. As a result, the corporate responsibility to respect human rights languishes as a social obligation rather than a legal one.[151]

CONCLUSION

The existing international framework, which is premised on state-to-state relations, does not efficiently tackle adverse consequences caused by the international operations of powerful TNCs. This failure has created a governance gap, wherein TNCs gain impunity due to overlapping jurisdictional issues. The policy-oriented process, as described in this chapter, provides a theoretical framework by which the international legal system may evolve to ensure corporate accountability for violations of fundamental norms of international law. Achieving this policy-oriented process requires a shift away from a state-centric perspective and towards polycentric governance that recognizes individuals, in this case victims of corporate human rights abuses, as international stakeholders. This chapter examined international and domestic frameworks that have sought to address corporate accountability for human rights violations. In doing so, this chapter has discussed the international instruments created to address the existing governance gap, the domestic forays into implementing such international instruments, and attempts to regulate transnational corporate wrongdoing through domestic civil actions. The analysis suggests that while the corporate responsibility to respect human rights is on its way to becoming a norm of international law, corporate accountability for human rights violations still faces hurdles to complete development. Instead, the lack of political will by states and legislatures to implement measures to facilitate findings of corporate liability, as well as the procedural and substantive obstacles to holding corporations liable for human rights violations in court, threaten to undermine the progress made in affirming the corporate responsibility to respect human rights.

This chapter discussed how domestic implementation of the Guiding Principles, as well as the trend exemplified in the settlement of *Garcia* that sees corporations adopt human rights policies and due diligence following transnational human rights litigation,[152] is entrenching Pillar 2 of the Guiding Principles (the corporate responsibility to protect human rights) as a customary norm. Despite the advancement of Pillar 2, Pillar 1 (the state responsibility to respect, protect, and fulfill human rights and fundamental freedoms) and Pillar 3 (the need for rights and obligations to be matched to appropriate and effective remedies when breached) are not experiencing the same level of success. Mechanisms that would allow victims to access effective remedies for corporate human rights violations have yet to be established; this, in turn, undermines Pillar 1. Indeed, the Guiding Principles state that "[u]nless States take appropriate steps to investigate, punish and redress business-related human rights abuses when they do occur, the State duty to protect can be rendered weak or even meaningless."[153] As discussed in Section 2 of this chapter, while claims have been brought before domestic courts, no corporation has yet been found liable for human rights violations committed abroad in Canada's existing legal framework. Furthermore, legislative bodies are hesitant to implement legislation that would facilitate foreign victims to bring claims in home countries of corporations.

The question remains as to whether it is enough that the corporate responsibility to respect human rights becomes a norm of customary international law, without the principle of corporate accountability for human rights violations following suit. While it is conceivable that the existence of such a norm of customary international law would reduce corporate human rights violations, can the corporate responsibility to respect human rights truly be considered a norm of customary international law where there are no consequences for those who violate it? Perhaps that in itself is a criticism of international law, generally.

NOTES

1 John Gerard Ruggie, "Multinationals as Global Institution: Power, Authority and Relative Autonomy," *Regulation & Governance* 12, no. 3 (September 2018): 317.

2 See e.g., Erica Sandhu, "Closing the Accountability Gap? Early Lessons from the Canadian Ombudsperson for Responsible Enterprise," chapter 11 of this book.

3 United Nations Human Rights Office of the High Commissioner, *Guiding Principles on Business and Human Rights: Implementing the United Nations 'Protect, Respect and Remedy' Framework* (United Nations, 2011), 13, https://www.ohchr.org/documents/publications/guidingprinciplesbusinesshr_en.pdf.

4 Nadia Bernaz, "Enhancing Corporate Accountability for Human Rights Violations: Is Extraterritoriality the Magic Potion?" *Journal of Business Ethics* 117, no. 3 (2013): 493–4.

5 Florian Wettstein et al., "International Business and Human Rights: A Research Agenda," *Journal of World Business* 54, no. 1 (January 2019) 55–6.

6 Anita Ramasastry, "Corporate Social Responsibility Versus Business and Human Rights: Bridging the Gap Between Responsibility and Accountability," *Journal of Human Rights* 14, no. 2 (Winter 2015) 237–59.

7 Wettstein et al., "International Business and Human Rights," 55.

8 Ibid., 57; Federica Nieri and Elisa Giuliani, "International Business and Corporate Wrongdoing: A Review and Research Agenda" in *Contemporary Issues in International Business: Institutions, Strategy and Performance*, edited by Davide Castellani et al (Palgrave, 2018) 35–6.

9 Ibid., 55.

10 Ibid., 58.

11 John Ruggie, "'For the Game. For the World': FIFA and Human Rights," Harvard Kennedy School, 2016, 36, https://www.hks.harvard.edu/sites/default/files/centers/mrcbg/programs/cri/files/Ruggie_humanrightsFIFA_reportApril2016.pdf.

12 Ibid.

13 Fleur Johns, "The Invisibility of the Transnational Corporation: An Analysis of International Law and Legal Theory," *Melbourne University Law Review* 19, no. 4 (1994): 897.

14 Ibid.

15 Larry Catá Backer, "Multinational Corporations as Objects and Sources of Transnational Regulation," *ILSA Journal of International & Comparative Law* 14, no. 2 (February 2008): 502.

16 Johns, "The Invisibility of t he Transnational Corporation," 897.

17 Ruggie, "For the Game," 321.

18 Johns, "The Invisibility of t he Transnational Corporation," 904.

19 W. Michael Reisman, Siegfried Wiessner, and Andrew R. Willard, "The New Haven School: A Brief Introduction," *Yale Journal of International Law* 32, no. 2 (2007): 577.

20 Paul Schiff Berman, "A Pluralist Approach to International Law," *Yale Journal of International Law* 32, no. 2 (2007): 301, 306.

21 Ibid., 324–5.
22 Reisman, Wiessner, and Willard, "The New Haven School," 576. For criticisms of the policy-oriented approach's Western focus, see Johns, "The Invisibility of the Transnational Corporation," 920–1; Backer, "Multinational Corporations as Objects," 20, 25; Berman, "A Pluralist Approach," 309.
23 Johns, "The Invisibility of the Transnational Corporation," 919–20.
24 Reisman, Wiessner, and Willard, "The New Haven School," 577.
25 Laura A. Dickinson, "Toward a 'New' New Haven School of International Law?" *Yale Journal of International Law* 32, no. 2 (2007): 549; Harold Kongju Koh, "Is there a 'New' New Haven School of International Law?" *Yale Journal of International Law* 32, no. 2 (2007): 567.
26 Radu Mares, "Decentering Human Rights from the International Order of States: The Alignment and Interaction of Transnational Policy Channels," *Indiana Journal of Global Legal Studies* 23, no. 1 (January 2016): 172; Berman, "A Pluralist Approach," 304.
27 Stéphanie Bijlmakers, *Corporate Social Responsibility, Human Rights, and the Law* (New York: Routledge 2019), 67–8.
28 Backer, "Multinational Corporations as Objects," 507.
29 Mares, "Decentering Human Rights," 196–7; Bijlmakers, *Corporate Social Responsibility*, 64; Berman, "A Pluralist Approach," 304.
30 Berman, "A Pluralist Approach," 304.
31 Marianne Thissen-Smits and Patrick Bernhagen, "Outsourcing Global Governance: Public-Private Voluntary Initiatives" in John Mikler, ed., *The Handbook of Global Companies* (John Wiley & Sons 2013), 325; see e.g. OECD, *OECD Guidelines for Multinational Enterprises: 2011 Edition* (Paris: OCED Publishing 2011).
32 Johns, "The Invisibility of the Transnational Corporation," 902; Surya Deva, "Global Compact: A Critique of the UN's 'Public-Private' Partnership for Promoting Corporate Citizenship," *Syracuse Journal of International Law and Commerce* 34, no. 1 (Summer 2006): 109, 143; Thissen-Smits and Bernhagen, "Outsourcing Global Governance," 316–17, 320.
33 United Nations Economic Commission for Europe, *Guidebook on Promoting Good Governance in Public-Private Partnerships* (New York: United Nations 2008), 1.
34 United Nations Global Compact, "17 Goals to Transform Our World," accessed 19 August 2021, https://www.unglobalcompact.org/sdgs/17-global-goals.
35 Deva, "Global Compact," 108–9.
36 John Gerard Ruggie and Beth Kytle, "Corporate Social Responsibility as Risk Management: A Model for Multinationals," *Corporate Social Responsibility Initiative Working Paper* 10 (March 2005): 8.

37 United Nations Global Compact, "The Ten Principles of the UN Global Compact," accessed 19 August 2021, https://www.unglobalcompact.org/what-is-gc/mission/principles.
38 Ibid.
39 Ibid.
40 United Nations Global Compact, "Our Mission," accessed 19 August 2021, https://www.unglobalcompact.org/what-is-gc/mission.
41 United Nations Global Compact, "UN Global Compact Academy," accessed 19 August 2021, https://www.unglobalcompact.org/academy.
42 United Nations Global Compact, "About Local Networks," accessed 19 August 2021, https://www.unglobalcompact.org/engage-locally/about-local-networks.
43 Global Compact Network Canada, "About the Global Compact Network Canada (GCNC)," accessed 19 August 2021, https://globalcompact.ca/about_gcnc.
44 United Nations Global Compact, "Our Integrity Measures," accessed 19 August 2021, http://unglobalcompact.org/about/integrity-measures.
45 Ibid., 3.
46 Deva, "Global Compact," 148.
47 John Gerard Ruggie, *Protect, Respect and Remedy: A Framework for Business and Human Rights: Report of the Special Representative of the Secretary-General on the Issue of Human Rights and Transnational Corporations and Other Business Enterprises* (Geneva: United Nations 2008), https://digitallibrary.un.org/record/625292?ln=en.
48 United Nations Human Rights Office of the High Commissioner, *Guiding Principles*.
49 Ibid., 1.
50 Ibid.
51 Larry Catá Backer, "On the Evolution of the United Nations' 'Protect-Respect-Remedy' Project: The State, the Corporation and Human Rights in a Global Governance Context," *Santa Clara Journal of International Law* 9, no. 1 (June 2010): 43.
52 Ibid., 68.
53 Ibid., 69.
54 United Nations Human Rights Office of the High Commissioner, *Guiding Principles*, 27.
55 United Nations Secretary-General et al., *Human Rights and Transnational Corporations and Other Business Enterprises Note/By the Secretary-General* (New York: United Nations 2017).
56 Ibid., 13–16.
57 Ibid., 18–20.

58 MiningWatch Canada, "Brief on Concerns Related to Project-Level Non-Judicial Grievance Mechanisms," 23 October 2014, https://miningwatch.ca/publications/2014/10/23/brief-concerns-related-project-level-non-judicial-grievance-mechanisms.

59 United Nations Secretary-General et al., *Human Rights.*

60 Nadia Bernaz, *Business and Human Rights: History, Law and Policy – Bridging the Accountability Gap* (New York: Routledge 2017), 97.

61 Ibid., 154.

62 Ibid., 139, 143.

63 Humberto Cantú Rivera, "The United Nations Guiding Principles on Business and Human Rights in the European Union: From Regional Action to National Implementation," in *The Business and Human Rights Landscape: Moving Forward, Looking Back*, edited by Jena Martin and Karen E. Bravo (Cambridge University Press 2015), 498–500.

64 Foreign Affairs Council, European Commission, "Council Conclusions on the Action Plan on Human Rights and Democracy 2015–2019," 20 July 2015, https://ec.europa.eu/anti-trafficking/eu-policy/council-conclusions-action-plan-human-rights-and-democracy-2015-2019_en.

65 Council of Europe, "National Action Plans," accessed 19 August 2021, https://www.coe.int/en/web/human-rights-intergovernmental-cooperation/national-action-plans.

66 Shift and the Institute for Human Rights and Business, *Oil and Gas Sector Guide on Implementing the UN Guiding Principles on Business and Human Rights* (European Commission, 2013), 8.

67 Directive No. 2014/95/EU, European Parliament and the Council (22 October 2014), *amending* Directive 2013/34/EU.

68 Bijlmakers, *Corporate Social Responsibility*, 176.

69 Foreign and Commonwealth Office, "Good Business Implementing the UN Guiding Principles on Business and Human Rights," last modified 12 May 2016, 20, https://www.gov.uk/government/publications/bhr-action-plan.

70 *Bribery Act 2010*, *UK Public General Acts* 2010, c. 23, https://www.legislation.gov.uk/ukpga/2010/23/contents.

71 *Modern Slavery Act 2015*, *UK Public General Acts* 2015, c. 30, https://www.legislation.gov.uk/ukpga/2015/30/contents/enacted.

72 Ibid., 20.

73 Ibid., 21.

74 Ministry of Foreign Affairs of the Netherlands, *National Action Plan on Business and Human Rights,* April 2014, 38–9, https://media.business-humanrights.org/media/documents/files/documents/netherlands-national-action-plan.pdf.

75 *Lex loci delicti* is a choice of law rule which holds that the law of the place where a tort occurred is the one applied in the adjudication of the claim.
76 Ministry of Foreign Affairs of the Netherlands, *National Action Plan*, 33. See also Bernaz, *Business and Human Rights*, 278–84.
77 Ministry of Foreign Affairs of the Netherlands, *National Action Plan*, 33.
78 Ministère de l'Europe et des Affaires Étrangères (Ministry for Europe and Foreign Affairs, government of France), "National Action Plan for the Implementation of the United Nations Guiding Principles on Business and Human Rights," accessed 19 August 2021, 49, https://www.diplomatie.gouv.fr/IMG/pdf/pnadh_version_finale_en_cle8ffacb.pdf.
79 Ibid., 50.
80 Ibid., 50, 53.
81 Rivera, "The United Nations Guiding Principles," 523–4.
82 Federal Government of Germany, "National Action Plan: Implementation of the UN Guiding Principles on Business and Human Rights" (Berlin: Federal Foreign Office 2017), 24, https://globalnaps.org/wp-content/uploads/2018/04/germany-national-action-plan-business-and-human-rights.pdf.
83 Ibid., 25.
84 United Nations Human Rights Office of the High Commissioner, *Guiding Principles*, 27.
85 Ibid.
86 Ministère de l'Europe et des Affaires Étrangères, "National Action Plan," 52.
87 Federal Government of Germany, "National Action Plan," 9, 28, 36, 39.
88 Bijlmakers, *Corporate Social Responsibility*, 64.
89 Ibid.
90 Mares, "Decentering Human Rights," 177–8.
91 Judith Schrempf-Stirling and Florian Wettstein, "Beyond Guilty Verdicts: Human Rights Litigation and its Impact on Corporations' Human Rights Policies," *Journal of Business Ethics* 145, no. 3 (October 2017): 546.
92 Ibid.
93 United Nations Human Rights Office of the High Commissioner, "Statement at the End of Visit to Canada by the United Nations Working Group on Business and Human Rights," 1 June 2017, https://ohchr.org/EN/NewsEvents/Pages/DisplayNews.aspx?NewsID=21680&LangID=E.
94 Bijlmakers, *Corporate Social Responsibility*, 70.
95 United Nations Office of the High Commissioner, "Statement at the End of Visit to Canada."
96 *Garcia v. Tahoe Resources Inc.* [2017] 5 WWR 631, 2017 BCCA 39.
97 *Choc v. Hudbay Minerals Inc.* [2013] OJ No. 3375, 2013 ONSC 1414.
98 *Araya v. Nevsun Resources Ltd* [2018] 2 WWR 221, 2017 BCCA 401.
99 *Nevsun Resources Ltd v. Araya.* [2020] 4 WWR 1, 2020 SCC 5.

100 *Garcia v. Tahoe Resources Inc.*; *Choc v. Hudbay Minerals Inc.*; *Araya v. Nevsun Resources Ltd.*
101 *Garcia v. Tahoe Resources Inc.*
102 *Choc v. Hudbay Minerals Inc.*
103 *Araya v. Nevsun Resources Ltd.*
104 *Garcia v. Tahoe Resources Inc.*
105 Ibid., 45, 49, 70, 96.
106 Ibid., 130–1.
107 "Canadian Mining Firm Apologizes to Protestors Shot Outside Guatemalan Mine," *CTV News*, 30 July 2019, https://www.ctvnews.ca/world/canadian-mining-firm-apologizes-to-protesters-shot-outside-guatemalan-mine-1.4530358.
108 Pan American Silver, "Pan American Silver Announces Resolution of Garcia v. Tahoe Case," *Business & Human Rights Resource Centre,* 30 July 2019, https://www.business-humanrights.org/en/latest-news/pan-american-silver-announces-resolution-of-garcia-v-tahoe-case/.
109 Ibid.
110 Ibid.
111 Ibid.
112 *Choc v. Hudbay Minerals Inc.*
113 Ibid., 49, 55.
114 *Choc v. Hudbay Minerals Inc.*, 67–8.
115 *Caal Caal v. Hudbay Minerals Inc.* 2020 ONSC 415.
116 John H. Currie, *Public International Law,* 2nd ed. (Irwin Law, 2000), 187.
117 *Nevsun Resources Ltd v. Araya*, 99–103.
118 Ibid., 107.
119 Ibid., 108–11.
120 Ibid., 90–5, 114.
121 Ibid., 112–14.
122 Ibid., 113, 122.
123 Miranda Lam, Meghan S. Bridges, and Edmond Chen, "Supreme Court of Canada Cracks Open the Door for International Human Rights Tort Claims in Nevsun Resources Ltd v. Araya," *McCarthy Tétrault*, 9 March 2020, https://www.mccarthy.ca/en/insights/blogs/canadian-appeals-monitor/supreme-court-canada-cracks-open-door-international-human-rights-tort-claims-nevsun-resources-ltd-v-araya; *Nevsun Resources Ltd v. Araya*, 122–5.
124 *Nevsun Resources Ltd v. Araya*, 125.
125 Niall McGee, "Canadian Miner Nevsun Resources Settles with African Workers over Case Alleging Human-Rights Abuses," *The Globe and Mail*, 28 October 2020, https://www.theglobeandmail.com/business/article-canadian-miner-nevsun-resources-settles-with-african-workers-over-case.

126 Ibid.
127 Ibid., 132.
128 Rivera, "United Nations," 527.
129 Jodie A. Kirshner, "A Call for the EU to Assume Jurisdiction over Extraterritorial Corporate Human Rights Abuses," *Northwestern University Journal of Human Rights* 13, no. 1 (2015): 6.
130 *Nevsun Resources Ltd v. Araya.*, 125.
131 Ibid.
132 Schrempf-Stirling and Wettstein, "Beyond Guilty Verdicts," 558–9.
133 Amnesty International, "Injustice Incorporated: Corporate Abuses and the Human Right to Remedy," 2014, https://www.amnesty.org/en/documents/POL30/001/2014/en.
134 Ibid., 84, 86.
135 Ibid.
136 Ibid., 94.
137 Samuel Farkas, "Araya v Nevsun and the Case for Adopting International Human Rights Prohibitions into Domestic Tort Law," *University of Toronto Faculty of Law Review* (2018), 130, 160–1; Rivera, "The United Nations Guiding Principles," 521–2.
138 Farkas, "Araya v Nevsun", 160–1. Such concerns were also raised in *Choc v. Hudbay Minerals Inc.*, 39; *Araya v. Nevsun*, 196.
139 Farkas, "Araya v Nevsun," 161.
140 *Nevsun Resources Ltd v. Araya*, 262–3.
141 Ibid., 70.
142 Ibid., 161–2.
143 Bill C-331, *An Act to amend the Federal Courts Act (International Promotion and Protection of Human Rights)*, 1st sess., 42nd Parliament, 2019, https://openparliament.ca/bills/42-1/C-331.
144 Farkas, "Araya v Nevsun," 162–4.
145 Ibid., 163.
146 Ministry of Foreign Affairs of the Netherlands, *National Action Plan*, 38–9.
147 *Kiobel v. Royal Dutch Petroleum Co.* 569 US 108 (2013), 6; *Alien Tort Claims Act*, 28 USC § 1350.
148 *Kiobel v. Royal Dutch Petroleum Co.*, 5, citing *EEOC v. Arabian American Oil Co.* 499 US 244 (1991), 248.
149 *Jesner v. Arab Bank, PLC* 138 US 1386 (2018), 13–14.
150 Ibid., 14.
151 Bijlmakers, *Corporate Social Responsibility*, 80.
152 Schrempf-Stirling and Wettstein, "Beyond Guilty Verdicts," 549, 556, 558–9.
153 United Nations Human Rights Office of the High Commissioner, *Guiding Principles*, 27.

Contributors

CRISTINA BORBELY is an associate at Gowling WLG's Toronto office, practicing in the areas of commercial litigation and investigations. She attended Trinity College at the University of Toronto where she studied international relations and graduated from the Peter A. Allard School of Law, University of British Columbia, in 2019. While at law school, Cristina was a member of the 2018 Allard team for the Jessup International Law Moot Court Competition, bringing home the First Place Memorial Prize. She was also involved with the *University of British Columbia Law Review* as an associate editor. In her third year of law school, Cristina participated in the Corporate Counsel Externship at a national telecommunications company.

SELENA CHEN is an associate with MLT Aikins LLP in Vancouver, BC, practicing in the areas of corporate/commercial law with a focus on corporate finance, securities, and mergers and acquisitions. Selena advises clients across various industries, including financial services, technology, and cannabis, and has assisted in a number of initial public offerings for such clients. While attending the Peter A. Allard School of Law of the University of British Columbia, Selena was the recipient of the Society of Trust and Estate Practitioners (Canada) Prize in Succession. Prior to attending law school, she completed her Bachelor of Arts with a major in history and politics at New York University, graduating magna cum laude in 2012.

BLAIR FELTMATE is an associate at JFK Law Corporation, a boutique Aboriginal law firm located in Vancouver, BC. At JFK, Blair works for Indigenous governments in a variety of practice areas, including assisting First Nations to navigate the regulatory and consultation aspects of resource extraction, supporting First Nations engaged in the modern-day treaty process, and facilitating economic development for First Nation governments. This work is focused primarily on ensuring that Indigenous Peoples' constitutional rights are preserved and protected, while supporting the resurgence of Indigenous governance systems and law. Prior to his legal career, Blair worked in public consultation and community engagement supporting government and industry. Blair lives and works on the unceded territories of the xʷməθkʷəy̓əm, Sḵwx̱wú7mesh, and səlilwətaɬ.

CATHERINE L.H. LEE is an associate at Terra Law Corporation in Vancouver, BC, where she works in various aspects of commercial real estate including acquisitions, dispositions, development, leasing, financing, and corporate structuring. In addition to commercial real estate, she also has experience acting for institutional and private lenders in general corporate and commercial matters, including corporate governance, reorganizations, and the purchase and sale of businesses. Prior to joining Terra Law Corporation, Catherine practiced as a general solicitor at Kahn Zack Ehrlich Lithwick LLP, a full-service firm in Richmond, BC. She particularly enjoys working with local real estate developers on sustainable building and affordable housing projects. In her spare time, Catherine enjoys baking and spending time with her two adorable poodles and her family.

JULIE LIANG obtained her Juris Doctor degree from the Peter A. Allard School of Law at the University of British Columbia, specializing in business law by completing the Business Law Concentration. Previously, she obtained a Bachelor of Commerce with Honours majoring in accounting and international business, also from UBC. After articling and briefly practicing in-house at FortisBC, a natural gas and electric utility company, Julie joined the Canada Revenue Agency to learn more about Canada's tax system from the regulatory perspective. In her spare time, she enjoys watching sports, watching Asian dramas, and listening to music. She can read and speak multiple languages, including English, Chinese (Mandarin and Cantonese), and Korean.

CAROL LIAO, PhD, is associate professor and director of the Centre for Business Law, Peter A. Allard School of Law, University of British Columbia. She is the UBC Sauder Distinguished Scholar of the Peter

P. Dhillon Centre for Business Ethics, UBC Sauder School of Business, and principal co-investigator of the Canada Climate Law Initiative. Carol is an internationally recognized and widely published scholar in the field of corporate law and sustainability, and has delivered over one hundred invited talks around the world on sustainable business. She is the co-author of a leading business organizations text in Canada and is a past Bertram Scholar of the Institute of Corporate Directors. Prior to academia, she was a senior associate in the New York mergers and acquisitions group of Shearman & Sterling LLP. In 2021, she received the Influential Women in Business Award from *Business in Vancouver* and was named as one of Canada's Top 100 Most Powerful Women by the Women's Executive Network.

OLUDOLAPO MAKINDE is a PhD candidate and Liu Scholar at the University of British Columbia. Her doctoral research investigates the practicability of adopting an integrated approach that fuses corporate governance and corporate social responsibility measures with artificial intelligence tools to effectively tackle corruption involving Canadian multinationals doing business in the Global South. Oludolapo also obtained her LLM at UBC and a Bachelor of Laws from the University of Lagos, Nigeria. Her other research interests include race and law, and business and human rights. Prior to pursuing graduate studies, she worked as an associate at the law firm of Kenna Partners where she provided corporate governance advisory services to the firm's clients. She has also worked as a researcher with the Cullen Commission of Inquiry into Money Laundering in BC. Oludolapo is also a member of the Daughters of Themis International Network of Female Business Scholars, the Liu Scholars Network for Africa, and Transparency International Canada.

MEGAN PARISOTTO is legal counsel in the Resource and Environment Group of the BC Ministry of Attorney General. In this role, Megan assists natural resource ministries with a wide range of matters, including drafting contracts and interpreting legislation. Megan's first two years of law school were spent at the University of Victoria, where she participated in a law co-op program. Prior to attending law school, Megan completed the BC Legislative Internship Program, during which she wrote speeches and media releases for members of the Legislative Assembly. Megan also obtained a Bachelor of Arts in political science from the University of Northern British Columbia. Outside of work,

Megan can be found exploring coffee shops, bookstores, and bakeries with her husband and their labradoodle puppy in Victoria, BC.

BIKARAMJIT S. SANDHU is an associate with Bennett Jones LLP in Toronto, ON, practicing in the areas of corporate law with a focus on corporate finance, mergers and acquisitions, private equity, and shareholder activism. Prior to his legal career, he completed his Bachelor of Arts with a major in political science at UBC Okanagan. In his free time, he assists with his family business of growing and exporting cherries around the world.

ERICA SANDHU practices union-side labour law in Vancouver, BC. She completed both an undergraduate and a Master's degree in political science at the University of British Columbia. Erica is committed to social justice; during law school she was the student coordinator for the Centre for Feminist Legal Studies and volunteered with Lawyers' Rights Watch Canada. As a union-side labour lawyer, she is committed to advancing the rights of workers. In her spare time, Erica enjoys running and biking along the seawall in Vancouver.

SAUL WANG is an associate at Dentons Canada LLP, a global law firm, where he regularly advises clients on corporate finance transactions, mergers and acquisitions, corporate and commercial matters, and securities compliance matters. During his time in law school, Saul participated in the publication of the second and third editions of *Trusts in Common-Law Canada*. He was also the lead mooter representing the Allard School of Law in the 2019 Ian Fletcher Insolvency Moot, where the Allard team placed second in the global competition. Saul previously interned at SAP SE, one of the world's largest enterprise software companies, where he advised the company's software development teams on licensing issues related to open-source software and commercial web services. Outside the practice of law, Saul is interested in finance and data science.

ASHA YOUNG is a lawyer in the Business Law Group at Lawson Lundell LLP in Vancouver, BC, on the unceded territories of the Coast Salish Peoples, including the Squamish (Sḵwx̱wú7mesh Úxwumixw), Tsleil-Waututh (səlilwətaɬ), and Musqueam (xʷməθkʷəy̓əm) Nations, where she maintains a general corporate and commercial practice. She holds a BA from the University of British Columbia Okanagan and a

JD from the University of British Columbia. She is a past recipient of the Law Foundation of British Columbia Public Interest Award and the prestigious Raymond G. Herbert Award for Best All-Round Graduating Student. In addition to practicing law, Asha is passionate about art and works as an artist in Vancouver.

SHERRY YU is a lawyer called to the Bar of BC. Driven by her ideals in the realms of public policy and social reform, Sherry looks forward to pursuing a career in labour and employment law. During her articling year, Sherry worked closely with a management-side employment lawyer at a full-service law firm, where she discovered her passion for solving workplace problems. Currently, Sherry is the labour relations advisor for a large public sector employer. Prior to articling, Sherry enjoyed a yearlong stint at the City of Vancouver where she was a compliance analyst. After obtaining her Bachelor of Commerce from the University of Toronto (St George), Sherry relocated to Vancouver to attend law school at the University of British Columbia. In her personal time, Sherry enjoys reading fiction novels, eating her way through the city, and getting strong at the gym.

Index